Growth and Governance of Canadian Universities

Howard C. Clark

Growth and Governance of Canadian Universities: An Insider's View

UBC Press · Vancouver · Toronto

09 08 07 06 05 04 03 5 4 3 2 1

Printed in Canada on acid-free paper

National Library of Canada Cataloguing in Publication Data

Clark, Howard C.
Growth and governance of Canadian universities : an insider's view / Howard C. Clark.

Includes index.
ISBN 0-7748-1023-8 (bound); ISBN 0-7748-1024-6 (pbk.)

1. Universities and colleges – Canada. 2. Education, Higher – Canada. 3. Clark, Howard C. I. Title.

LA417.C52 2003 378.71 C2003-910152-5

Canada

UBC Press gratefully acknowledges the financial support for our publishing program of the Government of Canada through the Book Publishing Industry Development Program (BPIDP), and of the Canada Council for the Arts, and the British Columbia Arts Council.

UBC Press
The University of British Columbia
2029 West Mall
Vancouver, BC V6T 1Z2
604-822-5959 / Fax: 604-822-6083
www.ubcpress.ca

Contents

Acknowledgments

To many, many colleagues and friends with whom I have worked at the University of British Columbia, the University of Western Ontario, the University of Guelph, and Dalhousie University, I owe far more than can be expressed in words. Your ideas, suggestions, and criticisms over the years have stimulated my thinking and have helped create that supportive and intellectually exciting environment that is at the heart of any university. My gratitude is owed to you all for a wonderfully rewarding thirty-eight years in Canadian universities. I hope that in this book, I have offended none and can still count on you as my friends, although on many issues discussed here we may well disagree.

My deepest thanks are due to those who willingly agreed to read various versions of this manuscript, and to offer comments. In particular, I thank David Murray of the University of Guelph, and Denis Stairs of Dalhousie University, who have been especially forbearing and long-suffering. In particular, Denis Stairs provided at the critical moment that detailed and impartial analysis of the text that only the few experienced and highly respected academics can provide; without his assistance, this book, such as it is, would not have been possible. Lest they inadvertently be associated with views expressed in this book, I claim full and sole responsibility for such views and opinions, none of which should necessarily be attributed to those who have assisted me. I am also most grateful to Reuben Cohen for his friendship and support in making the publication of this book possible.

Finally, I offer my greatest thanks to Joy Dickson-Clark, with whom many aspects of this book have been discussed during our odyssey from coast to coast, and who has also had to endure the many unspoken vicissitudes of that journey.

Introduction

In many countries, the university as an institution is currently under attack, not so much for the quality of education it provides as for a perceived rigidity and resistance to change, and for a lack of accountability. Critics of the university attack its supposed inability to set priorities or to engage purposefully in strategic planning. They also attack its lack of financial accountability and especially its reluctance to engage in any robust assessment of performance and quality. They question the established dogma that research necessarily complements and strengthens the teaching function. In short, there is a skepticism about the traditional role and mission of the university, a skepticism that is only increased by what some label as the commercialization or privatization of the universities, and by the objections of many to continually increasing tuition fees.

That such doubts and questions are arising now is perplexing yet understandable; perplexing in the face of the widespread recognition of the increasing value of, and need for, higher education in a knowledge-intensive economy, understandable because of the rapidly increasing cost to government and particularly to individuals that such education and research now implies, especially at a time of greatly expanding participation by all sectors of society. Whatever the reasons for the skepticism, its reality has been very evident in the lack of government confidence, often expressed, especially in the 1990s, through limited or reduced funding, More recently, specifically targeted funding has again reflected low confidence, while public concern over rising tuition fee levels and their effect on accessibility for the less privileged has steadily increased.

Much of this alienation of the university from the society that supports it stems, on the one hand, from a lack of understanding of the way in which universities operate internally and their consequent style of administration, and, on the other hand, from the unwillingness of academics to recognize and modify the weaknesses in governance and management that have become evident. The way in which universities in many countries are structured, governed, and managed shelters their staff from the economic realities of the wider community and provides a seemingly comfortable existence in which there is little internal incentive for change. Canadian universities have not escaped such criticisms and have certainly not been immune to some of these problems, although their achievements over the past decades have been very substantial.

The intent of this book is to consider some of the changes and accomplishments of Canadian universities in coping with the remarkable growth in enrollment during the past forty or so years; to raise some of the major issues that the universities have confronted, in some cases successfully and in other instances with less success; and to offer some comments about the present state of the universities and the challenges currently facing them. Not surprisingly, in view of some of the public concerns that are voiced about universities, much of the discussion focuses on their internal affairs: How are they governed? How are they managed? Are university leaders well chosen? And, of course, such fundamentally important and perennially debated issues as: Is tenure necessary? Should universities train or educate? What is the quality of the education they provide? What, indeed, is their primary educational function? And how can the educational and research missions attain real complementarity? Many such questions inevitably have no final answer, nor do I make any claims to provide them; they must continue to be at the centre of the academic debate into the foreseeable future. It is nevertheless useful to examine periodically the state of our universities in light of changes that have occurred, and to consider the factors, internal and external, that have brought about those changes.

Surprisingly, there have been relatively few accounts, of a scholarly or more personal nature, of the remarkable changes that have transformed Canada's universities since 1950. Yet it is fair to suggest that these universities have achieved more and progressed further than their sister institutions in many other countries. Canadians should take great pride in their universities, and should be much more aware of the enormous transformations of the last fifty years, and of the international recognition that Canadian universities rightly now receive. Similarly, those outside the university, as well as many within, would benefit from a greater understanding of the processes by which Canadian universities are governed, and of the significant governance changes that have occurred since 1950. It is my hope that this book will at least contribute to such greater understanding.

Any commentary on such changes, and any discussion of current issues and challenges, might of course be undertaken in a purely scholarly fashion. A literature search would be made; literature references, government documents, and university archives would be consulted, as well as a variety of other materials; and factual statements appearing in the text would be supported by the appropriate references in an often long bibliography. Any subsequent commentary on actual issues or perceived problems would still remain subjective, however. More importantly, since such sources have only a very limited ability to convey to the reader how Canadian universities actually operate in real life today, the discussion would likely seem abstract and theoretical. It could also be dull reading.

For these reasons, I have chosen to introduce the various issues and themes in a chronological sense based on my own experiences in Canadian universities. A chronological framework is essential since in many instances the university debate of issues over time has changed considerably as circumstances, both internal and more often external, have changed, often very rapidly. Considerable justification for the use of what may seem to be an autobiographical structure for this book lies in the fact that, by happenstance, my career in Canadian universities has been more diverse than most: I began as a green, young assistant professor and finished some thirty-eight years later as a president and vice-chancellor. Geographically, I held academic positions in universities from coast to coast, commencing at the University of British Columbia and retiring from Dalhousie University in Halifax, with some twenty intervening years at two Ontario universities. This depth and variety of personal experience provides, I would suggest, at least a comparable, if not superior, base for the discussion of current university issues than would an abstract scholarly analysis of the literature, which is necessarily several steps removed from the realities of academic life. At the same time, the book does make systematic reference to a bibliography of relevant references, but no claim is made that this is comprehensive in the scholarly sense.

The book is not intended to be an autobiography. While the reader may have to progress beyond the first chapter to be well convinced of this, some early biographical material has been included only so that the reader can be aware of my background, especially educationally, and thus be better able to assess my later comments on the universities. Moreover, universities do not exist in isolation but are part of comprehensive educational systems; education is a lifelong process and these early chapters place my university experiences in some context. Indeed, since the only aspects of my life mentioned in the book are those to do with universities, the volume just does not qualify as an autobiography; it is simply that my own career in Canadian universities happens to span a remarkable, recent period of growth and change in the universities and thus provides a good chronological time frame for its discussion.

Inevitably, this approach, like any other, has its own difficulties. Some critics, especially those who will not agree with my views, will immediately assert that my commentary on the Canadian university scene is too subjective. Throughout, however, I have endeavoured to avoid what might be regarded as "cheap shots" directed at faculty members, or boards, or faculty unions, or anyone else. All my comments are based on fact, drawing directly from my own experiences. Opinions or views that are attributed to faculty are based on comments made to me, and reflect actual facts, events, and experiences. I have made every possible effort to recount these as accurately and impartially as possible, and to present arguments from both sides. Moreover, many of my colleagues who have served in senior administrative capacities in other Canadian universities have had similar experiences and would report similar events.

A remarkable characteristic of the university community in Canada, and in much of the Western world, is its ability to dismiss or ignore criticism, valid or otherwise, using such reasoning as "academic freedom is threatened," or the criticism is "subjective" and therefore hardly valid, or that it is not sufficiently "scholarly" and therefore not worthy of consideration. Yet the fundamental mission of the university is the search for, and transmission of, knowledge and truth, which must include self-analysis and criticism. Surprisingly, it is difficult to identify another institution or community that is so resistant to rigorous self-examination and assessment.

As indicated, the first chapter describes my personal background and education in New Zealand through to the completion of a Ph.D. degree in chemistry, and postdoctoral experience at Cambridge University. The personal details are not important in themselves; what is significant is that this background is remarkably similar to the backgrounds and early education of many of those recruited to Canadian universities in the period from 1955 to 1970. This was the time when Canadian universities were transformed from often small, essentially undergraduate colleges to real universities fully engaged in both teaching and research. The fact that so many of the young recruited faculty, including those who were Canadians, had such similar backgrounds, based on the British university model, certainly made the transformation easier, but also put a particular stamp upon it. It is also important to point out that there were essentially two quite different waves of faculty recruitment to Canadian universities. The first, in the 1950s and 1960s, was largely, although not exclusively, from Britain and Commonwealth countries, with Canadians in the minority. The second, in the 1970s and early 1980s, was much more heavily American. It was the first wave that so influenced the shape and governance structure of Canadian universities, while the latter probably had a much greater impact on the curriculum and on what was viewed as the Americanization of the universities.

In Chapter 2, some aspects of life as an assistant professor are described, in the context of the University of British Columbia from 1957 to 1965. Then, as now, the junior faculty member was preoccupied with initiating a good teaching and research program, especially the latter, and had little time for what occurred outside the academic department. What was important was the internal functioning of the department or equivalent unit, and the role of the department head or chair. It was at this level that the significant governance changes of Canadian universities began during an era of unrestricted growth.

The next two chapters concern the eleven years, from 1965 to 1976, that I spent at the University of Western Ontario. This was a time of faculty and student unrest, and to the outside observer was dominated by student activists and their efforts to have students play a significant role in decision making. More apparent to those within the universities were the much more successful efforts of faculty to both limit student activism and gain for faculty the decisive decision-making role, with the power and influence of both administrations and boards greatly reduced. It also happened to be a decade during which I served as a department head, gaining much experience in wider university matters and university governance. These involvements occurred over the years during which the University of Western Ontario became the first major Canadian university to introduce significant governance changes that were reflective of those turbulent times. The events and climate of that time also led to greater concern on the part of many, including myself, for the quality and nature of undergraduate education.

By the mid-1970s, the faculty and student radical movements had contributed perceptibly to the diminished generosity of governments in their financial treatment of the universities. A period of restraint, commencing at somewhat different times in various provinces, began to take its toll. From 1976 to 1986, I was vice-president academic at the University of Guelph, and by the nature of the position had to take a broad institutional view of university issues and of budgets, a position that often put me in opposition to one or other of the many groupings of faculty. Because of growing financial constraints, there came about a reluctant acceptance of the concept of strategic planning, and the word "priority" began to be heard. In Chapter 6, some of my experiences in such areas are mentioned, along with comments about the educational mission of the university, the meaning of liberal education in today's university, and the attitudes and policies that affect the faculty member's career, particularly through the granting of tenure and promotion.

Chapter 7 offers more general comments on the, at best, very limited success that Canadian universities have actually achieved in strategic planning. Some of the factors at play within the institution that encourage undirected growth and prevent the identification of specific, non-universal priorities and the elimination of academic programs are discussed. Governance of the institution is at the heart of these difficulties and is treated more specifically.

In 1986, I became president and vice-chancellor of Dalhousie University in Halifax, one of Canada's oldest universities, with long traditions and many Maritime characteristics. I arrived there at a time of severe financial crisis and weak morale, largely attributable to the powerful presidential role of one of my predecessors, which had led ultimately to faculty unionization and confrontations between the union and the board. In Chapters 8 and 9, some of this history is examined from the viewpoint of governance, as well as the difficult financial and political steps that were needed for change. There is a discussion of the effect of faculty unionization at Dalhousie and elsewhere in increasing still further faculty control of the university. Chapter 10 considers university governance in relation to the issues surrounding government funding over the past years, and also looks at Nova Scotia's attempts in the 1990s to rationalize its universities.

Chapter 11 deals with issues of accountability. It discusses various approaches that governments in Canada have taken to influence the development of universities, at first through funding formulae, then through targeted funding and more recent initiatives. The vagaries of funding and threats of more direct government intervention undoubtedly encouraged the move towards faculty unionization that surged across much of Canada in the 1970s. Some effects of unionization are discussed, especially the negative impact it has had on attempts at institutional planning and program reductions. Tenure provides a further protection for faculty, and the manner in which it has come to be equated with job security is considered. These and other factors all contribute to the significant resistance to internal change that characterizes today's universities, which is also very evident in the failure of various attempts to rationalize universities and avoid duplication.

In Chapter 12, some comparisons are made of the universities in New Zealand and Canada today, of their accomplishments and current challenges, and of how different governments have attempted to increase accountability. In both cases, only limited success has been achieved, but there appear to be grounds for the conclusion that the more directly intrusive approach taken in New Zealand has been more successful. Certainly the emphasis there on enhancing the power of the university board, and at the same time requiring greater accountability of it, appears central to solving current problems in Canadian universities.

In conclusion, I emphasize that while it will always be possible to find problems, nothing should diminish public recognition of all that Canadian universities have accomplished. They have demonstrated a considerable resilience towards survival while achieving very significant growth and undergoing remarkable transformation. Yet they have changed fundamentally in nature and mission, and are faced now with a further challenge in dealing with the opportunities and temptations that commercialization and privatization offer. This and other challenges will be overcome only if the universities fully understand how they have changed, and in doing so determine what they wish to become.

1
Similar Beginnings

Before the Second World War, New Zealand was a remote and isolated place, more than a thousand miles distant from its nearest neighbour, Australia. Settled by Europeans for less than a hundred years but with a proud and unsubdued Maori population, the country's ties in terms of culture, society, and the economy were with Great Britain, from which nearly all migrants had come. At that time, when international air travel was in its infancy, a journey to Britain needed at least twenty-eight days by sea, with the only sight of land to break the monotony of shipboard life being passage through the Panama Canal. Not many New Zealanders travelled abroad and, not surprisingly, the country's society was inward-looking and still bound to a considerable degree by the customs and behaviour of the Victorian and Edwardian eras.

The lifestyle of New Zealanders was relatively simple. Blessed with a temperate climate that contained nothing of the Arctic cold or summer heat and humidity of North America, surrounded by an ocean that, although often dangerous, still encouraged swimming and boating, and blessed with an abundance and diversity of foods and many natural products, New Zealanders played sports, especially rugby, sailed, swam, hiked and climbed the New Zealand Alps, and enjoyed the diversity of the country's natural setting. Family ties were strong, and family values, as they are now called, governed society. Visits to relatives, events centred on the church or school, or especially sporting organizations, were the mainstay of social life. While there were numerous amateur musical and theatrical groups, some of outstanding quality, no professional theatre, orchestra, or ballet existed then, although infrequent visits by touring artists filled some of this gap.

In its broad aspects, life in New Zealand at that time was not unlike that experienced in Canada, especially Western Canada, or in Australia, or in most provincial centres in the United Kingdom outside of London. There were, of course, major climatic and oceanic differences, and centres such as Sydney or Melbourne, or Toronto or Montreal, or Manchester or Edinburgh were relatively more sophisticated and cultured than any New Zealand city, yet the general circumstances, lifestyles, and outlooks were quite similar. It was true, however, that a New Zealander always experienced a greater sense of isolation and separation, and perhaps deprivation, than others.

Family Background and Early Education

I was born in 1929 into a very typical middle-class New Zealand family, the second of three sons. My mother had emigrated with her family from Great Britain in 1911, and remained very English throughout her life: she never quite accepted that colonial New Zealanders could be the equal of Englishmen! My father was born of a large family in New Zealand. Both families were much involved in the central Methodist church in Auckland, through which my mother and father first met. Their marriage was delayed until 1921 by military service in the First World War. My brothers and I had a peaceful childhood in a very traditional family. Father was clearly head of the family, the financial support and breadwinner; mother ran the home, provided the meals, and was the chief caregiver. Our social life centred on church and church events, and family visits, although father had a wider range of interests, especially in music. My family background and early childhood experiences were therefore typical of their time, with the exception that there was more family interest in music and culture than in sports. While this tended to set us apart in a country devoted to outdoor life, it would also have been true in many other countries.

Early school experiences were unexceptional. At that time in New Zealand, some but not all children attended kindergarten, and then commenced primary school at age five. That was my experience, after which I spent about one and a half to two years in Primers 1 to 4, then a year in each of Standards 1 to 4. The quality of education in New Zealand elementary schools at that time was good, although probably not remarkably so: the basics of reading, writing, and arithmetic were certainly well covered, even though the last included rote learning of the multiplication tables, much valuable mental arithmetic, and interminable calculations in the nonmetric English measurement systems, and also in pounds, shillings, and pence, an experience that even many Canadian contemporaries had to endure! These school years were moderately happy, despite my reluctance to participate in the usual extracurricular activities of rugby and cricket, and I obtained a solid foundation for further education.

In the early 1940s, New Zealand, like Canada, was developing junior high schools, known in New Zealand as intermediate schools. I had the good fortune, at my father's insistence, to attend one of the first, Kowhai Intermediate School, in 1941-42, a superior school for its time. In distinct contrast to the Standard 5 and 6 programs of the elementary schools, Kowhai provided an introduction to Latin and French as well as excellent science and mathematics teaching that made those two years exciting and stimulating, and that gave its pupils a decided advantage as they moved on to secondary education.

My years at Kowhai coincided with the crucial years of the Second World War. The war was an utterly transforming experience, just as much for those living in remote parts of Canada or in the isolation of New Zealand as it was for those closer to the conflicts. It separated completely the first four decades of the century from those that followed. It was a time of awakening and change for all. In New Zealand, people had slumbered in a remote ocean fastness for a century; their isolation gave them a sense of complete security, to which was added the reassurance that Great Britain, the founder and mother of the British Empire, would always be there to defend and support them. When war broke out in 1939, New Zealanders were stunned by the series of reversals and defeats that marked the first two years: Dunkirk, the Battle of Britain, the German occupation of Europe, vicious fighting in retreats from Greece and Crete in which New Zealand troops took part, the see-saw battles across North Africa that eventually took Rommel to the gates of Cairo.

While we quickly learned geography that had never been covered in school, there was little here to reassure New Zealanders as we sat glued to our radios. British supremacy and support seemed, and indeed was, a thing of the past. But then came the sudden entry of Japan into the war, the attack on Pearl Harbor, the lightning Japanese advances across the Pacific, the fall of Hong Kong, Singapore, and what is now Indonesia, advances into Papua New Guinea and the Solomon Islands. For Australia and New Zealand, the enemy was at our gates, and we had only our own meagre resources on which to rely, although it was not long before the United States came to our defence.

These events, and those of the remaining war years, caused a profound shift in New Zealand thinking and attitudes. The place of New Zealand as a Pacific country, and more especially Polynesian in terms of much of its history and culture, is now at the heart of New Zealand thinking and of its domestic and foreign policy. The Second World War brought to New Zealand a more realistic understanding of its geographical position, and of the need to create a distinctive New Zealand culture, society, and economy, less dependent on the United Kingdom or even the United States. Again, such traumatic changes in outlook and policy, while having some characteristics unique to each country, were also experienced in Australia and Canada as well as in other countries.

The end of the war was greeted with enormous celebration in New Zealand as elsewhere. Yet it took years for life in New Zealand to return to something like normal, and in many ways, it never really did, since life in all countries was changed irrevocably by those years of conflict. While the rationing of food and petrol was phased out only slowly, there was nevertheless a steadily growing feeling of optimism and of growth. As the direct effects of the war fell away, that optimism led to new forms of thinking in a variety of fields, and across the world many of the wartime scientific discoveries were being adapted to imaginative peacetime uses. By 1950, there was a general air of intellectual excitement, of financial stability, and of general social confidence. It was over those years, just after the Second World War ended, that I and many others who were later to become faculty members in Canadian universities completed high school, studied for undergraduate degrees, and took our first steps into graduate work and research.

The high school that I attended, Takapuna Grammar School, was one of five such grammar schools in Auckland. Modelled on the English grammar school although well adapted to the New Zealand climate and culture, it was the only one that was coeducational. It was also the smallest of the five grammar schools, a fact that was often reflected in our limited success in rugby or cricket competitions, but more seriously in the more limited choice of subjects available, especially in the upper forms.

The school was quite a typical New Zealand secondary school, although with a more academic emphasis than comparable district high schools across the country. Participation in sports was compulsory, as was involvement with military cadets, although a few exceptions were allowed in the latter case on conscientious grounds. Prefects appointed by the headmaster had considerable authority and helped maintain discipline; caning by a teacher was not common but certainly occurred. The wearing of school uniforms was absolutely mandatory: boys wore navy flannel shirts and navy shorts, with knee-length socks and black shoes, while girls wore a white blouse under navy gym dresses, socks, and black shoes. It is probably almost impossible for today's Canadian high school student to imagine a seventeen-year-old being required to wear navy shorts to school, let alone contemplate the punishment that befell such a student who was seen on the street in uniform but not wearing the school cap!

The curriculum was that to be expected of a grammar school – a strong emphasis on English and mathematics, the commencement of Latin and French, with science taught as a single subject for two years then becoming specialized into chemistry, botany, zoology, and, in some schools, physics. Here I was at a disadvantage in that my school was too small to maintain a sufficient enrollment in physics, which I was therefore not able to take until I entered university. Some physical education was compulsory, as was woodworking for the first two years, while geography and history could also be taken. After three years of this curriculum, all students were expected to write government-sponsored examinations in at least five subjects. These constituted the School Certificate Examination, which was intended to provide a national standard for high school achievement and to be an indicator of competence for future employers. Many students ended their schooling at this stage, but not those intending to proceed to university or teachers college.

While the university entrance qualification could be obtained after one year in the sixth form, the best students heading towards university were encouraged after completion of the School Certificate Examination to spend two years in the sixth form. Such was my experience, having been among the top two or three students in each of my first three years at Takapuna Grammar School. These last two years consisted of special teaching and coaching in preparation for writing the University Scholarship Examinations, which were highly competitive and written by only the best students across the country, probably some 250 or so at that time. English was a compulsory subject, but otherwise each student chose the remaining subjects governed only by the requirement that the total of possible marks in all the subjects written by that student had to reach a certain figure. Only the top thirty students received scholarships, although a further 100 received bursaries, which were still quite valuable. To compete in these examinations was both a challenge and an incentive; to actually win a scholarship was an outstanding honour.

The standard of teaching that my contemporaries and I experienced was, on the whole, very high, since it was the respected senior teachers, the heads of subject departments, who taught at the scholarship level. These were teachers with considerable experience and real enthusiasm for their subjects. For the average student, however, the level of teaching was probably less satisfactory, and there certainly were some, well known among the pupils, whose lack of teaching skills was all too obvious. Some fifty years later, I still retain a great deal of respect and gratitude for many of those who taught me, especially at the scholarship level. Neither they nor their colleagues who helped set and mark scholarship examination papers awarded marks easily. Any mark above 50 percent was respectable; to obtain a mark over 80 percent was outstanding, and only very rarely indeed was a mark over 90 percent ever awarded. In my second writing of these examinations, I received marks of 67 and 68 in the two mathematics papers. Not only did I feel quite satisfied with these results but my feeling was confirmed when I met my mathematics teacher on the street after the results had been released. He congratulated me on doing well overall in the scholarship examinations and said that I had done better in the mathematics papers than he had thought I might!

Those marks in mathematics need to be placed in some perspective, however, in order to appreciate the marking standards at the time. My other marks were of the same order in two other papers, two others were in the 70s and two were in the low 80s. While I did not win a scholarship, my total marks placed me in the top forty-five students in New Zealand. The very solid education that I received at Takapuna Grammar School was probably a little better than average by New Zealand standards, and it certainly served me well as I went on to university.

A University Student

No one in my extended family had been a university student, and any perceptions of universities and university life came from reading and from conversations with former school acquaintances one or two years ahead of me. I knew that I wanted to continue studies in science, preferably chemistry, and I knew that to do so I had to attend university, but beyond that my understanding of universities was limited. My first association with a university began in February 1948, when I was one of several hundred students matriculating, or registering for the first time, at what was then Auckland University College, a constituent college of the University of New Zealand. I enrolled for the B.Sc. degree, which would require three years of study during which eight units had to be completed, each unit consisting of one full year of study of a particular academic subject. Chemistry I, II, and III would be taken consecutively over the three years; a course in physics was required, as well as at least one course in mathematics. An elective from the humanities or social sciences was not a requirement, although it could be included in the choice of eight units.

A student at Auckland University College in 1950 found a small and struggling college with little more than the basic subject areas covered and with only about seventy permanent teaching staff; no single department had more than ten faculty members.[1] This meant that class sizes, particularly in first-year courses, could be as large as 150 to 200, but in second- and third-year courses, it was rare to encounter a course with more that twenty-five or so students. A major factor in this was the high failure/drop-out rate, which was probably on the order of 40 percent. In my final year of chemistry, we had a tight-knit group of eighteen who knew each other well; in a real sense, we were the survivors. Those lecturing us were, on the whole, competent and knowledgeable, although we still had our share of poor lecturers, those who spoke to the blackboard rather than the class, or those whose voice trailed away into inaudibility towards the end of a critical sentence. Our only means of expressing displeasure at such inadequacies was through a collective class hiss, since of course student evaluations or comments on teaching were inconceivable. However, others of the faculty had just returned from graduate work, usually in Britain, and were full of exciting research ideas and enthusiasm, while many others without doctoral degrees were still competent and dedicated teachers. I have never subsequently felt that an undergraduate education in New Zealand in any way shortchanged us; on the contrary, it seemed that very conscious efforts were made to offset the New

Zealand isolation and to make the curriculum as relevant and up-to-date as possible.

In some other respects, however, we were much less fortunate. The physical facilities at the college had received little maintenance and no additions during the Depression and Second World War. The library, administrative offices, and some arts and related departments were quite comfortably housed in a well-planned, permanent building that is still at the centre of the campus. Its "wedding cake" clock tower is a well-known Auckland landmark and has been a climbing challenge for generations of students. A number of other departments, such as Botany and Zoology, also occupied a relatively new, adequate building, but the physical sciences and engineering were housed in old, inappropriate buildings long converted from their original purpose.

Chemistry, Physics, and Geology were the principal occupants of what had been Auckland's Choral Hall, designed for choral concerts and other musical events. The main auditorium had been fairly readily converted to make two reasonable lecture theatres, but much of the rest of the building was a maze of corridors and odd-sized rooms quite unsuited to scientific laboratory work. A small laboratory block had been added, probably around 1930, which contained on the ground floor a first-year laboratory consisting of two large rooms fitted with benches and lockers and separated by a balance room. On the upper level was a laboratory for organic chemistry and several offices and small rooms. We were, in fact, educated in facilities that would never have met today's environmental and health standards. In the first-year laboratory course, which was largely qualitative analysis using hydrogen sulfide, the fume hoods were woefully inadequate both in number and efficiency. At the end of a three-hour class, it was barely possible to see across the room due to the chemical smog! Official recognition of these inadequacies did exist, and at the beginning of our second year, we found two prefabricated huts erected on the tennis court next to the Choral Hall, both well equipped and to be used for advanced inorganic and physical chemistry. It was the late 1960s, however, before permanent buildings specifically designed for chemistry teaching and research were provided.

Library facilities also were barely adequate. The main College Library was rapidly becoming overcrowded for both books and users, and the modest acquisitions budget could not cope with the burgeoning number of new journals and books. To some degree, this was offset by the large number of departmental reading rooms or libraries. In Chemistry, the reading room contained all of the essential chemical journals, and rarely was it necessary to go through the lengthy procedure of obtaining copies of papers or books through interlibrary loan. Many of the journals were part of the holdings of the central College Library, but others had been the personal property of faculty members who donated them to the reading room. There remained, however, a shortage of monographs and texts, and if this was the case in a science subject, it was probably a much more serious problem in the arts subjects. We just did not have access to a library containing anything comparable to the vast holdings of today's Canadian universities.

The enrollment of the college was small; more part-time students took evening courses in accounting or law than there were full-time students. The latter numbered only about 800 in 1948, out of a total enrollment of about 2,500. One knew by name many other students regardless of the subject being taken, since social life tended to focus on the cafeteria and common room or on the various sports clubs. With only one small hostel and no true university residence, however, the college was essentially a 9 AM to 5 PM institution, with the vast majority of students living at home and commuting from various suburbs. Most students from rural areas lived in rooming houses, or "digs." As a result, the social and cultural life of the college was severely limited and probably resembled that of a British "red-brick" university of the day. True, a good number of students did take part in university sports and athletics, but by and large most lived at home and maintained their previous social involvements.

Graduate Studies

Completion of the B.Sc. degree provided an opportunity to leave university and work as a chemist in industry. In my final undergraduate year, however, I had been especially excited by a portion of the course that was based on Linus Pauling's book *The Nature of the Chemical Bond:* it seemed to me to be so full of new ideas and original and provocative thinking that I wanted to be further involved with it, and I chose to undertake graduate work. To obtain an M.Sc. degree required a minimum of one year of further study with the satisfactory completion of lecture courses and the submission of a thesis. Although there had been for some years a strong research and graduate program in natural-product chemistry at Auckland, there had been few graduate students in other fields of chemistry. The recently appointed head of the department, F.J. Llewellyn, who quickly revitalized and rebuilt the department, was establishing a significant research group in X-ray crystallography, and students were beginning to enroll for M.Sc. and Ph.D. work in physical chemistry, but I was only the second student to undertake an M.Sc. degree in inorganic chemistry. At my request, the lecturer who had given the lectures on Pauling's book agreed to supervise my thesis research. The facilities available for such research were decidedly primitive, and the work that I did was relatively simple, but I was able to attain the degree in one year and began thinking immediately about going straight into a Ph.D. program. At that time, it was the general view that research and graduate experience overseas, usually in Britain, were essential, especially if one was inclined towards an academic career. Indeed, the unspoken implication was that graduate work done just in New Zealand could not really be of sufficiently high quality! Thus, after obtaining their M.Sc. degrees, students usually proceeded to British and, increasingly, American universities to undertake doctoral work. In the early to mid-1950s, however, I and an increasing number of others decided to complete the Ph.D. in New Zealand and then travel elsewhere for postdoctoral work.

There continues to be considerable debate over what constitutes the ideal doctoral experience, especially regarding the extent of supervision that should be provided. In my own case, I was continuing research under the same supervisor: he had never previously supervised Ph.D. students, and indeed did not hold a Ph.D. degree himself. Nevertheless, as I commenced my work, he posed an interesting question relating to several points in Pauling's book and directed me to the library. There followed a very intensive literature search, from which an appropriate line of investigation seemed to suggest itself; other than reporting to him the results of this search, the direction of the research was left entirely to me, although there were frequent chats about day-to-day work and support was always available. There was, in fact, considerable emphasis on the Ph.D. student as an independent investigator, more so than is commonly the case in North America, at least in the sciences. After I had completed almost two years of laboratory work, my supervisor left Auckland for University College London to undertake his own Ph.D. studies, and the completion of my experimental work and preparation of my thesis were unsupervised. Some fifty years later, I am still impressed by the quality and sophistication of the research done at Auckland at that time: much was accomplished despite inadequate facilities and inexperienced supervisors.

Upon completion of my thesis, a fairly standard examination process ensued. Several examiners were appointed, one from the department at Auckland, one from another New Zealand university, and the third overseas, almost certainly in Britain. A written report was received from the overseas examiner, although as usual this took several months, and then the two New Zealand examiners conducted an oral examination. This was quite formal, far more so than I later experienced in Cambridge, and was both probing and lengthy. A considerable period of time then elapsed before I received official notice in 1955 of being awarded the Ph.D. degree.

During the time that I was writing my thesis and after my supervisor departed for Britain, I was appointed a temporary junior lecturer in the department. While this was of great benefit financially, the workload was not onerous and easily allowed for completion of my thesis. The work involved delivering a small number of lectures and supervising some laboratory classes. What was striking was that no one gave me advice on lecturing, and certainly no one really evaluated my ability as a lecturer; the overly simplistic view held then and still strongly entrenched in most universities that a Ph.D. graduate would automatically make a good lecturer obviously applied at Auckland.

The vast majority of students then, as now, knew almost nothing of the inner workings of the university as an institution. We knew that Auckland University College was governed through a council that included both university and appointed community representatives and one or two professors, and that the president of the council, a city lawyer, effectively ran the college, at least until 1950, when a full-time principal was appointed. However, the relationships between the council, its president, and the chancellor and Senate of the University of New Zealand were completely mysterious to us. Indeed, we were quite indifferent to university politics. We did, however, realize that it was a period of major transition, with the breakup of the University of New Zealand already being planned, and leading to the creation in 1961 of a number of separate and quite autonomous universities, including the University of Auckland. Somewhat closer to the students was the Professorial Board, consisting largely of the heads of departments: this board might be viewed as the equivalent of today's Senate, at least in the sense that both held the responsibility for academic matters. However, the senates of most Canadian universities today have a majority of elected faculty members, as well as a number of students and perhaps alumni representatives, whereas the Professorial Board at Auckland then consisted only of those holding professorial appointments, usually one per department, and their membership on the board continued indefinitely. Even at the working level of the department, my contemporaries and I knew little of its actual operations. We certainly held the head of the department, Professor Llewellyn, in great respect, and we knew without any doubt that he had complete and undisputed authority over the department. This was fully confirmed during the eighteen-month period that I served as a very junior member of the department; in fact, I have no recollection of there even being a departmental meeting during that period. Chemistry was not at all unusual; every department was under the authoritarian control of a head appointed for an indefinite term.

Students knew even less of the financial affairs of the college: we knew that essentially all funding was provided by the national government and we knew that all the colleges throughout the country were "underfunded," even though that clever and ambiguous word had not yet been created. We complained, although only very mildly and politely, about the level of fees we had to pay (in 1948, I paid fees of approximately $100), but all students were in fact very heavily subsidized through government funding and many such as I received bursary or scholarship support that often substantially exceeded fee levels. And, of course, there were no student representatives on either the council or the Professorial Board.

Postdoctoral Pleasures

Early in 1955, after completing all of my Ph.D. work, I received word that I had been awarded a fellowship for study overseas. With no prospects of an academic position in New Zealand in the foreseeable future, this was the opportunity of a lifetime, and an especially important one for me since I had married in 1954. After some consultation with Professor Llewellyn and others, I quickly decided that I wished to work with H.J. Emeleus at Cambridge, even though this would mean a complete change in research interests. Since I would be there for two years, the minimum time required to complete a Ph.D. degree, I decided to register for the degree, which also meant my becoming a member of a college, in my case, King's College. For two young and green New Zealanders, the sea voyage around Australia to Ceylon, through the Suez Canal to the Mediterranean, with calls at Naples, Marseilles, and Gibraltar, was an eye-opening and fascinating experience, as was shipboard life itself. But even more so were the two years that we spent at Cambridge. Although we were both students, my spouse being registered for the Part II tripos in botany, we were necessarily at the periphery of Cambridge life, since we belonged to but did not live in a college. In fact, as married students rather than single, we were quite unusual. Nevertheless, those two years enriched our lives enormously, not just through the Cambridge experience but also through the opportunities we had to travel in Britain and Europe, and to meet so many remarkable and fascinating individuals.

My experience of supervision as a graduate student at Cambridge was quite different from that in New Zealand. Professor Emeleus, a Norwegian by birth, had become a true English gentleman. He had been appointed to a personal chair of inorganic chemistry at Cambridge in 1947 and had developed a substantial program of research in fluorine chemistry. It was in this field that I worked, and although it required me to become quickly adept in a number of new techniques, such as glassblowing, I was able to produce worthwhile research results quite rapidly. It was not the Cambridge practice to spend long hours in the laboratory, and Emeleus did not encourage evening work, in part, I suspect, because of the dangerous nature of some of the work we did. If he did find us in the laboratory in the evening, he would politely remind us that we had wives at home and that we should pack it in and depart. He was an excellent supervisor, never too obtrusive or overly insistent, but visiting the laboratory at least once each day, usually with quiet comments about what I was doing or suggestions for other experiments that might be worthwhile. He took a genuine personal interest in each of his students, and would often interrupt our work with an invitation to go immediately to watch the cricket at Fenner's or go to the Lion for a beer. Supervision by an experienced and gifted scientist such as Emeleus was a new and very beneficial experience for me.

Between September 1955 and June 1957, my research progressed rapidly to the point that the results were sufficient for a Ph.D. thesis. In the summer of 1957, I therefore found myself again having to face a Ph.D. external examiner, and discovered that it was a very different experience from that in New Zealand. The Cambridge regulations stated that gowns were to be worn at examinations, and I asked Emeleus if this was necessary. He dismissed this with a laugh and told me to just be at his office at the appointed time. I was, and after a ten-minute wait, Emeleus emerged to apologize and explain that they were waiting for the tea to arrive! In a few minutes, I was in his office and was introduced to the examiner; we then spent at least thirty minutes having tea and discussing cricket before the examiner apologetically suggested that we proceed with the examination. There followed about a dozen questions, all direct and straightforward and based on the thesis, and at the end a more indirect but obviously important question. The moment I answered it satisfactorily, the examiner smiled and congratulated me; the whole affair was concluded in well under ninety minutes. In both formality and severity, the Cambridge Ph.D. oral examination was certainly at a lower level than my previous New Zealand experience, but it was much more enjoyable!

Interestingly, my experiences at Auckland and Cambridge were similar with respect to the physical facilities in which I worked. My first year at Cambridge was spent in the old laboratories on Pembroke Street while the magnificent new University Chemical Laboratory on Lensfield Road was under construction. The Pembroke Street laboratories were antiquated and inadequate, with undergraduate teaching laboratories being taken over one by one for research purposes. They were also unsafe and a health hazard because of the research being done. The wooden floorboards were worn with age and use, and liquid mercury frequently disappeared through their cracks. The small room off the main laboratory in which Emeleus's group used a fluorine electrolytic generator had only one exit despite the fact that the generator not infrequently discharged molten fluoride electrolyte onto the floor, and the few windows were etched and quite opaque due to the high concentration of hydrogen fluoride in the atmosphere. We were in fact working with some of the most violently reactive compounds known, and we were taking considerable risks with only minimal personal safety protection. It is interesting to read now of the major refurbishing in the last few years of what were in 1956 the resplendent new laboratories on Lensfield Road.

Beyond the laboratory, Cambridge has always been remarkable for the intellectual and cultural riches it offers to students. There was a great diversity of students, not only in Emeleus's research group but also at King's College. Advanced-standing students were expected to dine in hall at least once per week, and these occasions, despite the need to be appropriately garbed in a gown and the necessity of eating inedible beef and overboiled Brussels sprouts, provided some insight into college life and into the history, wealth, and idiosyncrasies of the various colleges, and led to friendship with other students. An advanced-standing student had little status at Cambridge, however; I and others in the same position were referred to as "Mr.," since only degrees from Cambridge, Oxford, or Trinity College Dublin were officially recognized. Such lowly status provided little opportunity for us to understand complex college politics, or the structure and operations of the School of Chemistry. As one of the largest such units in the United Kingdom, the latter had moved away from the traditional departmental structure of a single professor with a number of readers or senior lecturers, and lecturers. There were then chairs of Organic Chemistry, Inorganic Chemistry, Physical Chemistry, and Theoretical Chemistry, with Lord Todd, a Nobel Prize winner as head of the entire School of Chemistry. One had the impression that, within his own operation, each professor functioned in a fairly autonomous way, but often there was a strong hierarchical structure under each professor. Lord Todd, for example, had several lecturers who clearly functioned as his research lieutenants, each supervising the work of a number of Ph.D. or advanced-standing students from overseas but still reporting directly to Todd. Subsequent scientific publications were under Todd's name but, of course, included the names of the lieutenant and of the individual research workers. It was, indeed, the era of large research groups working under a scientific star.

Those two years at Cambridge changed our lives. Our perspectives were broadened to a very considerable degree, and totally new dimensions were added to our understanding of universities and university life. In mid-1957, we knew we must move on; my fellowship was ending, but the prospects for a suitable position in New Zealand, in a university or elsewhere, were extremely remote. To remain in the UK held little attraction for us, and while further postdoctoral experience in the United States was readily obtainable, there was a growing need for a permanent position and the opportunity to establish a career. My response to an advertisement in the journal *Nature* for assistant professors in chemistry at the University of British Columbia was based as much on concern over the limited number of possibilities open to me as it was on fragmentary knowledge of Vancouver and UBC. The matter was settled by return mail, with its offer of a position at UBC; since it seemed to be about halfway back to New Zealand, and since no other offers arrived, it was quickly accepted, and by August 1957 we were en route to Vancouver.

The Unifying Effect of the Commonwealth

I have given this detailed description of my personal and educational background not just because of an irrepressible urge to be autobiographical but for several other reasons. First, as suggested in the introduction to this volume, a description of my early background and qualifications may help provide some credibility to my later discussion of Canadian universities. At least it may give my critics some reason to pause before they launch their attack! More importantly, circumstances now are so very different from those in the 1950s that the reader may well need this description to maintain a reasonable perspective.

But there is a much more important reason. The Second World War was the watershed of the twentieth century, forever separating the first four decades, with their Victorian, Edwardian, and even colonial customs and outlooks, from the profoundly different postwar world. In the 1930s, the Western world especially suffered the privations and hardships of the Great Depression, a decade of unemployment and social and economic stagnation. During that decade, universities suffered badly and what limited resources were available had to be directed to other, more pressing priorities. In many countries, university staff was reduced, as were salaries. Physical facilities were neglected and expansion could rarely be contemplated. Only the commencement of the Second World War relieved these constraints to any degree, and then only to the extent that recruitment of university staff and the use of university facilities could enhance the war effort. This was the case across Canada, and it was only with the end of hostilities and the return of veterans seeking university qualifications that the neglected state of universities in many countries became all too apparent.

In Canada, as in New Zealand, the late 1940s saw universities struggling desperately to cope with the flood of veterans with woefully inadequate resources and facilities, and with small numbers of faculty. That they were so successful says much for the ingenuity and dedication of faculty and administrations. By the early 1950s, however, the global mood was one of optimism and expansion, and the intellectual and academic worlds were abuzz with the excitement of new thinking and new research. Whether it was in education in the schools and universities, or in health care in the hospitals and other institutions, expansion and growth became endemic. It was time for universities to plan for their long-term future. For universities, especially in Canada but also in the UK, Australia, the US, and many European countries, demographic projections showed unambiguously that explosive growth in university enrollments would occur throughout the 1960s and into the 1970s, and would require massive investment in new facilities and additional staff. Inadequate though they were, Canadian projections in 1956 predicted that over the next decade, faculty numbers would have to double, with the salary bill of the universities expected to triple or quadruple. The contrast between the first four decades of the twentieth century and those from 1950 onward was, for universities, especially marked.

The period of enormous growth and expansion of Canadian universities probably began about 1955, although much less visible politicking and planning had commenced much sooner. From 1955 onward, Canadian universities were completely transformed from what had usually been, with only one or two exceptions, small, struggling undergraduate institutions into large, diverse universities with wide ranges of undergraduate and professional programs and, in most instances, an impressive array of graduate programs. Existing institutions from Quebec westward rapidly doubled, tripled, or quadrupled their enrollments, and the campuses sprouted an impressive variety of new facilities, sometimes temporary but from at least 1960 onward usually permanent. Institutions such as the University of Toronto or UBC (whose origins had been as a distant, small daughter of McGill) were rapidly and completely transformed, and new institutions such as the University of Waterloo, York University, or Simon Fraser University were miraculously brought into being.

The essential ingredient for the creation of the needed new physical facilities for the universities was money, and for fifteen or so years from about 1960, provincial and federal governments were quite willing to provide it. Capital funding was increased substantially; between 1952 and 1957, federal grants to universities, calculated on a per-student basis, typically increased from $120 to $221. Hundreds of millions of dollars were generously provided, and the universities created some excellent facilities, many of them world-class. To find the necessary faculty so that the burgeoning undergraduate student body could receive quality instruction was another matter entirely, however. It was well recognized that prior to the 1950s, existing Canadian graduate programs had been small and few in number, producing only a very modest stream of Ph.D. graduates. These numbers were totally inadequate for the vast expansion of faculty that was required, and the only solution lay in recruitment from other countries. During the 1950s and 1960s, and to a lesser degree in the 1970s, Canadian universities recruited an enormous number of faculty members who were non-Canadian. The extent of this recruitment, the fact that Canada encouraged and benefited enormously from this "brain drain" from other countries, and the fact that without this recruitment Canadian universities would have been in continuing and serious crisis seem now to be scarcely remembered.

That Canada was able to succeed in such recruitment was not due to any government intervention or incentives, although certainly government funding was essential to the offering of substantially improved salaries. It was successful only because Canada was such an attractive country to which to migrate. At that time, the US appeared to be the only more attractive country, but for many of us who came here, Canada had nearly all of the advantages of the US and few of the disadvantages. Canada had limitless space and vast resources, and appeared to offer unlimited opportunities. Those who deplore the present brain drain from Canada to the US and the negative effects it may have on social and economic life in Canada might pause to consider the massive brain drain from many countries into Canada that has occurred over the last fifty years and still continues, and to contemplate the social and economic impact of those losses of talent on countries much less developed than Canada.

In the 1950s and 1960s, where did these recruited faculty members come from, and what were the numbers? Accurate answers are not easily found, particularly since most of those who settled in Canada at one point or another have became Canadian citizens. Specific examples can be given, however. I joined the Chemistry Department at UBC in August 1957. At that time, of 19 faculty members, 9 were Canadians, 1 was from the US, 7 from the UK, 1 from Australia, and 1 from New Zealand. Significantly, only two of those faculty members had been at UBC since before the Second World War; there was virtually a completely new faculty body. By 1964, of 36 faculty members, 15 were Canadians, 13 were from the UK, and there were 3 Americans, 2 Australians, 2 New Zealanders, and 1 European; only the same two had been at UBC before the war. These numbers were not atypical for other departments, perhaps especially in the sciences: for example, in 1964 the Physics Department had 37 faculty members, of whom 16 were Canadians while 13 were from the UK, 4 from the US, 2 from European universities, 2 from New Zealand, and 1 from South Africa. An examination of the UBC calendars of the early 1960s suggests that perhaps 30-40 percent of the faculty represented a brain drain from other nations, particularly from Commonwealth countries; it is also evident that the vast majority of Canadians had obtained their graduate degrees from British or American universities, and only a small number from European or Canadian universities.

That such large numbers of non-Canadians were recruited to UBC and other Canadian universities was not a reflection of the excellence of Canadian universities on a global scale. The attractiveness of Canada relative to other countries lay in the availability of jobs when none, or at least very few, were available elsewhere. And Canada was seen by all of us who migrated to it as a stable, rich, democratic country with a future of great promise, and yet very similar to our own native land whether that be the UK, Australia, New Zealand, or South Africa. Clearly these similarities arose from the common British heritage we shared, even as that heritage was being rapidly discarded. In addition, while we did not know a great deal about Canadian universities, their histories, traditions, and academic standards were seen as comparable to those from which we came. Canada was attractive and the transition could be smooth and comfortable.

It might have been expected that, with such large numbers of non-Canadians joining the faculty ranks of Canadian universities, the institutions would have become cosmopolitan, and socially and racially diverse. In fact, this did not occur because of the simple fact that we, the recruited faculty, were not particularly diverse. Yes, we came from different parts of the world, and, yes, the much smaller number recruited from European and to an even lesser extent American backgrounds brought quite different cultures, traditions, and expectations. But any thoughtful examination of my own biographical background, as sketched out earlier, must lead to the conclusion that most of it could have been equally well the background of an English-speaking Canadian, an Australian, a South African, or a new faculty member from the UK. Of course, there would be significant geographical differences, and we would have had different experiences of climate, topography, and recent history. But we all came from societies that were strongly British in tradition and social culture, and we generally tended to be of middle-class background.

Our families had all been greatly influenced, moreover, by prewar values and the Great Depression, and the school systems through which we had passed were really remarkably similar. Most of those recruited even from Britain came from middle-class families and had been educated at grammar schools or their equivalents. Canadian high schools of that era were more similar to the grammar schools of Britain, New Zealand, or Australia than they are now, with much greater discipline, tougher grading, and higher failure rates. The universities we had attended were all modelled essentially on the British university, although those in Canada reflected also some influence from the US. Whether that university had been in New Zealand, the UK, or Canada, during the war and immediately thereafter, it would probably have been quite small, struggling financially, and equipped with inadequate facilities and limited libraries. In the late 1940s, there was little difference between UBC, Leeds University, and Auckland University College. Very importantly, nearly all of us had attended university as commuting students, attending institutions that were largely 9 AM to 5 PM universities with little by way of a residential component. Moreover, after graduation from those "home" institutions, each of us had chosen to follow one of two academic paths: either we went, if we were Canadians, to a British or American university for graduate work, or we did graduate work at the home institution and then went abroad for postdoctoral experience, again usually to a university in the UK or the US.

Also very importantly, all of our doctoral or postdoctoral work, which influenced us greatly, was carried out at a major research institution. It was these institutions, more than our undergraduate universities, that shaped our opinions and concepts of a university. While in most cases we had been only at the periphery of a large residential institution, whether it was a Cambridge or a Berkeley, we had worked in a research-intensive atmosphere and we had been thoroughly indoctrinated with the research ethic. Across all these institutions, with perhaps the exception of those in the US, the degree patterns, the subject content, and the academic standards were surprisingly similar. This is not to argue that there were no differences – of course, there were! But in essence, our backgrounds and university experiences were remarkably alike. Hence, we simply did not bring to our new work in Canadian universities a strong diversity of backgrounds or a variety of opinions as to the essential nature and role of the university as an institution. Nor, in general, had we really experienced the life-changing impact of exposure to the true residential university.

The history of faculty recruitment in the US was very different. Not only were American universities historically older and better established prior to the Second World War than those in Canada, so that there was much greater continuity between the pre- and postwar eras in terms of both tradition and faculty culture, but throughout their history they had also recruited far more faculty members from a variety of European countries than from Britain or other Commonwealth nations. American universities have always been much more diverse in terms of the composition of the faculty body than those in Canada, a reflection not only of immigration and recruitment patterns but also of the sheer size and population diversity of the US. This was emphasized in the late 1960s and into the 1970s, when a considerable number of Americans were recruited to Canadian universities, especially in the social sciences. An extreme example is that of sociology departments across Canada: no such departments existed in 1960, and those created in the late 1960s and early 1970s were staffed entirely by Americans and a few expatriates from Britain. This later wave of "Americanization" led to political controversy arising from fears about its possible impact on the curriculum, but it did introduce much greater intellectual diversity into those fields than had resulted from recruitment of the 1950s and 1960s.[2]

The similarities in background described here made it quite easy for two New Zealanders to adjust to UBC. Allowing for Canadian culture and customs, UBC seemed much the same as our home universities, and new recruits such as I saw others who had also arrived recently from the UK or Australia as kin; we talked the same language and had much in common, whether it was chemistry or cricket. This was not so with the few Americans recruited, with whom there were more obvious educational and cultural differences. By and large, however, we all settled into a new department quickly and smoothly; we accepted that our views of universities were much the same and did not require debate. We all implicitly understood that we were responsible for training future chemists, for conducting vigorous and continuing research programs, and for recruiting as many graduate students as possible. No one called us to a discussion of the role of science in a liberal education, or of our responsibility to the institution as distinct from the department. The great similarities in our previous experiences made assimilation smooth and imperceptible.

A further point is perhaps equally important. As some of the figures presented above show, by the late 1950s, at UBC and probably most Canadian universities, recently recruited faculty constituted almost the entire faculty body. Very few faculty members remained who had served and struggled in those institutions in the 1930s and during the war years. There was in many cases very little continuity, so that those of us who made up the faculty by 1960 shaped our department and the university in accordance with our own opinions and with little encumbrance from the history and limiting traditions of the prewar era. The shape and nature of Canadian universities today was to a considerable degree determined by the generation of faculty members who were recruited through the 1955-65 period, largely free of history, biases, and consequences from the past. And, of course, this major influence was only strengthened by the fact that the considerable recruitment created a demographic bulge in the faculty body that has slowed more recent appointments, especially as finances have become more restricted. It is only now, at the beginning of a new millennium, that large numbers of retirements are enabling a demographic change in faculty composition.

A final comment concerns the views and attitudes of those of us who constituted that large recruitment. As already indicated, we had no direct understanding of the universities of the 1920s or 1930s, and by the late 1950s there were few in our midst to remind us. We did, however, have vivid memories of the Second World War and of the significance of the tremendous scientific advances that it produced. We knew that scientific research, whether it be British such as the development of radar, or German such as rocket science, or American such as the Manhattan Project leading to the atomic bomb, had been absolutely central to the outcome of the war. In the immediate postwar years, we could also see the benefits of this avalanche of scientific discoveries in peacetime, as their commercialization led to the marketing of new products and robust economic development. And at a personal level, these impressions had been further strengthened by our experiences in major research-oriented universities, perhaps as Canadians at Harvard, Berkeley, or Illinois, or as New Zealanders at Cambridge or University College London. We came as eager, young faculty members, largely from Commonwealth backgrounds and similar educational experiences; we came from the major research institutions of the UK or the US, convinced that fundamental research was basic to the role of the university in the postwar period. With little to guide us in terms of the earlier history of Canadian institutions, we shaped the growth of Canadian universities during the critical period from 1955 to 1975.

2
The UBC Experience

Arrival at the University of British Columbia gave us our first taste of Canadian academic life and of the North American lifestyle. Both have given us much for which to be eternally grateful, although in 1957 I was still a green, young faculty member who knew nothing of the inner workings of a Canadian university, and little of the machinations involved in academic politics. Eight years at UBC were to remedy that very effectively.

Our first impression of UBC was of the beauty and natural magnificence of the campus located at the end of Point Grey, looking across the Strait of Georgia to the snow-capped coastal mountains and, further to the west, at a greater distance, the mountains of Vancouver Island. Clearly, here was the opportunity, with careful planning and a concern for architectural excellence, to develop one of the world's most beautiful university campuses, but even then it was apparent that this opportunity was being lost.

The university was not that large, with an enrollment in 1957-58 of approximately 9,000, and because of the Depression and the Second World War, the number of permanent buildings on the site was not great. They included the Buchanan Building, Wesbrook Building, Biology and Physics buildings, Engineering, the Library, the Student Union Building, and, of course, the Chemistry Building. In addition, a large number of Second World War prefabricated army huts provided space for an assortment of academic and administrative units, as well as faculty and student housing. Even the central administration was located in a somewhat more substantial but nevertheless prefabricated "temporary" building. While these ex-army huts played an absolutely essential role well into the 1960s, their rate of demolition and replacement by permanent buildings was disappointingly slow. A few of these old prefabs, gracefully changed by renovations, probably remain to this day. They speak eloquently of the all-too-common belief in many Canadian universities that all existing physical space must be retained, that there will always be an insatiable demand for more space, and that growth, especially in terms of the erection of new buildings, is an end in itself. Both my eight years there and numerous visits since then suggest that the past fifty years have entrenched these views especially strongly at UBC.

Over that period, the campus has grown enormously, and some architecturally significant buildings have been erected. Nevertheless, there is an impression of an unplanned and, in places, crowded campus, giving the sense that the natural beauty of the site has not been well matched by orderly, planned development of very high quality. In too many locations, the siting of buildings has clearly been hasty, and the architecture and construction of only mediocre quality.

In 1957 the Chemistry Department was housed in what had been the Science Building, the first permanent building to be erected at the Point Grey campus when the university moved there from central Vancouver in the 1920s. So, on the whole, we were well housed in a solid, permanent building, although the fittings and services provided in a 1920s building often did not meet the demands of the 1950s. Many rooms had to be substantially altered and upgraded to accommodate new research uses, and rapid expansion of the department quickly put pressure on available space. In 1957 the conversion of a washroom to a research laboratory led to newspaper publicity, with photographs, which lent support to requests for a new building. The department itself was not overly large; in 1955 it had only sixteen faculty members, but in the next few years growth was very rapid. There were three additions in 1956, and I was one of six new faculty members to join the department in 1957; many more appointments were made in the next years.

In 1957 the university was under the leadership of Norman A.M. MacKenzie, who had been recruited as president in 1944.[3] A graduate of Dalhousie, he had served with distinction in the First World War before returning to Dalhousie to complete a law degree and going on to Harvard for his Master of Law degree. After fourteen years at the University of Toronto, he had served as president of the University of New Brunswick for four years, until 1944. W.N. Chant was dean of the combined Faculty of Arts and Science, which had about two dozen departments, and within that faculty were several forceful and dominant individuals who greatly influenced the university over several decades.

Notable among them was Gordon Shrum, a remarkable person who appeared to function for many years as MacKenzie's right-hand man. In 1957 Shrum was head of the Physics Department, dean of graduate studies, president of the British Columbia Research Council, and chair of the University Housing Committee, and he probably had other official tasks as well. In today's Canadian university, it is inconceivable that one person should hold more than one of these positions! At the end of the war, it was very largely Shrum who had the audacity to commandeer army huts from abandoned military camps across BC, often obtaining official permission post facto, thus enabling the university to cope with the influx of returning veterans and other new students. Shrum was almost Mr. UBC, and certainly Norman MacKenzie's principal lieutenant. Ian McTaggart-Cowan, head of the Zoology Department, was a formidable and respected figure on campus, and later became dean of graduate studies. The head of the Chemistry Department, Charles McDowell, became powerful and influential in the late 1950s, and continued to be a major force on campus until the end of the 1970s. Other strong leaders included people such as historian F.H. Soward, Rocke Robertson of Medicine, J.J. Deutsch in Economics, C.E. Dolman in Bacteriology, George Curtis of the new Law School, and Earl McPhee in Business.

The decades of the 1950s and 1960s saw phenomenal growth, during which UBC struggled to keep up with the demands of rapidly expanding enrollment, burgeoning research initiatives, and the introduction of numerous new graduate programs. Such a time encourages strong academic leaders and forceful personalities to compete for growth opportunities and new resources, often with little restraint from preoccupied institutional authorities. Indeed, the pressures of the time left little opportunity for long-term institutional planning, and the spoils of growth went to the bold and the aggressive. Many strong deans and department heads operated very effectively in this way as "robber barons," and were able to achieve much for their own units. This remains evident, in my opinion, in the somewhat unplanned appearance of the campus, in the relatively low sense of institutional coherence, and in the solidity and isolation of individual departments, which in turn inhibited the development of interdisciplinary research and graduate programs.

The Chemistry Department languished after the war until the mid-1950s; in fact, it deteriorated to the point that the National Research Council (NRC) quietly intimated to the university that there would be few if any research grants coming to it unless the department was strengthened. This led to the appointment of McDowell as head in 1955. McDowell, a graduate of Queen's University, Belfast, had been teaching at Liverpool University; he had also spent some time at the National Research Council laboratories in Ottawa and was well connected there. He went to UBC with a clear mandate and the intense determination to create a world-class department, and to do so as quickly as possible. Combining ambition with ability and aggression, he was most capable and very tough. He appointed 3 new faculty members in 1956, and, as already mentioned, I was one of 6 additional faculty members appointed in 1957. In 1958 there were 6 more new faculty members, and in 1959 another 4. Indeed, by 1965, when I left UBC, the Chemistry Department had grown to a total of about 45 faculty members. Similarly rapid growth occurred in the Zoology, English, and, to a lesser degree, Physics and many other departments. Such growth has not been seen since and may not be seen again in any Canadian universities. Today's young faculty members and recent Ph.D. graduates, all of whom have to search diligently and often frustratingly for secure academic employment, must view those times with amazement and even incomprehension.

Growth was also very evident in the UBC campus in terms of construction of physical facilities, and again the Chemistry Department provides a useful example. In 1957 the department was the major occupant of the old Science Building, along with Chemical Engineering. Within a year, Chemical Engineering had vacated its space to Chemistry, and plans were being developed for an addition to the building for teaching laboratories. No sooner was it completed and occupied than plans were under way for a new research wing at the other end of the old building. Its construction proceeded rapidly, and it was in use by 1962. When I left UBC in mid-1965, a third new wing was under construction, to be used for more teaching laboratories and some specialized facilities. Three building additions in eight years – it is true that only limited additions for Chemistry were erected in the subsequent thirty years, but that exceptional expansion during 1957-67, which continued at a declining rate into the 1970s, was astonishing in retrospect. Not surprisingly, those buildings today have an appearance of mere functionality, and only the original Science Building, built in 1923, has any style or architectural significance.

It was certainly not that the Social Credit government of the day was sympathetic towards the university, nor was money from any source obtained easily. Among faculty members, there was unconfirmed gossip about President MacKenzie having appointments with Premier W.A.C. Bennett in Victoria to discuss the university's budget and capital needs. The premier, so it was related, often did not keep such appointments, and the frustrated president vainly sat outside his office most of the day, eventually returning to UBC empty-handed, never having met with the premier. In fact, the university was not held in high regard by the conservative Social Credit government, which was, however, a government that understood the political value of building roads and erecting public buildings. For this reason, therefore, capital expansion still occurred even though many Social Credit supporters looked on the university as a den of radicals and communists.

The Assistant Professor's Life

In the 1950s, the development of an academic career by a new faculty member was left very much to the individual. On arrival in the Chemistry Department, we were each told of the course we would teach in September. If the course was taught in a number of sections, as were the first-year chemistry courses, one worked with colleagues in deciding on course content and lecture sequence. If one taught third- or fourth-year courses, as I did, the organization of the curriculum, the type of examination, and the academic standard to be achieved were left entirely to the one lecturer.

Remembering that in September 1957, 25 percent of the Chemistry faculty had never before taught in a Canadian university, that our ability to lecture undergraduates had never been assessed, and that we had received no orientation to the Canadian educational system and were given no indication of the expected academic standards, it is surprising, perhaps remarkable, that there were so few problems. Because of our very similar backgrounds, we did fit together as a department easily and well, yet I recall few, if any, departmental discussions about the overall design of the chemistry curriculum as an educational experience. Certainly, we discussed content, or more specifically how we could increase the content as new fields opened up: there was never any doubt that we were training future chemists who would be mirror images of ourselves.

Little interest was taken in students who were not pursuing the Honours Chemistry program; the teaching of chemistry to engineering students, for example, was still done conscientiously but was seen as a necessary chore. There was no formal evaluation of our teaching skills, nor were there programs available anywhere in the university to improve those skills. We were each required to give in our first year a research seminar, but while this was viewed critically by McDowell and others in the department as a source of evidence of future research potential, the question of whether it demonstrated our ability to lecture well to undergraduate students did not seem very relevant. At the end of each teaching year, there was usually a departmental meeting to review all marks for the graduating honours students, and any marks that seemed particularly out of line in comparison with those in other courses might receive some adjustment, but generally the failure rate, the median mark in a large-enrollment course, and the overall mark distribution were left entirely to the individual faculty member, even where this might lead to some unfairness to students.

With the postwar perception of the value of scientific research, and with the Sputnik era of the Cold War, remarkably rapid growth occurred in the research activities and funding of faculty members in science departments at most North American universities. The Chemistry Department at UBC was no exception, as my own case showed. In April 1958, I received an NRC grant of $2,500 – a princely sum indeed! This rapidly paled into insignificance compared with funding from US agencies. To my astonishment, I quickly found that the US Office of Naval Research, the US Air Force, and the US Army Research Office all wished to fund my research, and I quickly had funds available totalling $50,000 or more annually. While this was due to the US military's interest in fluorine chemistry in the context of the development of new potential rocket fuels for both civilian and military use, others at UBC working in very different fields were equally or more fortunate. Total research funding in the department grew very rapidly, and despite continuing complaints about the inadequacies of Canadian support for research, the UBC Chemistry Department was, by the mid-1960s, equal to the best in Canada in terms of research activity and external funding. Moreover, McDowell fought remarkably successfully to obtain large equipment grants, and in only a few years we had all the essential major instrumentation for an internationally respectable chemistry department. Over the same period, there was enormous growth in the number of scientific publications from the department, a fact that caused much pride in us all, particularly McDowell.

There were, however, negative aspects to life in the Chemistry Department at UBC. McDowell's view of the academic discipline of chemistry placed major importance on physical chemistry, and the majority of faculty members were recruited into that field. Organic chemistry was, in his view, next in importance, with my own field of inorganic chemistry a fairly distant third. Due to the then common perception that the field had stagnated, analytical chemistry was not taught at all. This fundamentally wrong view of analytical chemistry, which many chemists shared, led to considerable criticism and a serious worldwide shortage of analytical chemists in the 1970s, when environmental issues came to the fore. McDowell's personal views were also reflected in his efforts to recruit all of the best incoming graduate students into physical chemistry research, and to allow only limited scope for inorganic chemistry (and none for analytical chemistry!) within the undergraduate curriculum. That he could, and did, impose his views on what rapidly became a very large but somewhat unbalanced department, and was able to do so without substantial discussion and with little outward dissension, reflected his firm interpretation of his position as head of the department.

His attitude on financial matters was identical. At no time while I was at UBC did I have any knowledge of the departmental budget. This was information that McDowell retained exclusively for himself, and the decisions on its distribution were his alone. Since I was responsible for the major inorganic chemistry laboratory course, I was asked each year to provide a list of chemicals and apparatus that would be required for the following year, and while in one or two instances some reductions were requested, in general we obtained what was asked for but had no means of knowing whether twice as much could have been sought just as successfully! This handling of the departmental budget was fully consistent with practice at UBC: it was the rare department head who shared any budgetary information with faculty members, and we knew even less of the university budget.

At another level, those of us in the Chemistry Department worked in splendid isolation from our faculty colleagues in other departments. It was made quite clear to us by McDowell, especially those of us who were junior faculty members, that we should not waste our time on university activities outside the department. Participating in the work of university or faculty committees was, in his view, quite unnecessary if not useless, since our role was to do research and teach. In retrospect, there was some validity in his view, at least as far as the department was concerned, but it had the effect of reducing interest in, and loyalty to, the well-being of the institution as a whole. We were indoctrinated in the view that the department was more important than the university itself. In practice, virtually no one went against McDowell's vigorously expressed views, and our participation in university-level activities was low; this made those of us in Chemistry even more isolated than other colleagues. Even in the Faculty Club at lunchtime, the chemists usually tended to sit together, with little conversation with others.

It will be clear by now that Charles McDowell interpreted very firmly his position as head of the department. He was autocratic and tended to hold very firmly fixed ideas, to the extent that it was often difficult to discuss an issue rationally with him. He believed that, as head, he had and would retain indefinitely full and complete control over the department. This became abundantly clear to me and others during my first year at UBC. In the fall of 1957, my fellow chemists and I had, as was the custom, submitted our applications for individual research grants to the National Research Council. We expected to be formally notified of awards in February 1958, but February came and went without such notification. This was even more surprising when we realized that colleagues in other science departments at UBC had received notification of their awards at the customary time. To the complete astonishment of all Chemistry faculty members, we then received notice, not from the NRC but from McDowell, advising us that the NRC had decided to give a block grant to the department, to be administered by McDowell, rather than individual grants. From the NRC's viewpoint, this was rationalized as a way to reduce NRC bureaucracy and paperwork. From the viewpoint of the individual faculty member, given the Canadian and North American practice of awarding individual grants, as distinct from the British practice of awarding a single block grant to the department head, it was totally and completely unacceptable. Quite apart from the principle of research independence for the individual, we knew that we would be entirely subject to McDowell's opinions and biases in the allocation of those funds.

A departmental revolution quickly began, with attempts, at first unproductive, to discuss the issue with McDowell, and then deputations to the dean of science, President MacKenzie, and the NRC. All of us assumed that McDowell must have encouraged the NRC to take this step, presumably arguing that it would be in the best interests of the department; why the NRC would make such an abrupt policy change, unannounced and for one department only, was and still remains a mystery. Characteristically, at the height of the controversy, McDowell attempted to gather support by calling each new junior faculty member one at a time, including me, into his office and saying: "Well, Howard, you are quite new here and I am sure that you don't really understand all of the aspects of this matter. Surely you don't really have any difficulties with the idea of my managing a block grant for the department?"

Despite such coercive pressures, virtually the entire department stood firm and the NRC eventually backed down, promising never to award such a departmental block grant again. However, this incident, the playing out of which occupied several weeks, caused enormous tension within the department and showed clearly how McDowell interpreted his position as department head. Even for those days, it was a rather extreme interpretation, but if such a complete change in NRC policy had been successfully brought about, many believed that other heads at UBC and elsewhere would have quickly followed suit.

To the chemistry faculty in those years, with few exceptions, the governance of the university was a relative mystery. None of us knew anything of the activities of the Board of Governors other than reports we might read in the press or in the university newspaper. Nor was there any inclination to delve into this mystery – we were generally uninterested, other than in decisions of the board about salary levels! It was a different matter with regard to the Senate, the senior academic body. We recognized that new academic programs and modifications to existing ones required Senate approval prior to implementation, making Senate decisions very relevant to us. For most chemistry faculty members, however, participation in university governance translated into nothing more than attendance at periodic meetings of the Faculty of Arts and Science and, much more importantly, at departmental meetings. In 1957 pressures for the breakup of the historic Faculty of Arts and Science were already evident. The actual separation into distinct faculties of Arts and of Science occurred several years later, after a period of often acrimonious debate between the two sides. In the late 1960s, I was fascinated to see the same course of events, and to hear the same arguments, as the single Faculty of Arts and Science at the University of Western Ontario split into three separate faculties of Arts, Social Sciences, and Science. Remarkably, the same process, with the same arguments pro and con, occurred while I was president of Dalhousie, leading in this case to the formation of a Faculty of Arts and Social Sciences and a Faculty of Science.

Several factors lie behind these organizational changes that have occurred in so many Canadian universities. Rapid growth in terms of both student and faculty numbers, combined with the need in any organization to have administrative units of a manageable size, certainly provided some valid justification. Some of the other arguments that were often advanced were far more self-seeking, however. Among the scientists, in an age when science and technology are of increasing importance, there was, and remains, the strong feeling that separation and the creation of a separate Faculty of Science would be beneficial in terms of gaining a larger share of the university's resources. And, of course, the single-minded emphasis in science departments on research and graduate studies has increasingly given scientists a different perspective on academia than their colleagues in the arts. In addition, very fundamental pressures arising from the ever-increasing need for greater research specialization have led worldwide to an unhealthy degree of isolation between the science disciplines themselves. More recently, there has been some coming together again as the need for interdisciplinary research has gained better recognition.

Nevertheless, from all three debates on faculty separation that I have listened to and participated in, it appears to me that in every case it was the undergraduate student who was likely to be shortchanged, and that any resulting benefits would accrue largely to the faculty. Such organizational divisions make it much more difficult to provide the broadly based but rigorous undergraduate education that is so badly needed at present, and was just as badly needed in the 1960s. Separate faculties decrease substantially the level of academic dialogue between the "two cultures," and this is inevitably reflected in the education and learning experiences of undergraduates. The view held strongly by many that science and engineering graduates tend to lack literacy and communication skills stems directly from the highly technical and all-too-often content-driven training they usually receive. And this has been encouraged and emphasized by the creation and isolation of separate faculties of science over the last forty years. In the late 1950s and early 1960s, however, there was little doubt in our minds that a separate Faculty of Science at UBC would be a good thing, and so it happened. I do not think, however, that there is any evidence at all to show that science departments subsequently gained a greater share of the university's resource pie! With a separate faculty, we certainly were able to go about our own business without having to take into account the views of others, and at UBC and Western there was a clear feeling of being much closer, in terms of governance matters, to the dean. He was, of course, a scientist and it was just assumed that he was much more understanding and sympathetic to the scientists' cause.

But where, at that time, did the real power within the university lie? Was President MacKenzie in full control of the university and able to make, if necessary, unilateral decisions? Was the group of faculty deans powerful enough to effectively determine the president's decisions? And to keep the departments they were responsible for under control? The answer to these questions is largely, although not entirely, "yes." For the last point relating to the individual departments, the answer is unambiguously "yes." This exception is important, since at that time UBC had a very powerful group of department heads who genuinely functioned as heads, without term, and not as chairs of departments for three- or perhaps five-year terms, as is the practice today. They did indeed manage their departments as they saw fit, with a degree of consultation within the department, or lack of it, that they alone determined. Their decisions, often taken unilaterally, were based on their personal judgments of what was in the best interests of each department. A group of such strong department heads could, and in some cases did, effectively control the dean, and could have an equally substantial influence on presidential decisions.

Department Head or Chair?

The fact that departments had heads without term, rather than chairs with term as in the United States, was very much a carryover from British universities, in which traditionally each department had a single professor who acted as head and had complete and absolute control of the department and its resources. Over the past forty years, however, the trend in Canada has been to abolish the position of department head, except in a few professional faculties such as Medicine, and to replace them with chairs for a set term, often of three years. In British and New Zealand universities, the trend has been towards the establishment of several professorial positions in each department, with the administrative management of the department rotating perhaps every two or three years among the professors. In the 1950s and early 1960s at UBC, there were the first obvious signs of the postwar movement towards greater faculty involvement in university governance, and this was initially directed at the role and responsibilities of the department head.

Three or four years after my arrival at UBC, the Faculty Association, which was becoming increasingly active and militant, produced a major report recommending sweeping changes to the internal governance of the university. One of the key proposals was that department heads in the Faculty of Arts and Science should all voluntarily resign and be replaced with elected chairs with terms not to exceed five years. The arguments on which this was based included the fact that, as had been evident in many British universities, a department head could be an insufferable dictator, adversely affecting the careers of any subordinates he disliked. Conversely, he could also with age decline into senility yet still remain in the position, with dire consequences for the department. In contrast, so the argument went at UBC, American universities had chairs with defined terms who were selected democratically and who operated consultatively. All of the British disadvantages were thus avoided. What was not mentioned in the Faculty Association report was that in many American universities, a department chair was often appointed and not elected, and often had the same powers as a British or Canadian head. Moreover, a chair in the US in many cases was appointed without term, or to a term of not less than five years. In fact, the differences between a head and a chair were greatly exaggerated, and the disadvantages of a chair with a short term of office were ignored.

As it happened, the report elicited a vigorous reaction but was largely rejected by those in authority. In Chemistry we were especially interested to know of Charles McDowell's opinion, since he was the quintessential department head. A week or so after the report was released, he called a departmental meeting at which we guessed there would be some comment on the report. Not surprisingly, nearly every faculty member was present, and after transacting other items of business, McDowell faced us all and said: "I expect you will all have read the Faculty Association report that recommends that all Heads in the Faculty of Arts and Science should resign and be replaced by elected Chairs. I want you to know that this has been discussed by all of the Department Heads in the Faculty and has been rejected by a vote of 23 to 1. If any of you have the idea that I am going to resign, forget it!" That ended the meeting and he left the room, but we never did discover who was the brave, lonely soul who voted against the other twenty-three determined department heads.

Although this particular governance change did not occur then at UBC, it has taken place at virtually all Canadian universities since, and is at the heart of many current difficulties in university governance. In my opinion, the change that has occurred from head to chair has been based on judgments about two issues that have become inappropriately confused. The first issue is that regarding the length of appointment of the head or chair; the second is that of the responsibilities to be exercised by the head or chair.

There is much to be said for appointment for a set period of time, especially when it is coupled with an effective performance review process at the end of that period to determine whether reappointment is or is not desirable. Appointment for a defined term avoids essentially all of the problems that can otherwise arise; any undue dictatorial tendency, any apparent slide into neglect or semi-senility, indeed, any serious lack of leadership or administrative ability can in most cases be borne for the remaining two or three years of a five-year term. But while term appointments are therefore entirely appropriate, the length of the term needs much more thought; indeed, it is on this point that I think Canadian universities have gone wrong.

A widespread practice across Canada today is to appoint chairs for only three-year terms. This has occurred with the acceptance of the view that a chair is to be seen as just one among academic equals, with the responsibility to administer the department according to the consensus view of the department. While there can be no objection to such a view, it has led to at least two undesirable consequences. First, it causes too many faculty members to view the task of the chair as an undesirable, short-term position to be avoided as long as possible; being chair for just three years entails constant effort to obtain and maintain departmental consensus on all major issues if significant changes are to occur, often with little if any thanks. The remaining responsibilities are largely administrative; there seems little opportunity for creativity and initiative, and for many faculty members, being chair for three years is little better than acting as departmental secretary. Moreover, being chair reduces the time available for the scholarship and research on which one's career ultimately depends. Why, then, would any ambitious academic be willing to serve as department chair? Second, and very importantly, such short-term appointments often remove much of the continuity in the administration of the department. This can cause a number of problems, perhaps the most important of which has to do with personnel management or, in today's terms, human resource management.

Neither term is used or accepted by academics; they are used in Canadian universities but only in relation to the support staff, the secretaries, technicians, and so on. Academics will argue that such a concept may well be appropriate in the world of business but has absolutely no relevance to the faculty within a university, who constitute a self-governing professional body, or so it is claimed. Yet this completely overlooks the fact that in all but the very smallest departments, there is at least one secretary, and large departments not uncommonly have twenty or more support staff. Every one of these needs some degree of supervision, as well as periodic performance review and perhaps career counselling. But the central personnel office at any Canadian university is quite incapable of providing these for the large numbers of staff involved, and they must come primarily from the department chair. Given the current views that academics hold regarding the responsibilities of department chairs, no one should be surprised at the almost total absence of such supervision. The regrettable fact is that universities do almost nothing for the career development of their staff. The result is that there is essentially no career mobility within the institution except on the basis of individual initiative, and in most universities performance reviews of staff either do not take place or are patchy and perfunctory. The prime cause is the entrenched view that chairs have no role in human resource management – indeed, are not seen as part of management at all. Nor has the institution insisted on appropriate training for chairs, either in personnel management or in any other area, although some Canadian universities do offer voluntary courses. It can, of course, be argued that in many departments, especially in the arts and social sciences, it is actually the departmental secretary who manages the department and provides continuity. This is quite true, but the fact should then be openly acknowledged, allowing administrative staff with appropriate management skills to be given a title such as department manager, at an appropriate salary level. The chair's role should then be confined to academic issues only.

Even more important is the need for better mechanisms to deal with personnel matters affecting the faculty. At present, such matters are dealt with only under extreme circumstances. Yet their seriousness and the impact they can have on students, either directly or through their effect on the atmosphere and morale of any department, cannot be denied. Problems may arise because a faculty member has become stale, has lost enthusiasm for the subject, is not attending to grading responsibilities or meeting with students, is demoralized by family or marriage problems, or, in the extreme, is quite unable to meet reasonable professional standards of performance. In other cases, there are such severe personality clashes between two or more faculty members that the work of the entire department is disrupted. Considering just the case of a faculty member not performing at the appropriate level, it is virtually certain that, in every university in Canada, it would be possible to identify, with widespread agreement, a small handful of such faculty, who at the very least require thoughtful counselling and at the worst should be considered for termination. The contributions they make professionally and intellectually to their departments are recognized to be well below an acceptable standard. The taxpaying public, and more importantly the students who suffer, wonder why no action seems to be taken, and suspect that the existence of tenure may be the reason. The issue is much more complex, and the first point that needs to be understood is that there is no requirement for the chair of the department to do anything at all, and little by way of pressure that the dean can apply to force a chair to act.

There are, of course, other factors as well, and one of them stems from current societal concerns about due process and natural justice. In the university setting, especially where unionization of faculty has occurred, these concerns as they apply to the dismissal issue have led to such complicated, time-consuming, legalistic processes involving hearings, often more than one appeal process, and usually arbitration by external arbitrators that only the bravest is prepared to launch into them. And to do so requires there to be a well-documented case of inadequate performance, with written evidence of periodic reviews and previous warnings of inadequacies to the individual concerned. Moreover, many such cases have failed purely on procedural grounds because it has been demonstrated that the legalistic process has been imperfectly applied.

Since chairs and sometimes deans lack understanding of personnel issues and have no legal training, this should not be surprising. In the business community, reasonably complete personnel files usually exist and the procedures required for dismissal tend to be much better known, but even so dismissal for cause is not a simple or easy option, as the substantial number of legal cases for wrongful dismissal confirms. In universities, it is extremely difficult at present to develop systematically detailed personnel files of faculty members. A chair who is in office for only three years and who does not consider the responsibilities of the office to include management has no incentive to maintain good faculty files; nor does the university require it. In addition, because chair replaces chair every three years, there is no continuity whatsoever. Under these conditions, it is unrealistic to expect personnel files to be consistently developed and maintained at the departmental level. Many universities, especially where there is a faculty union, require that such personnel files be maintained in the dean's office for each faculty member. Given the large size of most faculties, however, the dean's role can only be passive, involving little more than the filing of material sent to that office by the faculty member or the chair. There is usually no requirement for the chair to comment on performance, or even to pass on to the dean the complaints of students. A group of students dissatisfied with the quality of a course or with inappropriate grading has to be persistent and courageous to confront first the lecturer, and then the department chair, and then the dean to ensure that their complaint has been heard and recorded in the appropriate personnel file. In far too many cases, such legitimate concerns never get outside the department and are thus often not recorded.

Another, more recent factor now causes still greater difficulty. I refer to the issue of faculty unionization, which has now gained hold in many Canadian universities. Initially, faculty unions were not willingly admitted to the university scene, and a significant proportion of faculty still oppose them. The creation of faculty unions was strenuously resisted and led to several legal challenges. The judgments on those cases determined that university faculty members are indeed covered by provincial labour relations legislation, that faculty members are not "management," and that bargaining groups are to include all faculty and department chairs but not deans or more senior administrators. This has had a profoundly diminishing effect on the role of the chair and has contributed greatly to the usually confrontational relationship between the bargaining group and the administration. It certainly causes chairs to be extremely reluctant to become involved in any issue that might be regarded as personnel management.

The change from head without term to chair for a defined, often three-year term that has taken place in Canadian universities over the last forty years has solved some problems but probably created even greater ones. It has certainly given greater power to the collectivity of faculty members in relation to decision making at the departmental level, and, for the reasons mentioned above, it has also increased the degree of protection and security provided to faculty members. Whether or not this was needed, or can in general be justified, is another matter entirely; it certainly cannot be justified in the extent to which it has made universities less accountable for inadequate performance. On the other hand, these changes took place with the agreement of boards of governors.

The second aspect of the position of chair that needs urgent clarification is that of the responsibilities of the position or the job description. Some universities have general statements that apply across the entire institution, but this does not recognize that the task of chair of the Philosophy Department is totally different from that of chair of the Department of Medicine or the Department of Civil Engineering. The chair of Philosophy has a group of faculty and perhaps several secretaries to "manage," with the faculty regarding the chair as just the person who convenes the department meeting. The chair of Civil Engineering has not only a group of faculty members but also a number of secretaries and technicians to "manage," and he or she may also be responsible for major technical facilities and laboratories on which the teaching and research of the faculty depends; the management component is that much greater. The chair of Medicine may have all of the responsibilities of his or her colleague in Civil Engineering, together with significant responsibilities for clinical teaching in a major hospital affiliated with the university.

The position of department chair varies very widely across today's complex university. What is needed, then, is a detailed statement of the specific responsibilities for each such position, to be prepared by the dean in consultation with the incumbent chair, and that is subject to careful study and approval by the institution's board. However, the fact that under all faculty collective agreements the position of chair is included in the bargaining unit would make such action almost impossible. It would require negotiating a change to the collective agreement, the price for which would be another concession. Again, this is a situation for which the universities have only themselves to blame.

The Teaching-versus-Research Issue

Another major theme is brought to mind by my years at UBC – that of the appropriate balance between research and teaching, an issue that has been increasingly debated over the last two or three decades.

A useful starting point is to emphasize the realities of the Canadian university scene in the 1950s and 1960s. At the end of the Second World War, probably only McGill University and the University of Toronto were known outside Canada for research accomplishments, and even they did not rank highly among the world's universities. Other universities were little more than undergraduate teaching institutions, and Canada's research effort, such as it was, was conducted at the National Research Council and in other government laboratories. However, the war itself had produced a scientific revolution; atomic physics came into its own, many fields of science, including my own of inorganic chemistry, were completely revitalized, and many new fields such as computer science were created. Coming into the 1950s, therefore, there was a high degree of intellectual fervour and excitement, as well as the need to expand the universities, especially at the graduate level. The result at UBC and elsewhere in Canada was a drive to establish new, viable research groups, and to develop a wide range of new graduate programs. Such an emphasis was entirely appropriate for the time; if it had not occurred then, Canada would not be well placed technologically and scientifically today.

I have to concede that this heavy emphasis on research probably did get out of hand by about 1970, and continues to have some serious consequences for the universities that will be referred to later. At that time, however, certainly at UBC, there was no belief or recognition that research was being developed at the expense of teaching. A great deal of effort was devoted to updating the curriculum. Indeed, we seemed to be in a constant state of change with regard to the content of the undergraduate program, and on the whole, much attention was given to the preparation and delivery of lectures. These were viewed by all of us as an important part of our responsibilities, and I cannot recall any sign that undergraduates were shortchanged.

On the other hand, however, there were very strong pressures to publish; every faculty member in the Chemistry Department knew that he or she was expected to produce at least two or three papers every year. Here, in my opinion, is the crux of the issue: since the Second World War, there has been in all Canadian universities a constant pressure to publish that has not been matched by clearly stated expectations of teaching performance. It has been sufficient for faculty members to give the required lectures and to complete the accompanying responsibilities, such as marking examination papers, with little if any assessment of their teaching performance, but with much more clearly and positively stated expectations of their research performance. There is also, of course, the well-accepted fact that it is somewhat easier to evaluate the content of research publications than it is to identify excellent teaching, but this is getting into a topic that I wish to discuss more fully in a later chapter. Suffice it to say that during my time at UBC, there was certainly great emphasis on research and research capabilities, but I do not think that it was at the expense of undergraduate education. Indeed, I suspect that the chemistry curriculum then had greater relevance and excitement than previously, precisely because of the burgeoning research enthusiasm in the department.

Probably another factor was also involved here. In the late 1950s and 1960s, the view was still widely held that the university was quite a different place from high school, and that the role of faculty was to lecture, not teach. The view was propounded that a university degree involved much more than attending lectures, memorizing one's notes, and then passing an examination. Books were to be read, seminars attended, tutorials sought out, and so on. These views of a university emphasized individual learning by a variety of means. They spoke of lecturing rather than teaching, with the faculty as a resource rather than the final authority; most importantly, they represented a traditional view of the university from the 1930s and 1940s that considered the university to be an elite institution.

The reality, however, was that the world of education had changed entirely, and we faculty members were too slow in realizing this; we should have seen the smoke when in our first years at UBC, we expressed great irritation at students who repeatedly asked, "Sir, are we responsible for knowing this?" Not only were students respectful then but they wanted to know whether each piece of subject matter would or would not be included on the examination! In other words, they saw no difference between high school and the university. By the late 1950s, we had already begun university education for the masses. The university was no longer intended only for an elite, and participation rates would rise steadily over the next forty years until well over 40 percent of the 18-24 age group now attends Canadian universities. With this "massification" of university education, it was no longer possible to pretend that any such discontinuity existed between high school and university; indeed, every effort was made to make the transition seamless. Massification has meant that we do indeed teach at university, and that in the three or four years it takes to acquire an undergraduate degree the challenge is to assist the student in changing from a taught receiver to being an independent learner.

Effects of Growth

Another aspect of life at UBC deserves comment. As I have indicated, in the late 1950s and 1960s, there was a necessary preoccupation with growth. Student numbers were increasing rapidly and all the demographic projections indicated that this would continue for many years. It was essential that UBC and other Canadian universities provide the requisite physical facilities and have adequate numbers of faculty. Indeed, the major issue that all Canadian universities have had to deal with over the last forty years is that of growth. Can we provide facilities for an increasing number of students? Will we be able to hire enough highly competent faculty? Can we expand the institutional infrastructure rapidly enough? And so on. With growth as a focus over so many years, however, it was all too easy for growth to become an end in itself.

To varying degrees, this has occurred across the country's universities; for more than a generation, there was no experience of dealing with anything other than growth. It seemed to me that, at UBC in the 1950s and 1960s, growth was regarded as the norm and preoccupied many people. If enrollment did not grow annually by at least 4-5 percent, and if there were not large, impressive new buildings continually under construction on campus, then clearly something was wrong. The normal expectation of everyone was growth, and growth was and perhaps still is to a considerable degree an end in itself.

As I have said, the universities, including UBC, could meet their responsibilities to Canadian society only by unprecedented, rapid growth, and by and large they did an excellent job, for which they deserve better appreciation than they now get. The real purpose of the university as an institution, however, is not growth but rather academic excellence. Bigger is not necessarily better; in fact, bigger can sometimes lead only to mediocrity, not excellence, and an overly strong emphasis on growth can all too easily divert an institution from its true goals.

Institutional Politics

I have already discussed the necessary recruitment of non-Canadian faculty, especially from the UK and other Commonwealth countries, and the significant brain drain that this caused. From the viewpoint of the individual, the majority of those so recruited have become Canadian citizens and have benefited greatly from the privileges that such citizenship entails. We made the choice to come to Canada and become Canadians and have been exceedingly grateful for the opportunities that Canada has offered. As indicated earlier, it seems likely that 30-40 percent of university faculty in the 1960s and 1970s came from these sources, but that in itself raises another question.

Despite the fact that it was this group that made expansion of the universities possible over the last few decades, I have seen few of them appearing in the higher levels of university office across the country. Yes, many have served as department chair, and again it is not uncommon to find a non-native Canadian as a faculty dean. But as I have looked over the past decade at the individuals who have served as university presidents or vice-presidents across the country, virtually all have been native-born Canadians. It is not possible for me to identify more than five who have served as president anywhere in Canada in the last decade and who were born and educated in other countries. This very small number does not match the high percentage of non-Canadians who were recruited in the 1955-70 period and who are now in senior faculty positions and well-qualified for the top positions within the university. I do not wish to suggest that I have seen any evidence of overt discrimination in the selection of presidents and vice-presidents, but the facts themselves are interesting. Is it possible that members of search committees do not see candidates for senior positions who may be non-white or who speak with an obviously non-Canadian accent as the most effective advocate for the institution? Or have these originally non-Canadian faculty members just been less interested in senior posts?

Finally, let me comment on the internal political climate of UBC in those days. Probably the best impression I can give is to state that I arrived at UBC in 1957 as a green, naive young faculty member, and I left in 1965 with the feelings and outlook of a battle-scarred veteran. The Chemistry Department, with the aggressive personality of Charles McDowell as head, and with many other ambitious and forceful individuals, was a hotbed of political intrigue and internecine warfare, usually directed against McDowell but invariably easily deflected by him. The department was academically first class, but it could hardly be described as happy or content. This was true, I think, for much of the university; it was reflected in the quite bitter and protracted battle over the split into separate faculties of Arts and Science mentioned earlier, and it was even more evident in the late 1950s in academic battles in the Faculty of Graduate Studies.

As I have indicated, Gordon Shrum was then dean of graduate studies and had kept in place over the years a set of regulations for graduate students that were quite strict. They included, for example, the regulation that no UBC student could complete bachelor's, master's, and doctoral degrees at UBC. Shrum believed quite passionately, and perhaps quite rightly, that a UBC student should, on completion of the bachelor's degree or certainly of the master's degree, go elsewhere to study for the Ph.D. degree. However, many such as McDowell in Chemistry, Volkoff in Physics, McTaggart-Cowan in Zoology, and others were eager to build graduate programs as quickly as possible, and saw these regulations as barriers to expansion. McDowell became chair of a committee of the faculty that proposed new regulations, and these eventually came to a full meeting of the faculty for debate and decision. While Shrum chaired the meeting, McDowell introduced the committee's recommendations, which, not surprisingly, proposed much easier regulations. It was a simple, but quite vicious gladiatorial contest between the two principals, Shrum and McDowell. As chairman, Shrum used every procedural ploy that he could think of to defeat or delay McDowell, while McDowell was aggressive and persistent, knowing full well that on the essential issues he had the support of the majority. It was a considerable learning experience for young faculty members like me.

In many ways, academic politics at UBC reflected British Columbia society and certainly provincial politics. Academic politics were much more brutal and bruising than those I later saw at Ontario universities. The political game at UBC was played for keeps; it was not just an idle pastime or a diversion from the more serious work of academia. Like those of BC provincial politics, the more extreme aspects of academic politics were very evident. That there were considerable pressures at work internally at UBC was obvious from the fact that during my eight years there, at least three faculty members, including one dean, committed suicide. When I left in 1965, I felt that I was a seasoned veteran of the academic battlefield, and so it proved. Academic life at Ontario universities never seemed to have the same intensity, and certainly not the same vicious qualities as at UBC; only in my nine years as president at Dalhousie did I encounter anything approaching the same atmosphere.

3
First Step to the East

In mid-1964, with the UBC Department of Chemistry still developing, and with both it and the university itself beset by crises and numerous tensions, I applied for and was granted a six-month period of leave, during which my wife and I spent several months visiting and lecturing at universities in India. Although by then our time at UBC had stretched to seven years, the dilemma of whether we should stay in Canada or attempt to return to New Zealand remained unresolved. The issue was brought to a head just before Christmas 1964, when we were in Auckland en route back to Vancouver. Somewhat unexpectedly, I was offered the chair of the Chemistry Department at Auckland, and was able to meet with the vice-chancellor to discuss the possibilities before returning to Vancouver. This discussion was not at all encouraging, especially after my experience of the robust and boisterous growth at UBC in the preceding seven years. At that time, the universities in New Zealand had not begun to expand, and were still struggling with very limited resources and the lack of clear government policy decisions on future directions. Although the Hughes Parry Committee on New Zealand Universities, on which Geoffrey Andrews of UBC had served, had reported in 1959 and recommended the independence of the separate colleges, it was only in 1962 that the University of Auckland formally came into existence.[4]

It took until 1965 for government policies to adopt a more generous attitude towards the universities. This was not apparent in December 1964 when I met with the vice-chancellor, and he could only speak from experience over the preceding decade and with little reassurance for the future. While new physical facilities for chemistry were being planned, completion would depend on funding and that was uncertain. Research funds were meagre, even by Canadian standards, and he could see no means for their increase. As for postdoctoral fellows and means to support them financially, these were unheard of in New Zealand universities at the time, and the vice-chancellor did not see this changing in the foreseeable future. Although he may well have been totally realistic in his responses to my questions, my interview with him could only be described as pessimistic. Had it occurred a year or so later, my career might have been quite different!

While these discussions were proceeding, I received word from a former colleague advising me that the University of Western Ontario was about to appoint a senior professor in inorganic chemistry, and while this obviously complicated matters, I agreed to be a candidate. My initial response to the offer at Auckland was to say that I needed some time to consider it, and that I intended to return to Vancouver and provide my formal response in a few weeks' time. Early January found me back at UBC, with both the Chemistry Department and the university itself in even greater turmoil. President MacKenzie, who had expected to retire in 1964, had, to his chagrin, been forced by the Board of Governors to retire two years earlier, when he reached the age of sixty-five. While he had served UBC with great distinction, he had remained president a little too long and there had been growing criticism in the last two or three years. The new president, John MacDonald, a dentist, was at first favoured by the Faculty Association; also, he seemed decisive, forthright, and able, and quickly seized the initiative. After the eighteen-year MacKenzie era, long pent-up desires for change were released, as well as warranted and imaginary frustrations. There necessarily followed a period of change, uncertainty, and some turmoil. In the Chemistry Department, relations between some faculty members and Charles McDowell were even more strained, and there were some ineffective and unsuccessful political manoeuvrings to oust McDowell as head of the department. The atmosphere was tense and unpleasant, and it took only a few days for me to decide that a move to either London, Ontario, or Auckland was certain. But which would it be?

In mid-January, I spent several days in London, participating in a number of interviews and gaining first impressions of Western and the London region. The Department of Chemistry at Western was undergoing the same type of transformation that had occurred at UBC and other Canadian universities in the late 1950s. A vigorous new head, F.L.M. Pattison, had been appointed in the mid-1950s, and he had been able to achieve a remarkable coup in obtaining from the president, G.E. Hall, a commitment to provide $100,000, an astounding amount in those days, for rebuilding the department. Pattison then proceeded to create at first two, and later a third, senior professorships, and by 1959 had been able to attract two rising research stars to Western from the UK. It was around these that the department was to be rebuilt. At that time, Chemistry, Physics, Mathematics, and other departments were all occupying an increasingly overcrowded Science Building, so Pattison also gained approval to commence planning for a new Chemistry Building. By early 1965, the inorganic chemistry senior professor, who had been appointed along with his organic chemistry colleague in 1959, had resigned to take up a chair in the UK; the third senior professorship, in physical chemistry, had just been appointed; and the Chemistry Building was one of a number of new facilities on the Western campus rapidly reaching completion.

Within a few days of my visit, I was offered appointment as the Senior Professor in Inorganic Chemistry, a position in which I would be able to concentrate on teaching and research free of major administrative responsibilities; there would be a secretarial position available for my exclusive use; and, of course, I would be immediately assigned an entire suite of brand-new research laboratories. These looked like riches indeed, as they certainly were at that time in Canada, and the contrast they provided with the impoverished prospects at Auckland was quite startling. Although my spouse and I had strong family ties drawing us back to New Zealand, and although we knew that the decision we had to make was probably final, we felt that the position at Western offered much greater opportunity and future potential. I accepted the University of Western Ontario offer and submitted my resignation to McDowell, knowing that before long I would be a full-fledged Canadian. A former New Zealand colleague accepted the headship at Auckland but experienced great frustration, much as might have been anticipated from the vice-chancellor's comments at my interview.

My decision to move to Western rather than Auckland was based much more on my then substantial interest in pursuing further research. As department head at Auckland, I would immediately have become involved in considerable administrative work, whereas research seemed much more exciting. Ironically, within a year at Western, I would find myself in an exactly equivalent position.

Western in 1965

Upon my arrival at Western in mid-1965, everything was as I had been promised and had hoped for, with one startling exception. The exception stemmed from the fact that the head of the department, Fred Pattison, with whom I had completed negotiations for my appointment, advised me shortly before we finally left Vancouver that he had resigned and, at age forty-four, would be registered that September as a first-year student in medicine. A remarkable individual with an established international reputation as a chemist, he made the transition to medicine very successfully and subsequently practised medicine for a number of years with the Grenfell Mission on the Labrador and Newfoundland coasts before returning to Western as Director of Student Health Services. Although his departure from the Chemistry Department was a considerable loss, a successor was readily found in Andrew Scott, whom Pattison had brought to Western from Bristol, UK, as a chemist with substantial expertise in the design of new chemistry facilities and in overseeing their construction. This had been his major task in the preceding two to three years, and with the new building virtually complete, and with much Canadian and British experience, he was an obvious choice to be Pattison's successor. Moreover, with my own appointment, all three senior professorships were now filled, and within a very short time, it became clear that they brought with them new problems as well as some benefits.

Not least, they immediately led to the formation of three informal subdepartments, each headed by a senior professor and each corresponding to a particular field of chemistry. Human nature being what it is, there was instant competition between the three groups, and care now had to be taken to ensure a fair tripartite division of any spoils the department might gain. To have Scott as a neutral head was thus a happy solution, but unfortunately one that was not to last long. With new faculty being hired into most departments, there were also changes at more senior levels, including the loss of the associate dean of science. With other rapid changes under way, including the construction of new physical facilities for other science departments, and with a new Faculty of Science being created, continuity in administration was important and a successor needed to be appointed quickly. Because of his extensive involvement in planning and new construction, there was little surprise when it was announced that Scott had been chosen as dean of science. In Chemistry, however, there was immediate realization that a new head now had to be found. Moreover, since several senior appointments, including my own, had just been made, the new head had to be chosen from within the department.

Perhaps because competition was somewhat greater between the organic and physical chemists, leading to the suspect view that we inorganic chemists were moderate and neutral, there was eventually a strong but not unanimous move from within the department for me to be appointed. The actual recommendation officially came from a formally established selection committee, and it happened that two such committees had been established at the same time, one for the head of Chemistry and the other for the head of Mathematics. These were the first such selection committees at Western to have a majority of faculty members and the first to recommend to the board that I be appointed chair, not head, for a five-year term, with a similar recommendation for an appointment in Mathematics. Since the recommendations went to the board at the same time, the two committees apparently at least compared notes. To the astonishment of all, not least myself, the Board of Governors, for the last time, made clear that it alone had the authority to determine the terms and conditions of appointments, and accordingly my Mathematics colleague and I were appointed as department heads without term. We were almost certainly the last to be thus appointed at Western, and in fact my Mathematics friend remained unchallenged in that position for more than twenty years!

Although I had the title of Head, I knew that even if I had the inclination, it would be impossible to fill the position in the same manner as McDowell at UBC or Llewellyn at Auckland. In the mid-1960s, the pressures for greater faculty involvement in governance, which I also then believed in, were steadily mounting, and they were soon increased by the emergence of student activism. My task as head, therefore, was to provide academic and administrative leadership to the department, not by fiat but by ensuring that, on all major initiatives, a sufficient consensus was reached so that I could take the appropriate action.

The following ten-year period was for me, and I think also for the department, a happy and productive time. A few additional appointments were made in each of the three main fields, for a total of about thirty faculty members. The number of students taking chemistry did not increase greatly, since as the environmental movement grew, the public image and understanding of chemistry deteriorated. At the graduate level, vigorous recruitment efforts steadily increased enrollment until the early 1970s, when the total number of graduate students in the department stabilized and then slowly decreased. Research in the department, then, depended more on a growing number of postdoctoral fellows. We had excellent technical staff and during the late 1960s, with aggressive applications to the National Research Council (NRC) and the Natural Sciences and Engineering Research Council (NSERC), we were able to bring our major equipment to a level almost equal to UBC and Toronto.

Those years were very happy and the department most congenial; there were naturally differences of opinion and tensions arising from clashes between strong personalities, but these were usually resolved amicably and there was never the animosity and personal feuding that had been prevalent at UBC. To a considerable degree, this was a result of the friendliness and informality of the faculty coffee room. Most, but certainly not all, of the faculty used the room daily, and while much of the conversation was light and frivolous, many departmental issues were discussed frankly, informally, and productively. A successful coffee room, well used by faculty, can be an enormous asset to the serious work of any academic department.

The Research Emphasis

During my first years as head, the dominant academic philosophy of the day determined that prime emphasis should be placed on developing the research and graduate programs of the department. As at UBC, undergraduate teaching was accepted as a responsibility but it was not where the excitement and enthusiasm lay. We were quite successful, at least in terms of the measures that were then commonly applied. Our graduate student numbers at first grew steadily, there were healthy increases in research grants, new equipment was obtained, the output of research publications mounted impressively, and the department was rapidly recognized as one of the best in Canada.

Late in the 1960s, wiser heads in Canada began to appreciate that there could not be a never-ending spreading of research funds to a continually increasing number of university research enthusiasts; put in different terms, such widespread dispersion of funds might ensure an increasing quantity of research, but could not assure improved quality. It was not sufficient for a young and still developing country such as Canada just to support fundamental research, although that was certainly necessary; more important still was the need to support more than adequately the small percentage of leading-edge, truly innovative research that establishes new intellectual directions. Moreover, any single country could manage to sustain that leading-edge capacity in only a limited number of fields. The NRC, therefore, began to promote the concept of centres of excellence, creating at the outset considerable controversy. This was further amplified by the NRC's view that there needed to be stronger links between the developing research programs in the universities and Canadian industry, in order to gain economic benefits from fundamental research.

At the time, neither of these initiatives was welcomed in the universities; we much preferred to have increasing, unrestricted, individual research grants. That the links between academia and industry in Canada were not strong should not surprise anyone, even though, at the time, the universities were wrongly blamed. In Germany, the US, or Britain, the need to staff universities to meet the rapidly growing enrollments of the 1950s and early 1960s had been fairly easily met by those graduating from the already well-established graduate schools. This was not the case in Canada, where, as discussed earlier, there had been few graduate schools and where the demand for additional faculty could be satisfied only by immigrants from other countries. These faculty members, and I was one of them, certainly were able to provide the necessary teaching and to create and develop new research and graduate programs, but by and large we knew no one in Canadian industry. It was inevitable, then, that a much larger gap would develop between Canadian academia and industry, a gap that has been closed only over the last fifteen to twenty years.

One of the first targeted programs introduced by the NRC was the Negotiated Development Grant Program, under which the NRC would supply a substantial amount of special research funding over several years provided there was a sufficiently strong institutional commitment, including some financial support, and provided there was evidence that a strong "centre of excellence" could be created in a field that might be of industrial or economic benefit to Canada. At Western, we already had several well-regarded faculty engaged in research in photochemistry, and I proposed to them that they might form the nucleus for a centre of excellence with many long-term potential benefits. We had no difficulty gaining the unofficial blessing, indeed, the enthusiastic support, of the dean and the vice-president academic, but, we were told, official sanction could be given only by formal motion of the Senate and board. Unfortunately, this happened to coincide with the implementation of the 1967 University of Western Ontario Act, which completely changed the entire mode of governance of the institution. The new Senate had to be established, terms of reference for an entirely new committee structure prepared and approved, and the new committees constituted. There was, in fact, a period of more than a year of turmoil and inaction during which no new proposal or initiative, including ours, could be considered until the new structures and approval processes could be created and become effective. After much frustration, we did obtain official university approval in the form of formal resolutions of the Senate and the Board of Governors, although not a commitment to specific funding. It was also apparent, however, that no widely representative, democratically elected Senate committee could recommend such a financial commitment; not only would it favour one segment of the university at the expense of others but it also implied acceptance of the idea that photochemistry was indeed a centre of excellence in an institution in which all claimed to be excellent.

Our proposal to create the Photochemistry Unit required a site visit by an NRC committee of photochemistry experts. Their report, while very supportive of the concept and acknowledging the research expertise we already had, expressed concern that the university's commitment did not extend to any financial support, and recommended that we reapply when Western provided solid evidence of real support. This left us in a quandary, since internal politics and participatory democracy appeared to make this impossible. Then one individual, willing to take decisive action, stepped in and enabled us to proceed. The president, D.C. Williams, was sympathetic and arranged for me and our most prominent photochemist to meet with the chairman of the Board of Governors. A.E. Shepherd was a partner in one of the old respected law firms in London, and a blunt, rather hard-nosed individual. When we met, he was first at pains to point out that he had no time for any vague proposal that woolly-minded academics might put together; in fact, he clearly did not have much respect for academics at all. However, he said, if we had a proposal for some research program that might really be, in the long term, of benefit to Canadian industry and the economy, and if he could be convinced of its merits, then he was prepared to listen.

Apparently we succeeded in persuading him, because a day or so later, we received his letter containing a guarantee for, as I recall, $200,000. On the basis of that guarantee, we were then able to identify a particular photochemist of some distinction who would complement our existing expertise, invite him to visit Western, and, after extended negotiations, gain his acceptance of an appointment at Western for the next academic year. The renewal of our application to the NRC, with this evidence of an additional faculty appointment already made, was immediately successful and we received a grant over three years of approximately $750,000. In the midst of our delight at this success, and over the next few years, I recalled how much we owed to A.E. Shepherd. As it turned out, the university did fully fund the faculty appointment we made, and he did not actually have to make good on his guarantee. Nevertheless, if he had not been willing to consider our ideas and to take the decisive step of making such a guarantee, the Photochemistry Unit at the University of Western Ontario, which developed into one of the major successes of the NRC program, would never have come into existence.

Over the next three years, we did indeed create a centre of excellence that has brought Western substantial recognition. We also took seriously the NRC's wish to see much stronger ties between academic research and industry. That photochemistry has great commercial potential can now be seen from the successful development of Canadian companies such as QLT Inc. and others, mainly in the pharmaceutical field. In the early 1970s, the pathway from basic scientific research to marketable product was not well understood or even recognized in Canada, certainly not in the universities. Both Canadian government and industry had seen little value in basic research, and while the NRC's intent was excellent, even the NRC itself knew little of the commercialization process; its own connections had been largely as a problem-solver with well-established industries. We in the universities had essentially no understanding of the business world, and would have benefited greatly from working with an industrial partner. At Western, however, we really did try, and we quickly saw that the Photochemistry Unit had the potential to develop new varieties of photochemical research equipment that might well be marketed worldwide, thereby generating a profit that we would then plough back into the research programs. Little did we realize at the outset how complex the process of commercialization is, and how difficult it also is to make a profit!

Shortly after the Photochemistry Unit had been established, we created Photochemical Research Associates (PRA) as a company to try to achieve the above purposes, initially within the university's legal incorporation, and physically located in the Chemistry Department. After two to three years, we began to appreciate that if we were to have any chance of success, the company would have to be put on a businesslike basis, with full-time management. We realized that to go from a unique piece of laboratory equipment to a prototype to the final marketable product took expertise that we did not have, so we engaged a recent MBA graduate with some chemistry background to serve as manager and to move PRA off campus. This required the company to be separately incorporated, and subsequently it operated from London, owned 50 percent by Western and the rest by local London investors. PRA remained in operation until well into the 1980s, and in some years it did indeed generate a modest profit; it was in fact one of the early spin-off commercial undertakings of a Canadian university. Ultimately, however, its existence came to the attention of some business persons newly appointed to the board of Western, who did not understand why any university should be the major owner of an entrepreneurial start-up company. PRA was therefore sold to American interests and has since been completely absorbed.

PRA was well ahead of its time and in many aspects a forerunner of the spin-off companies that Canadian universities and government now so actively encourage. It is interesting to note that A.E. Shepherd played a very active role in the creation and work of PRA, and served as a director for some time; he was the ideal supporter of the commercialization of university research, with a keen business sense and critical judgment.

Training or Education?

As my involvement, even as head of the department, in teaching and research continued into the 1970s, I began to feel increasingly uneasy about much that we as professional chemists provided to our undergraduate students. During this time, there were fewer and fewer job openings for chemistry graduates – in fact, for any science graduates. Canadian universities had met the challenges of greatly expanded enrollment but the Canadian business community was not responding with sufficient jobs for highly qualified people, and especially with the creation and growth of research and development programs. Even more unfortunately, our graduates did not seem to believe that they had been trained for anything except a career as a professional chemist. They had little understanding that, in fact, they had a range of problem-solving skills that were valuable in themselves and that could be applied in many fields. And if they appeared to have missed this point, we as their teachers must surely be responsible. Over the next year or so, it steadily became clear that chemists in many other countries were raising these same issues. In 1970, I was invited to attend an international conference on chemical education at which many of the world's leading chemists were present. Again and again the same issues were raised. Were we just filling students with chemical content that, in any event, would be out of date within a few years? Or were we really providing, through chemistry, a genuine education with the development of identifiable skills?

I had to conclude that I and many others in the postwar expansion had not devoted sufficient thought as to what we wanted to accomplish, at least in an educational sense. In our enthusiasm to make students aware of all of the new science that came from the Second World War and the 1950s, we had not thought sufficiently about our primary role as educators. The curriculum in chemistry, and in most sciences, had increasingly been determined by the need to cover additional new material. I recalled that while my first year of chemistry at Auckland was very similar to that at Western in

1970, over the intervening years we had crammed an enormous amount of new chemistry into the curriculum of the three higher years, making it a burdensome and overloaded program. No wonder we were seeing no increase in the numbers of students wanting to enroll in the sciences! We were drowning them in an ocean of scientific theories and facts, an ocean that could only get bigger as time passed.

On my return from the conference, I immediately initiated departmental discussions about the curriculum, and, of course, was faced with the inevitable skepticism and reluctance to change. After several meetings, however, at which we could not agree on appropriate changes, we did agree that we should initially look at what we considered to be the absolutely essential minimum amount of material that had to be included in an honours program in chemistry. So the three divisions – organic, physical, and inorganic – went off to prepare their minimal lists. Not surprisingly, when we next met, it quickly became embarrassingly clear to all that the total of what was considered essential far exceeded what could be covered in a four-year curriculum! The fact that we, as teachers of chemistry, were driven by the need to cover content – content that was increasing and changing rapidly – was all too apparent.

After much discussion, we did make some significant changes that, in their time, were quite unusual. We introduced a half-year course in industrial chemistry at the third-year level that was probably the first of its kind in Canada. We also introduced a very different type of third-year course designed to illustrate how new chemical concepts had developed, and another dealing with the history of chemistry. And, at last recognizing its value, we introduced a course in analytical chemistry. These changes were possible only because we managed to whittle down substantially what we had previously regarded as the "essential" four-year core. We also commenced team-teaching of some courses so that a broader chemical perspective could be given, and we required more oral presentations from students to improve their communication skills. We created a new, revitalized curriculum and a department with a much clearer view of its teaching mandate.

Involvement in Governance

My time at Western also had me much involved in wider university affairs. For a number of years, I served as a member of the Senate and on several Senate committees, including being chair of the Operations-Agenda Committee. I learned much from these experiences, not least that others in the university had very different views about the nature and purpose of the institution, many of which revolved around the concept that the university was a scholarly community and that the faculty, as the most important element of that community, should be predominant in its governance.

Student activists had a different view. At a time when the debate on student participation in governance was probably at its height at Western, the Office of the President and the Senate were struggling with student demands that they be allowed to serve on the promotion and tenure committees, a demand that was completely rejected by essentially all faculty members. The students' arguments were simple: how could students actually know that their views on the quality of teaching were being taken into account if they did not participate in the discussions? Ultimately, in some desperation, the Senate agreed to establish a committee to consider the issue. It consisted of three faculty members (of whom I was one), three students, and, as nonvoting chair, the much respected vice-president academic, R.J. Rossiter.

Meetings were held weekly over what seemed an interminable period. The students would introduce a proposal, which we debated and then defeated on a tied 3-3 vote. The same happened to any proposal introduced by the faculty members, but I sensed increasing defensiveness in my faculty colleagues, combined with an unwillingness to consider seriously what appeared to me to be quite reasonable student proposals. At one meeting, there was, after much debate, a student proposal on the table to which I could take no exception, and to the consternation of my two colleagues and Dr. Rossiter, I voted with the three students. Needless to say, when the committee's report went to the Senate, it was immediately rejected, but in the meantime I was astonished at the degree of hostility and anger that I received from many faculty members. There was vehement, unthinking opposition to any degree of student involvement in promotion and tenure considerations. The fact that this position was logically inconsistent with the demand that faculty members should have the right to evaluate academic administrators never seemed to occur to them.

Much of this attitude remains, although there have been some gestures, such as the regular use at all universities of some form of student evaluation. I have often heard faculty say, rather sanctimoniously, that of course they have no objection to some form of performance evaluation and in fact are willingly and critically evaluated several times per year by students. In practice, however, little is accomplished by such evaluations unless they are seriously reflected in the faculty reward system, and all too often this is not the case. Today, students may be asked to complete ten or more such questionnaires each year, and tend to regard them cynically, since no one has convinced them that any serious action ever follows. Moreover, the questionnaires are seldom revised and tend to be used year after year without change. The hard fact is that Canadian universities have, by and large, not taken seriously the institutional responsibility to assess the value of the education they provide, especially at the undergraduate level.

It was at Western that I first became involved in what is now referred to as rationalization. By 1968, the Ontario government had become increasingly concerned at the proliferation of graduate programs. There were then fourteen universities in the province, and every one of them had made clear its intent to become the Harvard of Canada, with a full panoply of both master's and doctoral programs. The driving forces behind these unrealistic ambitions were twofold. First, the provincial funding formula provided six "basic income units" for each Ph.D. student versus only one for a general arts student, so the financial incentive was considerable. Second, faculty members wanted to be recruited only to institutions where there were substantial research programs, and where they would have the opportunity to supervise graduate students; the tacit understanding was that career advancement depended on research and research publications. Confronted with these overblown ambitions, the provincial government let it be known that if the universities did not curb this growth themselves, the government would. In fact, to make its point, in 1971 the government imposed an embargo on the application of the funding formula to new graduate programs. A massive meeting in Toronto was called by what is now known as the Council of Ontario Universities (COU), and I distinctly recall the blunt and forceful message that J.J. Deutsch, principal of Queen's University, presented to us, arguing that the universities had to solve this problem themselves.

The most significant outcome was the creation by the COU, through its Ontario Council on Graduate Studies, of the Advisory Committee on Academic Planning (ACAP), which was given the task of examining, by whatever means it thought appropriate, all existing graduate programs and all proposals for new ones with regard to both quality and need. At the request of Western's president, D.C. Williams, I served on ACAP for a three-year term, from 1969 to 1972. The creation of ACAP and the work it undertook were bitterly resented in many of the universities. After much acrimonious discussion, the committee developed a process in which all the supporting documentation for a provincial set of graduate programs (for example, in chemistry or sociology) would be placed in the hands of a group of international consultants who would visit all programs, engage in any other consultation thought necessary, and develop a report containing recommendations on the future of each program. On the basis of this, ACAP would develop its own report for submission to the COU.

Since both the COU and ACAP were voluntary bodies and had no legislative authority, it was first necessary to obtain from each university senate and board agreement with these procedures, and acceptance of the outcomes. This was difficult and time-consuming, and not all institutions felt bound by such agreements later on. ACAP then proceeded with its detailed review of each subject, eventually completing perhaps five or six per year, although each entailed at least two years of work. Although approximately twelve to fifteen such subject reviews were completed, there was much resistance, and efforts to undermine ACAP and its reports continued. ACAP's program was never completed, at least as originally conceived, and some feel that, despite a tremendous amount of work, ACAP accomplished little. I disagree: the work of ACAP did curb the ambitions of all universities and prevented the introduction of a flood of ill-conceived and hastily devised graduate programs. Only two or three existing graduate programs were closed, but it was the work of ACAP that eventually led to the fairly rigorous and continuing quality assessment of all Ontario graduate programs now conducted through the Ontario Council of Graduate Studies.

From my personal viewpoint, serving on ACAP was arduous but exceedingly interesting. It was made forcefully clear to me, and has since been reinforced by my experience in Nova Scotia, that a voluntary body such as the COU, by its very nature, can exercise little direction or control over universities that are completely autonomous and independent. For example, more than one ACAP discipline report proposed that on the basis of advice from internationally regarded experts, two existing programs should be combined to enhance quality. In every such case, the institutions objected strenuously and disagreed with the advice of the experts – and nothing happened. I vividly recall attending a COU meeting at which a particularly controversial ACAP report was to be considered; it was controversial because it was the first such report that was highly critical of an existing doctoral program at the University of Toronto. The outside experts had in fact recommended that a joint program involving several universities be created. During the discussion, the president of the University of Toronto vigorously asserted that every criticism of the Toronto program was factually incorrect, but then went on to describe steps that were being taken to correct them, so that there was clearly no need for a joint program. No further action was taken!

The COU's handling of ACAP's report on chemistry was equally remarkable. The international consultants were of the highest calibre and included a Nobel laureate. In their report, they presented numerous powerful arguments that high-quality graduate programs in chemistry required departments of at least a minimum size: twenty-five to thirty faculty members and about fifty graduate students. Departments that lacked this critical mass could not provide the equipment, the breadth of subject areas, and the vigorous intellectual climate that were essential for quality. As the COU discussion of the report began, F. Leddy, president of the University of Windsor, a distinguished classical scholar and a formidable public speaker, immediately attacked this concept of "critical size." "Why," he said, "I don't understand at all what this is all about. As far as I am concerned, good graduate work only requires one student, one supervisor, and a library. This report is nonsense!" And in that single sweeping generalization, all of the consultants' wisdom and conclusions on critical size were dismissed!

While the specific accomplishments of ACAP seem minor, especially in relation to the vast amounts of time, effort, and paper devoted to it, I had the opportunity to contrast it with a very different approach taken in New York. In 1972 I was approached by the New York State Department of Education requesting that I participate in a new program just being started to evaluate all existing Ph.D. programs. Chemistry was one of the first to be examined, followed by history and numerous other disciplines. In each case, about 24 recognized authorities would be appointed by the Department of Education, and from this group, teams of 4 or 5 would be selected to visit and examine each of the existing Ph.D. programs. In chemistry, there were as I recall some 15 or so such programs, so each consultant participated in visiting and writing reports on 3 to 5 programs. All 15 reports were then reviewed by an executive group of 7 or 8 of the consultants, and an overall final report was submitted to the Department of Education. Because of existing state legislation, this process could be applied to all institutions in the state, both public and private, so we examined chemistry Ph.D. programs at Columbia and Rensselaer Polytechnic as well as those at the State University of New York campuses, and so on. What particularly impressed me was the fact that the entire process for chemistry took less than one year from the creation of the team of consultants to the implementation of the Department of Education's final decision to immediately close three or four of the programs. Later, however, when the process was applied to existing Ph.D. programs in history, Syracuse University launched legal action against the Department of Education on the grounds that the department was infringing on the university's autonomy; the entire review process became mired in legalities and eventually disappeared.

Around 1974, the issue of merit salary increases became particularly contentious at Western, at least if one listened to the Faculty Association. For quite a number of years, a process had been in place whereby, within each department, the performance of each faculty member would annually be rated on a 1-10 scale, but the average on a departmental or faculty basis had to be 5. In the Chemistry Department, the senior professors and I determined these ratings; other departments used a variety of methods. Grumblings among faculty, encouraged by the Faculty Association, centred on the feeling that ratings below 5 inevitably meant an unsatisfactory performance, which was, however, quite different from "below average." Eventually, a committee was established, chaired by vice-president academic Grant Reuber, with six to eight faculty members, including me. There was clearly a strong push to do away with merit increases of any kind, on the grounds that they were divisive within the community of scholars. There was an even stronger push to abolish any form of numerical rating, on the grounds that these were mechanical, dehumanizing, and insulting to faculty. A number of committee members, certainly including Grant Reuber and me, were determined to keep some form of merit evaluation that differentiated between the performances of individual faculty members. This was reflected in the final report, which was ultimately accepted and put into effect.

During the committee's deliberations, however, it had been clear that the unit on campus that was perhaps most strongly opposed to merit increases was, remarkably, the School of Business. When the report was implemented, the School of Business at first submitted to Grant Reuber identical ratings for all its faculty members, which he refused to accept. He then withheld all merit salary increase funds from the school, had them held in an escrow account, and asked the school to think again. Ultimately, the business school did submit a set of merit ratings that differentiated sufficiently between individuals to satisfy Reuber so that the funds were released. What seemed so ironical to me was that Western's School of Business, a bastion of the free enterprise market, a believer in competition, and teacher of entrepreneurialism, should be so opposed to merit salary increases. Moreover, the school's argument that merit increases that differentiated between individuals would cause such disharmony in the school that they would adversely affect their team-teaching approach seemed shallow. A spirit of competition was apparently desirable everywhere except within the School of Business.

In Ontario, the era of rapid growth of the universities had ended by 1972. Certainly, enrollments continued to climb, and there were continuing construction projects on most campuses, but the provincial government made it clear that it could not, and would not, continue to provide the substantial annual funding increases that the universities thought necessary. Within the universities, however, there continued to be high expectations in terms of continuing expansion, addition of new programs, and annual increases to all salary scales. Not until at least the late 1970s was there any realization that, for Ontario universities, the next two decades would be very different from the preceding two.

4
Lessons from Western

The period from 1965 to 1975 was undoubtedly the decade of student activism at Canadian universities; but it was also the decade of faculty discontent and of faculty insistence on change, especially in terms of their involvement in governance. Around 1968, for example, I can recall the prevalent feeling among faculty that the University of Western Ontario was mismanaged and that significantly greater faculty participation in governance was urgently needed. In retrospect, when I ask myself why, it is hard to find a convincing answer.

Effects of Growth

The University of Western Ontario was typical of Canadian universities in that era.[5] G.E. Hall had become its fourth president in 1947, presiding over what was just a small college of arts and medicine. His style of presidential leadership was friendly and informal, as befitted a small institution. By the time he retired in mid-1967, however, Western had become a large multiversity, with numerous faculties, many new academic buildings, and an enlarged administration.

The rapidity of these changes is easily illustrated. In 1961, F.L.M. Pattison, then head of the Chemistry Department, was endeavouring to fill the first of the senior professorships in chemistry, and had brought over from Britain a prominent organic chemist for interview. During this visit, the invitee met with Hall and told him that a major concern was the limited number of chemistry journals being subscribed to by the library. Dr. Hall went over to another desk in his office, on which was a large ledger, the university budget, and responded by saying that he could provide an extra $1,000 per year for this purpose. Hall controlled the university's finances and made the key decisions personally. Six years later, in 1967, that was no longer possible: the institution was large and an expanded and professional administration had been established. While Hall still had the final decision, budget preparation and financial management were the responsibility of administrative professionals.

Faculty members did not understand this and resented the growth of a substantial administrative arm of the university, even though the academic side of the institution grew much more quickly. The resentment may well have been unjustified, but it was based on the common faculty perception that the rapid growth of the university had changed its fundamental character, as indeed it had. It had made the institution more impersonal, and had placed faculty more clearly in an employer-employee relationship. Rapid growth also seemed, in the minds of some, to emphasize the "administration" versus "faculty" distinction; many faculty members felt, and still feel today, that "administrators" have too much influence over academic decisions, even though academic administrators are now chosen from among academics by academics.

Another cause of complaint among faculty was the presence on the Board of Governors of local business persons, and their presumed influence on academic issues. Such a worry seems ironic today, when all Canadian universities seek to appoint to their boards as many prominent persons from business as they can, especially to assist with fund-raising and community relations; in fact, Western had historically benefited greatly from the active support and interest of local appointees. In addition, there were faculty dissidents who were highly critical of the "remoteness" of the governing structure of the university and the alleged unresponsiveness of its administration to faculty sentiment and aspirations.

I cannot help but conclude that, at the time, all of us seriously underestimated the complex effects of rapid growth on an institution, and while we fully appreciated the financial benefits that came with such growth, we somehow hoped that the more human, personal, and informal characteristics of a smaller institution could be maintained. The perception of the university as a small, elite institution still prevailed. While we made unceasing demands on the additional funds that growth brought, we gave too little thought to, and certainly did not articulate, the characteristics, the values, and the ethos that we wished the much larger institution to have.

It is difficult to justify now the resentment and antagonism felt towards administration and boards of governors at the time. It seems to me much more likely that faculty ambitions were more concerned with the rapidly increasing amounts of government funding being allocated to universities, and the wish to ensure that the faculty had the major say in how those funds should be distributed. To participate in the distribution of government funding that seemed to increase automatically each year, to thereby create new programs and expand existing ones, gave faculty a sense of power and of control over the institution that they had not experienced before.

There was also the tendency, supported by the booming economy of the 1950s and 1960s, to view government generosity to universities as a legitimate entitlement of academia that would continue indefinitely into the future. We were totally unprepared to even consider that such a level of support might be a temporary aberration rather than the norm.

Governance Transformed

By 1965, President Hall and the board accepted the inevitability of internal change, and the last two years of Hall's presidency were largely devoted to the drafting of the 1967 University of Western Ontario Act.[6] When his successor, D. Carlton Williams, took office in 1967, Western was in a fractious mood, and about to embark on major reorganization. Implementation of the 1967 act was just beginning, the Faculty of Arts was about to fragment into three separate faculties, student activism was rapidly increasing, and growth in student enrollment, faculty numbers, and new facilities continued apace. The changes in governance that were contained in the new act were much the same as those made at other Canadian universities, although Western was in fact the first university to make such significant modifications to its governing legislation.

The principal changes were essentially those recommended in the 1966 report by the Duff-Berdahl Commission, based on its study of university governance in Canada.[7] First, the roles and responsibilities of the Board of Governors and the Senate were changed to create more of a partnership, rather than leaving the Senate in a subservient role. This was based on the recognition that academic planning and financial planning and decisions cannot be separated and handled by different governing bodies. The Senate, which had not been overly effective previously, was reduced in size to approximately sixty-five, and now had a majority of elected faculty members; there would also be elected Senate representatives on the board. The Senate was given a network of committees, the most important being the budget and finance committee, the committee on admissions and academic programs policy, the committee on university development, and the committee on academic planning. At the lower levels, each faculty was required to have a Faculty Council, the composition of which was determined by that faculty, and each Faculty Council had a number of committees reporting to it. This was the period when "participatory democracy" was a popular cause, and the new, complex governing structures put in place at Western and other universities more than adequately reflected that.

To make the transition from old to new took immense resources and a great deal of time; hundreds of thousands of hours of administrative and faculty time were required for "participatory" consultation to spell out all details of the necessary changes. For well over two years, the new Senate met for three hours every two weeks, and what emerged was not always constructive. I recall complaining to the dean at the time when we were seeking official institutional approval for the creation of the Photochemistry Unit that under these new governing processes, the proposal would have to be considered by nine separate and independent committees! Governance certainly became participatory, but participation was often unnecessarily extensive and always demanding in terms of time and resources. Worse still, this type of governance encouraged committees to adopt a leisurely academic view of their task, so that it was not the least uncommon to find committees taking more than one academic year to complete a task that most would think required only a few weeks or one or two months. Unfortunately, this attitude has not changed in recent years.

Such changes have now been in place in most Canadian universities for over thirty years, and one may well ask how effective they have been. Under legislation such as the 1967 UWO Act, faculty and, to a lesser degree, students have gained considerable power in governing and controlling the Canadian university. The extent to which a president or a board of governors can determine the future directions of the institution has been severely curtailed, and of course many would assert that this is a major improvement. One must also examine the quality of the decisions that have been made, however. Decisions made by a committee are not necessarily the best possible; they often represent the minimum compromise view of those present, a compromise that might well have been different if other persons had been on the committee. Moreover, a persistent proposer of some new academic program or new research endeavour can usually, if sufficiently determined, ultimately gain a committee's approval; several attempts may be needed, but it is usually the committee that tires first.

The most serious deficiency in the governance of today's universities, however, lies in the sheer impossibility of defining any specific direction or objectives for the institution. The 1967 UWO Act illustrated this well; while it provided for Senate committees on both university development (SCUD) and academic planning (SCAP), only the first was effective in the years immediately following. Development implies growth and expansion, but academic planning might also imply terminations and reductions. Planning has never been a concept that rested easily with a university committee. In my years at Western, SCUD was powerful and dealt effectively with proposals for specific projects, whereas SCAP had difficulty agreeing on its mandate and achieved little.

Western was not alone in this. As will be discussed more fully in Chapter 7, many Canadian universities have devoted enormous efforts to planning and the development of mission statements. Unfortunately, in such endeavours, participatory democracy ensures that no segment of the university will be disadvantaged, that all will strive for excellence, and that "priorities" are changes or initiatives from which all will benefit.

Of similar long-term consequence has been the effect of participatory governance during the last two decades, when reductions in government funding to universities have been made in every Canadian province. Apart from its excessive bureaucracy and waste of time and resources, participatory governance worked reasonably well during the period, probably the anomalous period, when government funding was increasing rapidly. It provided some openness in the distribution of new funds, and it helped prevent possible arbitrariness in the introduction of new programs. When government funding is being reduced, however, participatory governance not only does not work but actually causes great harm. Under such governance, which can permit only a vague, generalized mission statement, budget reductions can only be across the board, applied equally to all academic units; since there is no basis for differentiation, there are no academic priorities. Certainly, in probably all Canadian universities, greater budget reductions have been applied to administrative units than to academic units, but in virtually every case the long-term health of the university would have been much improved by the termination of some weaker programs, allowing those units central to that institution to maintain financial health and academic vigour. Participatory governance has almost totally prevented this, and Canadian universities are the weaker for it.

Another change in governance in the 1967 UWO Act and elsewhere required the creation of search or selection committees for all academic administrative appointments, from chair, to dean, to vice-president academic, to president. In all such committees, except that for the position of president, the majority of members were to be faculty members, and in many universities, provision was made, either then or later, for some student representation. At most universities, the board has retained the right to appoint a majority of members to the selection committee for president. Also, as mentioned earlier, the governance changes of the late 1960s required that all future appointments to these positions be for a fixed term, although usually with the possibility of renewal. Such legislation also often required that departments had to be administered by chairs rather than heads.

These were very significant governance changes, and again one should ask whether they have been beneficial. For reasons already discussed, the requirement that there be term appointments to academic administrative positions has unquestionably been a considerable improvement, although the issue of the most appropriate length of such a term requires some rethinking, especially by boards of governors. Whether or not better choices of individuals have been made by selection committees is, however, a moot point. Especially when an outside candidate is being considered, and the choice is therefore made on the basis of a two- or three-day visit, a selection committee is just as likely as a president or vice-president to misread character. Many selection committees have enthusiastically recommended appointments that were later much regretted. My point here is that the use of selection committees, while it certainly gives credibility to the recommended appointment, does not significantly increase the proportion of successful appointees.

What has surprised me greatly, however, not only at Western but also elsewhere, is the faculty attitude towards appointments made in this way, that is, through selection committee recommendations. One might have expected this to reduce substantially any previously existing mistrust between faculty and administration. If anything, the reverse is true. In my experience, faculty today feel more cynicism and mistrust towards academic administrators than thirty years ago, even though the appointees have been selected essentially by faculty members. There seems to be a peculiar belief that individuals who have been highly regarded by their faculty peers, and who have been recommended by faculty-dominated selection committees for appointment as a dean or vice-president, suddenly undergo a complete change of character on assuming the administrative office. Indeed, faculty members have made exactly that comment to me on more than one occasion.

Even more baffling is the unwillingness of faculty members to accept responsibility for the recommendations these selection committees make. As already indicated, even selection committees with a majority of faculty members make mistakes, and an unsuitable person can be appointed. In such cases, it is usually the committee that has erred, and the committee and the constituency it represented must accept responsibility and live with the consequences of such a poor recommendation. In too many instances of which I have been aware, when it has become apparent that a poor choice was made, faculty are quick to demand that the individual be immediately removed or even terminated. But it was not the individual who made the mistake; it was the selection committee, and life generally requires that those who make such errors of judgment must carry the responsibility and suffer some of the consequences. In one instance in which I chaired a selection committee for a senior appointment, several committee members had been vociferously enthusiastic in support of one candidate. He was appointed, but within two months, two of the same committee members came to me demanding that the individual be removed from office. It was indeed an error of judgment on the part of myself and the committee, but the chosen individual could not be expected to bear the full consequences; the committee and the institution had to recognize their responsibility and had to live with their choice until a reasonably humane resolution could be found.

The changes and adjustments that followed from the UWO Act were simply enormous. In 1970, because of continuing concerns over the administrative issues at Western, the Board of Governors engaged a Toronto management consulting firm to study the entire administrative structure of the university. One of its findings was that during the preceding year, an estimated 33,000 hours of academic time was consumed by university committee activities! More importantly, the consultants reported that, in their view, the greatest need was the creation of a climate of mutual trust. This was true then for most Canadian universities, yet there is little evidence that the UWO Act, or similar legislation for other universities, has done much to create such a climate.

Teaching and Evaluation

My eleven years at Western were also often preoccupied by issues relating to the performance of faculty members and to controversy over performance review and the reward system. The small Western of the 1950s was a place in which faculty, deans, and president knew each other, and promotion and salary increases were based on personal judgments. By the time the UWO Act was implemented, growth had already been considerable and the much larger institution required an established and open process so that dissatisfaction and controversy over promotion, tenure, and salary matters could be minimized. Each department was therefore required to have a duly constituted promotion and tenure committee, all recommendations from departmental committees had to be reviewed by a similar faculty-level committee, and finally a university committee chaired by the vice-president academic would ensure that comparable academic standards were being employed across the university. There was also an appeal process, often complicated, on which I will comment later.

Like those of most Canadian universities, Western's policies stated that faculty members should be evaluated on the basis of their teaching, their research, and their other contributions to the university and the wider community. And, of course, just as these formal processes came into effect, student activism developed rapidly across Canada. While much of the student unrest was a product of the anti-Vietnam War era and was highly political, there was also a genuine wish to give students at least some voice in decision making, and especially with regard to the quality of instruction they received. By the early 1960s, student unions at several universities were producing unofficial evaluations of undergraduate courses; by the late 1960s, many universities had agreed to allow some form of teaching evaluation by students. In virtually all cases, this was done in response to student pressure; rarely was it an initiative of the institution. More usually, there was vehement faculty opposition, some elements of which still exist.

At Western, Chemistry and several other science departments were forerunners in the use of teaching evaluation questionnaires in all courses. We used a standard questionnaire, the results were readily available to all, and the data each year formed a substantial part of the information that was considered by the departmental promotion and tenure committee, not only for promotion and granting of tenure but also in the awarding of annual salary merit increases. However, several of us in the department felt that the questionnaires alone did not give us all the information that might be helpful in improving the curriculum and the students' experience of it. We therefore arranged for students within each year, first year up to fourth, to elect six to eight representatives, who then met with me as head and those faculty members lecturing in the appropriate courses. These were often quite lengthy discussions lasting one-and-a-half to two hours, but they were extremely useful and gave us genuine information from the students' perspective, which was often quite different from ours. It was quite a revelation to two faculty members teaching different courses to the same students to discover that they were scheduling mid-term examinations on top of one another, or were expecting several major assignments to be completed on the same day. Or that a change in the order of presentation of certain new material would be helpful to students.

By 1970-71, the same questionnaire was being employed throughout the Faculty of Science, well in advance of the rest of the university. Student activists were still beating at the gates of Canadian universities, however, with the wish to change the institution completely, or at the least give students a much stronger voice. As usual, the Faculty of Science held very conservative views of such activism, but on the issue of student evaluation of teaching and the subsequent use of evaluation results, some of us felt considerable sympathy with the students. They were, and are, the recipients of that teaching, and they had every right to expect the best possible instruction in their university courses. Today, as students pay a greater and greater portion of their tuition costs, that right must be respected and students should be convinced that they are receiving value for fees.

In the early 1970s, some steps were taken at Western and other Canadian universities; by and large, however, they were taken only reluctantly under vigorous student pressure, and there has not really been any major change in attitude in the universities on the whole issue of evaluation. At Western in 1971, the very militant student representatives on the Senate pushed successfully for the Senate to consider the use of a standard teaching evaluation questionnaire across the entire university. Naively, some science colleagues and I volunteered to draft such a questionnaire, drawing heavily on the one we were using in the Faculty of Science. When our draft was presented for discussion in the Senate, we were vigorously attacked, especially by those from the social sciences. They complained that we obviously knew little about the science of designing a questionnaire and that our questions were inappropriately slanted, forcing us to admit that we were not experts in such matters. Our draft was quickly discarded, and the task of developing an acceptable standard questionnaire was given to two colleagues in the Psychology Department, both of whom had substantial reputations across Canada for such expertise. Time passed and no report appeared before the

Senate; upon inquiry, the Senate was told that these two experts had been quite unable to agree on any questionnaire!

What is remarkable to me now is that universities to the present day continue to look with great suspicion upon the entire issue of evaluation, especially of teaching. When the evaluation of research by the peer review process is required and valued within academia, how can the faculty with any degree of intellectual honesty not take just as seriously the need for evaluation of teaching? The common argument is that evaluation of teaching, or, more appropriately, education, is exceedingly difficult and fraught with possible error. That is certainly the case, but since when has the difficulty of an intellectual challenge been a reason for not addressing it? All acknowledge that many factors influence the educational benefit that a student receives, but it is also well established, although still only reluctantly accepted, that if one single indicator of teaching quality is to be used, student evaluation is by far the most effective. Of course, other criteria can be used singly or in combination, but what is distressing is that one can find very little experimentation at present in universities to develop better and more accurate methods of evaluation. Certainly, some individual faculty members, and even some departments, take these issues very seriously and some new approaches can be found, but by and large the entire issue of evaluation of education is not seen as part of the institution's mandate.

Similar student pressures also occurred in the 1960s and 1970s in universities in Britain, Australia, New Zealand and elsewhere, and since then governments in these countries have required a much greater degree of accountability than is now the case in Canada. Regular formal evaluations of all aspects of a university's operations are required, with teaching being no exception. New Zealand has very recently established an independent body, the Quality Assessment Authority, to ensure that all programs in institutions of higher education are regularly examined for the maintenance of quality according to predetermined standards. Canada lags behind and is moving too cautiously on quality evaluation, although Ontario has made some recent moves in this area.

Assessment of Research

The one aspect of evaluation that faculty members generally support is that of peer review of research and research publications. The principle of peer review is important, and indeed fundamental to the advance of knowledge. Its application, however, encounters serious problems in today's university. In the early 1970s, Western's Chemistry Department required the use of outside evaluators of research, as most universities do now. At the time, however, those of us on the departmental promotion and tenure committee usually had some knowledge of the outside reviewers we were choosing, and of the academic standards they would employ. It was also possible for at least one person on the committee, perhaps several, to read knowledgeably the publications of any particular candidate. The extent to which this is still possible is now much reduced. In many instances, there is no one within the department who can read another area of research with any expertise, and none on the committee may know the names of those suggested as external reviewers. This is not due to any failing of the university, and it is certainly a worldwide problem, not just a Canadian one. It stems directly from the exponential growth of research in all fields over the last fifty years, and the growth of numerous areas of specialization within any one field. The volume and rate of production of new knowledge are so great that a single researcher can only hope to keep reasonably abreast of one specialized field. Over the past fifty years, promotion and tenure committees in universities worldwide have increasingly found themselves able to do little more than count publications and read the letters of referees about whom they know very little.

In spite of all the denials of academics, Canadian universities, like their counterparts elsewhere, place greatest value on the research activities of faculty, and this is reflected in the behaviour of the institutions themselves. This does not mean that teaching is necessarily undervalued; rather, it means that each faculty member knows that, provided teaching responsibilities are met satisfactorily, it is research results and publications that will bring tenure and promotion. This view permeates universities worldwide, and has some insidious effects. It has created an international publishing machine, largely in the hands of the commercial sector, which flourishes only because of the need to publish. It is highly questionable that a matching pressure to read much of this new material actually exists. In fact, in various articles in the *Chronicle of Higher Education* in the early 1990s, it was reported that 50 percent of all Ph.D. theses in the social sciences had not been read once in the first five years following their publication, and that in one twelve-month period, over 25,000 new journals began publication across all subject areas. It becomes harder and harder to believe that all of these research results have real significance, other than to meet the faculty need to publish, a need that faculty themselves have created.

There is, moreover, a secondary outcome that affects all universities. University libraries are increasingly unable to acquire the journal holdings that faculty deem necessary. There is a continuing and exponential growth in the number of new publications, a growth that is fed to a considerable degree by the need to publish and is encouraged by commercial publishers for their own profit. At the time of writing in 2000, when general inflationary increases are virtually zero, Canadian universities face an 18-20 percent annual increase in journal costs, and this has been the case over the past thirty years. Put simply, the pressures to publish are bankrupting the libraries!

While teaching and research are the major responsibilities of faculty at virtually all Canadian universities, it is also recognized that faculty are involved in other areas, such as continuing education, international activities, community affairs, and so on, which should also be evaluated. This is a matter that I will discuss later; for the moment, suffice it to say that, in practice, all too often little or no recognition is given for such activities when it comes to promotion and salary increases.

Any institution like the university is most unlikely to impose upon itself the formal discipline of evaluation processes that public accountability demands. Yet the past fifty years has been a period during which Canadian universities have benefited greatly from the generous financial support of both provincial and federal governments. While some in the university community will argue that government funding has been woefully insufficient in absolute terms, vast sums *have* been poured into the universities; at various points during this last half century, many universities were receiving more than 80 percent, or even 90 percent, of their revenues from government. While this percentage has been declining recently, only for a handful of the smaller Canadian universities is it now below 50 percent. While the need for universities to be proactive in demonstrating public accountability remains, performance evaluation of faculty rarely receives serious attention in today's universities, since the faculty generally control the institution. It should not surprise the universities, therefore, if sometime in the future, governments give them the same considerable attention in Canada as universities have received from governments elsewhere.

Salaries and Merit

The results of performance evaluation should, of course, ultimately be reflected in salary adjustments, which should reflect merit. In the 1950s and into the 1960s, this was, I believe, a widely held view in Canadian universities, which has since, however, fallen into disrepute for a variety of reasons. One major factor has been the widespread unionization of faculty in Canadian universities; faculty unions have argued strongly for, and have usually won, standard uniform step increases for all faculty members within each rank. Such step increases are therefore based on seniority or experience rather than on merit. In some instances, the collective agreement will provide for consideration of special salary increases in cases where faculty members have received more attractive offers from elsewhere. The union will usually require, however, that there be a written offer, and will usually negotiate strenuously to keep such increases to a minimum. This inability of the university to provide truly competitive salaries for really outstanding faculty members is a major factor in faculty mobility, and probably also in the loss of outstanding faculty to the United States and elsewhere.

The fact that all faculty members receive the same step increase makes a mockery of any recognition of merit, and yet this type of policy has become the norm. The argument that there is no universally accepted method of determining merit and of assessing the performance of faculty members is totally unacceptable. After all, there is no universally valid method of determining student performance, yet faculty members claim to do exactly that every academic year with the use of the grading system.

The University System and Rationalization

My experiences at Western while serving as a member of the Advisory Committee on Academic Planning (ACAP) brought home to me very forcefully the difficulties inherent in rationalization of universities, or, putting it more positively, in the creation of a genuine university system. Separate autonomous institutions do not willingly relinquish the least part of their authority, yet there are clear examples that demonstrate the considerable benefits that can result. When ACAP completed its report on chemistry, its recommendations, if implemented, would have severely restricted the possible range of Ph.D. programs at both the University of Waterloo and the University of Guelph. Realizing this, the faculty of both departments came together and eventually agreed on a joint Ph.D. program that has been remarkably successful, largely because of the maintenance of very high academic standards for both entering students and participating faculty members. A number of other such joint programs have also been very successful. All of these have come about as a result of initiatives taken at the faculty level, however; none have resulted from institutional decisions or by agreement reached in bodies such as the Council of Ontario Universities (COU). Rationalization, of course, also includes the possibility of terminating academic programs, but for reasons discussed elsewhere, very few individual universities have managed to do this and none has done it voluntarily through pressure from an organization such as the COU. While ACAP was my introduction to these issues, my much more substantial and frustrating involvement occurred almost two decades later at Dalhousie University.

There is another aspect of rationalization that deserves comment. Given the vast expansion of knowledge that has occurred over the last century, there is no school or department in any Canadian university that can now hope to have faculty expertise in all of its subspecialties. Few departments, however, have long-term plans identifying those fields to which they intend to give continuing emphasis as faculty members retire and are replaced. It is far better to have a very solid nucleus of researchers in a small number of interrelated specialties than to have faculty members working as individuals across a large number of specialties. There is much to be said for boards of governors requiring each and every department to have such a plan, which can be monitored and updated periodically as the entire research field unfolds, and which can provide continuity to the life of a department, especially when chairs come and go too frequently.

Other aspects of my experience at Western deserve further comment, and several, such as the university/business relationship and the nature of undergraduate education, will be discussed in later chapters.

5
Going to Guelph

By late 1975, after nine years as department head, I recognized that the University of Western Ontario, because of recent senior appointments, could offer few new opportunities. My administrative work and my research kept me quite content, but a time would come when changes would be needed. It was certainly not the routine paperwork of academic administration that interested me – that was just an essential part that one accepted. Rather, it was the opportunity to undertake new initiatives such as the Photochemistry Unit and to stimulate debate on fundamental academic issues such as the nature and objectives of undergraduate education that excited and interested me. It seemed to me that academic administrative positions were too often being seen as just administrative, and not as the opportunities to provide academic leadership that they really were. Since I had already been approached about other university posts, it seemed sensible to keep an eye on advertisements for such positions elsewhere.

The stream of such advertisements in the 1970s was considerable, but few did more than excite only mild interest until I saw the advertisement for the position of vice-president academic at the University of Guelph. It seemed quite a jump from department head to vice-president, but I thought that it might be useful to at least make some inquiries since I knew next to nothing about Guelph. People in other Ontario universities all seemed to look down on Guelph as little more than an agricultural college, although some more knowledgeable persons commented that it had some excellent people in administration and that some of its academic programs were beginning to attract attention for their quality. Consulting the university calendar was of limited help, so eventually, finding little that was discouraging, I prepared and mailed an application.

Within a short period, I was invited to visit Guelph to meet with the selection committee and the president and to tour the campus. This I did, and returned to Western much impressed by what I had seen. My meeting with the committee had appeared to go well, but I was completely surprised a few days later, when the president, D.F. Forster, phoned to tell me that the committee had unanimously recommended my appointment and to ask when I could return to Guelph to negotiate details. In fact, these discussions did not take long; my requests were relatively straightforward and Forster could quickly meet them, perhaps the most difficult being to have me appointed as professor with tenure in the Chemistry Department and to provide me with a research laboratory there. My previous involvements on ACAP had not made me popular with chemistry colleagues at Guelph or Waterloo.

Based on all the information I had been able to gather, my decision to accept the appointment as vice-president was relatively easy. It was clear to me that, while the institution was still often viewed as little more than an agricultural college, such views were outdated and based largely on ignorance. Guelph was in the middle of an enormous transition, and over the previous ten to twelve years, a very strong foundation had been laid on which it was possible to do new things in ways that could not be contemplated in the older Ontario universities. While perhaps still a little rough around the edges, Guelph was a solidly academic institution, and more concerned than most about ensuring the quality of its programs. Although it was hard to break from the very congenial atmosphere of Western's Chemistry Department, the opportunities offered at Guelph attracted me and I accepted the position.

In midsummer 1976, therefore, we moved from London to Guelph, and I began to acquaint myself with the internal workings of the institution. Even at an early stage of my discussions with Forster, he had made it clear that he was looking for someone to be an essentially independent vice-president academic; that he anticipated that the university would shortly undertake a major fund-raising campaign that would occupy most of his time, and that the vice-president, while keeping him informed of issues, would be responsible for internal operations. As it turned out, there never was a fund-raising campaign in Forster's time; nevertheless, he gave me a very free hand to deal with all internal academic issues.

As he had come to Guelph in 1975 after serving as vice-president at the University of Toronto, Forster was a seasoned administrator and completely committed to the concept of the independent vice-president academic. I learned a great deal serving under him; we got on well together, and while I kept him informed of what I was doing, he had numerous other sources of information both on and off campus. He believed very much in keeping his ear to the ground, and I have met few other presidents who were so skilled at it. Although there were certainly occasions when he disagreed with a particular position that I was taking, he would tell me so in private, in quite a mild fashion; in public he was always able to present an opinion that gave no appearance of contradicting or undermining me.

During his term at Guelph, Forster also participated in fewer social events than his predecessors, and often asked me to represent him. I would not have been viewed then as a particularly social person, but this made me participate and also gave me needed experience in public speaking, which I had avoided until then. Forster may well have done this deliberately in order to give me those experiences, although it may also have been related to the fact that he was not a robust person, and his health, which was never good, was not improved by his chain-smoking. I probably could not have found a better mentor and president under whom I could gain experience.

In 1976 the University of Guelph was somewhat anomalous. A major component, the Ontario Agricultural College, had celebrated its centenary in 1974, but the university itself, created by provincial legislation in 1964, was the newest university in Ontario.[8] Before 1964, the three existing colleges – the Ontario Agricultural College, the Ontario Veterinary College, and the MacDonald Institute (which offered degrees primarily in home economics) – were all part of the provincial Ministry of Agriculture, and for them the transition from the civil service to the university culture took some time. For a good many years, to support the teaching programs in these colleges, there had also been growing numbers of faculty teaching arts and science subjects. When the university was established, a single arts and science unit, named Wellington College, was created, but it was disbanded in 1970 to create units of roughly comparable size, with four new colleges added to the founding three: the College of Biological Sciences, the College of Physical Sciences, the College of Arts, and the College of Social Sciences. Each college had its own dean, so that with the dean of graduate studies, and a fairly recently established dean of research, nine deans reported to the vice-president academic, as did the chief librarian, the registrar, the director of continuing education, and the directors of several other units. On the administrative side, Guelph had inherited from the provincial ministry a strong and probably overly large administrative organization, which, particularly in the early years of the university, served it extremely well. Over the next couple of decades, this administration was substantially reduced as financial constraints took their toll, but the university has been well served by the quality of its administration since its foundation.

The first president of the university, J.D. MacLachlan, had been principal of the Ontario Agricultural College before 1964, and the continuity in office helped smooth the transition. He, and especially his successor, W.C. Winegard, who served from 1968 to 1975, laid the foundation for what the university has now become. Some of the innovative structural features are described in this and the next chapter, but one important aspect was the attention given to the physical planning of the campus. While the siting of older buildings could not be changed, long-term development was carefully planned around them with the creation of a ring-road system for vehicular traffic, and a university centre and cross-campus walkways restricted to pedestrians. At the same time, the planned planting of trees took place, and sizeable areas were deliberately kept as open, green spaces. While there have been a few exceptions, the original plan has generally been adhered to, giving Guelph one of the more attractive campuses in Canada. This appearance will be further enhanced in the future as the many tree plantings, especially in the Arboretum, come to maturity.

There were other unique aspects to Guelph in 1976. Because of its history and its original distance from the then small community of Guelph, it still had its own police force and fire station and engine, as well as an extremely large laundry. All of these, as well as other features, reflected the fact that in 1976 there were about ten thousand students enrolled, approximately four thousand of whom lived in residence, a far higher proportion than at almost any other university in Ontario. A strong emphasis had been placed, therefore, on the quality of student life. Consequently, the level of student activity and student programming, not only during the day but especially in the evenings and on weekends, was much higher than I had observed elsewhere. There was a real feeling of belonging to a community.

Early Experiences

I encountered other unusual features of Guelph as my first term began in September 1976. There was the orientation for new students held during the first week. Much of the program was organized through Student Services and so had a pretty solid academic purpose, but although hazing had long been banned, there was still much partying and the usual student high jinks. I was informed that, as a newcomer, I had to participate in a cow-milking competition, arranged of course by the "Aggies." I did not look forward to this, since despite my New Zealand background and my original thought of becoming a farmer, I had never been that close to a cow in my life, but Forster made it quite clear that no excuse was available for me to opt out. Accordingly, on the appointed day, I gathered with my two competing administrators, three cows, and a large crowd of cheering and jeering students in front of the library. We were given the signal to start. To my consternation and the merriment of others, on my first pull at the teats, my cow immediately began to produce streams of bright blue milk! This caused no harm to the cow, being produced by a simple injection given by the "Aggies" just prior to the competition. It did, at least momentarily, bring my milking efforts to a halt, but I was not totally disgraced since I was able to produce a larger volume of bright blue milk than at least one of my competitors.

The institutional culture at Guelph also seemed different, at least in some of the colleges. During the first few weeks, I devoted considerable time to visits around the campus, to Dean's Councils as well as to individual departments. I knew that I had much to learn, and that, as an outsider, I needed to make myself known. During all of these visits, I stressed that I viewed myself as an academic who had chosen to become involved in administration, but that I was certainly not just a paper-shuffling administrator, and that I intended to maintain an active research program with postdoctoral collaborators for as long as possible. With one exception, this was greeted warmly everywhere, and helped reduce the confrontational atmosphere that all too often seems to exist between faculty and senior administrators. The one exception was with the Dean's Council of the Ontario Agricultural College, where, when I explained my intention to continue my research involvement, there was a slight, awkward pause. But only for a moment, since the associate dean politely but bluntly made it clear to me that this Dean's Council expected me to be a full-time vice-president who would always be available to deal with the college's problems and needs! They did not want a vice-president who might be spending time away in his laboratory, even if that did help maintain his academic credibility.

In fact, I did maintain some research activity throughout my time at Guelph, but only through the work of some very able postdoctoral fellows. I attempted to continue research at Dalhousie, but the workload made it impossible to keep abreast of the relevant literature or to think deeply about the research itself. A single term of not more than five years is about as long as a senior academic administrator can also keep at the research front of an academic field.

My decade at Guelph taught me much. While I made mistakes, I enjoyed nearly all of the work, although occasionally I was frustrated by the amount of time consumed in committee meetings. More importantly, my position as vice-president kept bringing to my attention a number of issues about universities that seemed increasingly fundamental, and that also greatly influenced my subsequent nine years at Dalhousie. They are issues that are profoundly important for Canadian universities today, even though others might frame them differently or perhaps have a somewhat different list.

Central Issues

Let me briefly describe these issues here, since they not only provide the framework of my career at Guelph but also establish a convenient structure for the rest of this chapter and the next. Perhaps the most important issue or theme concerns the nature of the academic career in today's Canadian university. Much has been said in the oversimplified, often overheated, and continuing debate on "teaching versus research" or "publish or perish." It is generally accepted that there is a subtle continuum from the didactic teaching of first-year university courses to the more sophisticated requirements of advanced courses, where the instructor must at least be involved in regular reading of the recent literature, to final undergraduate year and graduate courses, which require a strong commitment to high-quality research and publications. But how substantial in the Canadian university is the recognition of this continuum that ranges from the pure, undergraduate teaching function, to what some have called contemplative research and advanced teaching, to active productive research and graduate teaching? Does the institution value these quite different activities equally, or does the faculty reward system place the greatest value on research and publications? Does the university provide guidance on the appropriate balance between these different activities in the individual's academic career? Does the institution use its most valuable resource, namely, the intellects and abilities of its faculty members, most productively by insisting that there should be the same balance between these various functions throughout the academic career of each and every faculty member? What is faculty development, and how can it be encouraged by the institution?

Second, many issues of institutional governance remained unresolved. The highly democratic and participatory structures created in the 1950s and 1960s were implicitly based on the assumption that the sole source of funding was government, with tuition fees as low as possible. The accompanying corollary was that government funding would annually increase by a percentage that equalled or exceeded the rate of inflation. Were these forms of governance just as appropriate in the 1980s, when, in a totally different economic and political climate, government funding had been substantially reduced whether in relation to inflation, or on a per-student basis, or both? Has participatory governance of the university been adequate in a period of limited or declining resources? Has it allowed hard institutional priorities to be set, or consideration given to the closing of long-established programs to enable the creation of new multidisciplinary teaching and research programs that can more effectively tackle the major intellectual issues of today's society? Have forms of university governance recognized the rapidity of change in a new millennium, and its demands for efficiency in decision making, even in a university? Does institutional governance encourage strong links with the major sectors of society, including business, rather than the isolation of the academy of the nineteenth century? Does it stimulate and support new forms of education to help address more complex societal issues, and does it provide incentives for the creation of new partnerships to engage in broad cross-disciplinary research questions and to help develop alternative sources of funding? Finally, does the nature of university governance today provide the transparency and accountability that society now requires, and can it demonstrate to taxpayers and students that they receive value for their money?

The third issue concerns the university's essential educational mission. Most Canadian universities assert that they provide, at the undergraduate level, a high-quality liberal education, but few define what this means and even fewer have in place any method of evaluating the quality of education that is actually provided. Ironically, since the early 1970s, at least ten articles have been written by Canadian academics about the dire consequences of underfunding for every one article on the meaning of liberal education for today's university. By what comparison are Canadian universities underfunded? By what measures could the Canadian public be assured that the nature, quality, and content of university education had actually been improved by the spending of more money? By what methodology are the effectiveness and value of a university education being determined, and how active are the universities in studying and improving that methodology? There is considerable onus on the institution, and especially its faculty members, to be able to explain to the taxpaying public the nature of the education that is provided. It is not sufficient to state merely that universities provide a broad liberal education. What is liberal education at the dawn of a new millennium, and how convincingly can it be shown that liberal education retains great value if the university itself has not maintained a very vigorous academic debate on this issue over the past several decades? Without such debate, does the university even have an educational philosophy?

Fourth, there is the issue of the relationship between the university and society, a relationship that has over the past two to three decades become steadily more important. During the period of very rapid growth in the 1950s and 1960s, Canadian universities were necessarily totally preoccupied with growth. This was as it had to be, but it helped produce an attitude within institutions of complete dependence on governments for financial support, and of detachment from society and society's needs. These factors help explain society's growing disenchantment with universities. I do not mean that there is actual dissatisfaction with the degrees that students obtain, but rather that there is dissatisfaction with the university as an institution. The media have increasingly described Canadian universities as remote and out of touch with society. Recently, the self-interest of economic survival has pressured universities to seek new partnerships, to engage the commercial world, and to be more dynamic, but this has revealed fundamental tensions concerning the nature of the university. How can the university extend itself more effectively towards society and be a real partner without weakening its autonomy, and its ability both to uphold academic freedom and to act as a critic of society?

An issue of equal importance arising from the financial pressures on Canadian universities in the 1980s concerns their ability to engage in strategic planning and in the setting of meaningful priorities. A separate chapter will be devoted to these topics, using both Guelph and Dalhousie as examples.

The Faculty Career

Much of my time at Guelph was eventually committed to matters that directly or indirectly concerned the nature of the academic career. The vice-president academic was expected to lead annual negotiations with the Faculty Association on salaries and related matters. Actually, since the association was not a formally recognized bargaining unit, we held "discussions" rather than "negotiations." While it was therefore possible for the president to recommend to the Board of Governors unilaterally determined salary increases, we knew that discussions leading to an agreement were important for campus peace. By and large, these annual sessions were not confrontational, perhaps because they were only discussions. Still, they were often stressful, and the Faculty Association representatives always pressed vigorously for substantial salary increases and improved benefits, as was their responsibility. There was never, however, any real animosity, and the association usually had a sufficient sense of reality to bargain and trade off one item for another.

As at all Canadian universities, there was the frequent charge that the administration kept secret many budgetary and financial details, so the association members claimed that they were disadvantaged by lack of information in these discussions. Historically, it was true that at most universities the board and the senior administration had not welcomed the increasing pressure for better public accountability, but by the early 1970s, university annual financial statements were generally public documents, and most board meetings became open to the public, with both Faculty Association and student members fully involved. It was therefore incorrect to claim that financial information was kept secret; it was readily available, although not easily digestible.

In responding to this frequent assertion at Guelph, we agreed at one point to compile statistical and financial information and provide it annually to the association to assist in salary discussions. Within two years, with changes in the association's executive, there were again claims that we were concealing financial information. In my experience, most Canadian universities fully recognize their responsibility to be held accountable on financial matters and to make financial information available to faculty, students, and the public, except where privacy concerns affecting individuals are involved. And even here, it needs to be emphasized that in several provinces, legislation requires an annual publication of all individual salaries that exceed $100,000. The real difficulty is that the budget of an institution such as Guelph or Dalhousie is presently on the order of $150 to $200 million (excluding research and ancillary operations), and at large institutions such as Toronto or UBC closer to $500 million. Such a budget is necessarily exceedingly complex, and a full understanding and appreciation of its details takes more time and experience than most faculty members or students are willing to devote.

On the whole, these discussions at Guelph were conducted responsibly, often assisted by the parallel formal negotiations at other Ontario universities which helped produce very similar results. Guelph discussions certainly never exhibited the same degree of animosity that I later found at Dalhousie, and that seems evident at other unionized universities. Occasionally, these semi-negotiations had their humorous side; in one session, the association representatives presented a request that, as an additional benefit, the university might demonstrate an interest in the health and well-being of faculty members, and thus contribute to their health and fitness, by charging minimal or preferably zero admission fees to the gymnasium or swimming pool. To their embarrassment, however, this request was accidentally juxtaposed with another that would have faculty members guaranteed reserved parking spaces immediately adjacent to the buildings where they worked, so that they would have to walk only a minimum distance between car and office!

It was also my responsibility as vice-president academic to chair the Faculty Policies Committee, which, as far as I can ascertain, is unique to Guelph. The faculties of most Canadian universities are now unionized, with the prominent exceptions of Guelph, Waterloo, Toronto, and McMaster in Ontario, and those in Alberta and British Columbia, where unionization of faculty members is forbidden by legislation. A major problem with unionization is that all matters relating to the terms and conditions of employment of faculty members then become issues for negotiation in a confrontational atmosphere. For an institution as complex and diverse as today's university, this is by no means conducive to the development of the best possible policies. A policy, or part of it, may well be traded off for a slightly larger salary increase, or a new policy may be too hastily drafted in the middle of negotiations. Good policy development, especially regarding the terms and conditions of employment of faculty, requires deliberate thought and discussion if the policies are to be in the best interests of the institution and the faculty.

The Faculty Policies Committee at Guelph had been established during W.C. Winegard's presidency in the early days of the university. It consisted of faculty representatives from each college as well as representatives from the Faculty Association, all deans, and both vice-presidents. The balance of membership was such that opinions were expressed thoughtfully and carefully, and there had to be a very clear consensus of opinion, determined by vote, before modifications to policies or new policies could be adopted. A draft of the proposals was distributed to all faculty members for comment before final approval was given, with the new or revised policy being published in the *Faculty Policy Handbook*.[9] Recent changes in composition now require the committee to elect its own chair, and have placed faculty members in a substantial majority. Although board approval is still required for all policy changes, these changes further weaken administration and board authority, and essentially give the faculty control over policy matters affecting their own employment. Under its original, more balanced composition, the committee had to proceed very deliberately, and it seemed to me that this resulted in policies that were generally sound and carefully crafted.

As a minor example, I recall a prolonged debate over the significance to be attached to the signature of a department chair on the list of marks determined by the faculty member responsible for teaching each course, before such lists were sent to the registrar. Did the signature indicate that the chair had actually approved the marks? Or did it mean that, while the faculty member had sole responsibility for determination of marks and for their distribution, the chair's signature merely indicated that the faculty member had indeed completed the task of submitting a marks list? Did the chair, in signing the list, have any responsibility to ensure that the distribution of marks was reasonable and roughly comparable to that of other courses? Clearly, the debate was concerned with the balance between the proper expression of academic freedom by the faculty member and the institutional responsibility to the student. Such a debate, which led eventually to a consensus, could never occur satisfactorily in the confrontational heat of the bargaining table, or even through the use of a side table. The range of issues discussed by the Faculty Policies Committee affected every aspect of the life and work of a faculty member, and I have yet to see a better model for dealing with complex issues of this kind that are central to the concerns of faculty members and to the long-term well-being of the institution.

A further defined responsibility of the vice-president academic was to participate in all college-level tenure and promotion committees. Tenure and promotion matters were first considered by an elected departmental committee whose recommendation (positive or negative) was passed on to the college committee, also elected. Both recommendations were then considered by the president, who made the final decision. There was an appeals process through a university-wide appeal committee. The dynamics that appeared to operate in these college committees was fascinating. While the vast majority of cases were straightforward and strongly supported by both committees, it was readily apparent that in most of those cases where there was a divided vote at the departmental level, the benefit of the doubt tended to be given to the candidate. This was not a surprise because the vote cast by each departmental committee member concerned a colleague with whom one rubbed shoulders every day; human nature determined that it was better to support one's colleague and leave the hard decision to a higher level. The college committee usually took a more distant and firmer line and might arrive at a negative recommendation, which the president would usually support. Of course, the department usually made the same recommendation the following year, and, provided there was some additional supporting evidence, the college committee might support it. Usually, however, the president had the final say, and during his first two years, D.F. Forster rejected at least one-third of the recommendations that reached his desk.

While the appeals process ultimately led to the approval of two or three more, he sent a powerful message across the university about the standards that he expected to see applied at Guelph.

The criteria that were considered for tenure and promotion will be fully discussed in the next chapter. Suffice it to say here that, generally speaking, the research contributions of the faculty member were given the most substantial weight. As discussed earlier, the diversification of fields of specialization within and across disciplines since the Second World War has been enormous, and has made the evaluation of research contributions, even with the use of external referees, less reliable. Moreover, the greater degree of specialization has meant that committees have had to rely increasingly on candidates to name suitable experts as referees, with impartiality all too often being compromised. There are also great variations in the nature and usefulness of referees' letters, quite apart from the ongoing debate over whether the requirement to reveal their authorship inevitably reduces their effectiveness. In the sciences and humanities, such letters, coming from experts nominated by the candidate or selected by a committee, tend to be detailed, covering several pages, and while on occasion there may be unnecessary nitpicking, they can provide fair assessments of scholarly contributions. This also appears to be true for most of the social sciences, but in more professionally oriented fields such as veterinary medicine or, as I later saw, in clinical fields of medicine, the letters tend to be much shorter, less analytical or critical, and in some cases quite personal. In such files, it is not unusual to see letters from outside experts consisting of only one or two brief paragraphs expressing the view that the candidate is a remarkably fine individual who would obviously be a conscientious teacher and a reliable professional! The underlying message seems to be that one professional makes only positive, noncritical remarks about another, and that negative aspects are kept within the profession.

Although no true negotiations were conducted with the Faculty Association, there were from time to time threatening noises about seeking a mandate to become a legal bargaining unit. In the early 1980s, the association requested that a so-called special plan agreement, similar to that at the University of Toronto, be put in place. Such agreements can cover in detailed fashion all or most of the articles that might elsewhere be included in a collective agreement, but without requiring certification under labour relations legislation. The drafting of such an agreement was entrusted to the president of the association and me, and we quickly agreed that such a document should be confined to generalities and should complement rather than replace the functions of the Faculty Policies Committee. While the draft was subsequently approved by both the association and the Board of Governors, a later revision has replaced it with a much more detailed and legalistic document that is much closer in style and language to the Toronto document and to a formal collective agreement. Although the unique role of the Faculty Policies Committee at Guelph, combined with a special plan agreement and work that will be described later under principles for faculty development, have probably worked to delay faculty unionization, there has been continuing drift in that direction.

Governance and Management Issues

The vice-president academic had more specific, day-to-day tasks, many of which required frequent meetings and discussions with deans. Individual issues would range from budgetary problems, to curriculum or program details, to personnel matters involving faculty or staff, particularly appointments and resignations, and even to external and alumni matters. As in most Canadian universities, deans tended to be primarily concerned with the welfare of their own college; in fact, before 1987, when Forster developed the Vice-Presidents' Advisory Council consisting of the two vice-presidents, all deans, and several other senior administrators, the deans had never met collectively together or functioned collectively to help fashion university policies. Constant pressure was needed to make them work as a team for the best interests of the entire university, but they became an effective central advisory council that has come to play a powerful role in university governance at Guelph.

Sometimes, however, the interests of a particular college took precedence. A noteworthy example was the occasion in the 1980s when the external accreditation of the Ontario Veterinary College was being reviewed. At that time, the physical facilities of the college were not outstanding, although they could not have been described as severely inadequate; moreover, budget cuts in the preceding years had reduced the number of faculty and constrained the operations of the college. The dean at that time, perhaps together with some of his senior colleagues, decided to use the occasion of the accreditation visit for political purposes, hoping that a less than positive accreditation report would embarrass both the university and the provincial government sufficiently to produce additional resources. I argued, perhaps naively and in any event to no effect, that the college should take a neutral, entirely academic approach to the accreditation visit and let the report be an accurate and honest assessment of the academic condition of the college. The university was indeed embarrassed by the report, but the government did respond with additional financing and capital funds. The college unquestionably put its own interests ahead of those of the university, but at the same time it helped to illustrate the self-serving ways in which accreditation can be used.

Besides the nine deans, six other senior academic administrators reported to the vice-president academic, and since all served on term appointments of usually five years, there was inevitably much turnover during my ten years in office. For each new appointment or reappointment, there was an elected selection or review committee with a majority of faculty members and one or two students, which I automatically chaired. Working with such committees was always interesting and sometimes unpredictable. One problem concerned the need to maintain confidentiality, especially as the committee reached the point of developing a final recommendation. In my experience, it is the rare case in universities where confidentiality is successfully maintained. There have certainly been a good number of presidential appointments across the country in which confidentiality has been well maintained right up to the official announcement by the Board of Governors, but there have also been embarrassing instances where the correct shortlist of the last two or three candidates was published in newspapers before the committee had made a final recommendation!

The potential for such embarrassment was brought home to me with one selection committee for a dean. The committee had met late one afternoon and into the evening to develop a shortlist of candidates. At nine the next morning, I met with a senior colleague who had returned overnight from a visit elsewhere in Canada. His first question was, "Would you like me to tell you the order of preference of the candidates on your shortlist for the deanship?" In utter astonishment, I listened as he gave me the correct information, which he said he had been told the preceding evening at a city very distant from Guelph!

There were other lessons from observing the work of these selection committees. While we always obtained letters of reference for all candidates, I found that it was essential to check these with other persons whom I knew personally across the country – in too many instances, I gained important information that either contradicted a letter of reference or had been omitted from it. Again, I found that selection committees, when asked to define the characteristics of the ideal candidate, invariably asserted that academic distinction must be the prime criterion, even though the position was essentially one that required good skills in dealing with people and a considerable capability in financial management. Moreover, letters of reference usually reflected this attitude by devoting the first page to a description of the candidate's scholarly distinction, with only brief reference to personal attributes and little if any comment on suitability for an academic administrative position. It is true that academic distinction gives a candidate for a deanship credibility with faculty members, but it does not necessarily bring with it the essential interpersonal and management skills.

There was always pressure to make these searches as open as possible, often by having each candidate give a public lecture. While this certainly increases participation in the process, it does not necessarily improve the process. In some instances, excellent candidates are lost because they are unwilling to participate in what can become no more than a performance, with too much emphasis placed on the candidate's ability as a public performer. Moreover, it encourages a committee to be overly influenced by the tally of votes after such lectures. Indeed, in some Canadian universities, the selection process is essentially determined by such a vote even when careful consideration of other criteria may be much more important.

There is no doubt that the use of selection or search committees is widely accepted across Canada and is perceived as a considerable improvement over methods in use up to the 1950s. Certainly, appointments based on the recommendations of such committees appeared to gain much wider initial acceptability, and this was a decided benefit. On the other hand, there is little hard evidence to indicate that this appointment method is as successful as its proponents claimed in the 1950s and 1960s. The fact is, it is exceedingly difficult to assess accurately the personality and administrative abilities of an external candidate whom one has not known previously, based on perhaps two days of contact, a committee interview, and a public lecture together with letters of reference and discreet inquiries. For many private sector positions, and certainly for university presidential appointments, the process is much more rigorous, involves much greater scrutiny, and usually involves professional consultants. Even for presidential positions, the level of "successful" appointments is well below 100 percent, and where external candidates are appointed as deans or chairs and the process is less rigorous, I would estimate that the success rate is not much greater than 75 percent, and may be even lower. And, as mentioned earlier, it is incredibly difficult to convince faculty members and students, who carefully choose their representatives to serve on these committees, that the committees do sometimes make recommendations that, with hindsight, were ill-advised and that the appointment is not "successful." The attitude then is to blame the appointee or the senior administration, rather than admit that the committee composed largely of faculty members made a mistake!

Other aspects of my participation in governance involved the Senate, where committee work was most important, and the Board of Governors. The Senate at Guelph, as at most Canadian universities, has the primary responsibility for all academic matters, a fundamental aspect of the bicameral form of university governance. At that time, the membership was quite large, exceeding 120, and the Senate usually met monthly. Since the creation of the university in 1964, the president had served as chair of the Senate, as was also the case at Western. This may well have been advisable during the era of student activism in the late 1960s and early 1970s, since it gave the president full control of Senate debate; the president could terminate discussion whenever it was deemed appropriate, and could usually without difficulty have a supporter move adjournment if a meeting was getting out of hand. However, as chair, the president could not participate in discussion. Senate debates at Guelph were rarely contentious, but on major issues the intensity of discussion was quite high. Inevitably, however, most key business was conducted in committee meetings, where disagreements tended to be resolved before a report went to the Senate, and in cases where a report still met criticism or opposition there, it was usually referred back to the committee.

Since the vice-president academic was not formally a member of the Board of Governors, my involvement there was less, although, as in most Canadian universities, vice-presidents usually attended and often participated in discussion. I began to appreciate the importance of the board, as well as the delicately balanced relationship between the president and the board on one side and the Senate, faculty, and students on the other. In most Canadian universities, board members are usually prominent alumni or influential persons in the local or regional community, although in Ontario, legislation requires that board members also be residents of the province. Guelph's alumni had traditionally been from the agricultural or veterinary fields, and since the board itself appoints all but four of its members, this representation has always been substantial. Of course, by 1976 the principle that there be faculty and student members on the board was well established, and these members were appointed through the Senate. On the other hand, I quickly learned that, with regard to the four members appointed by the Lieutenant-Governor in Council, it was not at all uncommon for there to be no prior consultation with the university, or indeed any advance notice before the public announcement.

The very nature of the university's history gave Forster some concerns about the composition of the board, especially in terms of its fund-raising capabilities or its ability to exert political influence other than in matters relating to agriculture. Over time, therefore, he took steps to have a number of prominent Toronto business people appointed in the hope that they might become active in fund-raising. All of them were effective and interested participants at board meetings, but they were also commuters from Toronto to Guelph, and just did not have the same solid links and commitment to the institution as alumni. Forster was thus unable to recruit sufficiently prominent persons to provide the leadership that a successful major financial campaign would require. Some twenty or so years later, the situation is very different, and Guelph now has well-placed alumni in a broad range of fields.

Liberal Education

At Western in the early 1970s, my views on the curriculum and the purposes of undergraduate programs in chemistry had changed considerably. The move to a position at Guelph with university-wide responsibilities encouraged me to think more broadly about undergraduate education, and this interest was quickly focused on the first version of Guelph's mission statement, which stated that a prime objective of the university was to provide an undergraduate liberal education of the highest quality. More will be said about the mission statement in the next two chapters, but the question that it raised in my mind was that of defining the meaning of liberal education for the 1980s and 1990s.

An early opportunity arose for me to raise that question with the Board of Undergraduate Studies, which has been another valuable feature of governance at Guelph. The Board of Undergraduate Studies, or BUGS, as it is more familiarly known, was established to ensure that there was good institutional control of all undergraduate programs and courses. All new undergraduate programs, all modifications to these programs, and all course additions, deletions, or modifications require the approval of BUGS, which in essence has functioned as a mini-senate. Perhaps more because of the particular individuals who were members of BUGS in the 1960s, its role has always been taken very seriously, and while the amount of detail examined is enormous, BUGS has never become a perfunctory administrative committee – it has maintained a clear academic focus. Over the last forty years, BUGS has done much to prevent unnecessary duplication and overlap of undergraduate courses, and has laboured to ensure the academic integrity of new and modified programs. It has also devoted substantial effort to important institutional issues, such as the need to assess the competence of entering first-year students in written and oral English and, where necessary, provide remedial instruction.

The existence of such a powerful institutional body is by no means unique to Guelph; similar boards or committees exist under other names at a good number of Canadian universities. But many others, both large and small, including Dalhousie's, have no such authority to ensure that on all matters relating to undergraduate education, the institution acts consistently and with integrity. In some institutions, there has been too much duplication of courses and course content with attendant waste of resources, and new programs have been introduced that would have served students much better if they had first been exposed to the thoughtful criticism of such a body.

After much debate in BUGS, an ad hoc committee was established in 1979 to examine the nature of liberal education at Guelph. I argued strongly for this, recognizing the significance of the debate that was then under way in the US, as evidenced, for example, by the Harvard Plan for General Education introduced in 1978. In 1980 the Guelph committee produced an excellent report, which was totally accepted by the Senate.[10] There have been many other instances across Canada of strong committees with a majority of senior respected faculty members producing similarly excellent reports that have subsequently died, especially in cases where an issue as old and as controversial as the nature of liberal education was being examined. Why, then, was Guelph able to gain great benefit from this study?

There were probably at least three reasons. First, the work of the committee benefited enormously from the debate and studies in the US that commenced in the preceding two to three years. Second, in my opinion, the timing was almost exactly right. There were legitimate grumblings at Guelph and elsewhere across Canada from very capable and senior teachers in universities that too much lecturing had become content-driven and provided training but little education. What, they asked, really were the objectives of a university undergraduate education? Third, and probably most important, the work of the committee and its report were taken seriously across the university because it was known that both the vice-president academic and the president were fully committed to the cause of liberal education.

For all of these reasons, the issue became an important one at Guelph and did a great deal to refresh the interest and enthusiasm of many faculty members in their undergraduate teaching tasks. The debate and the emphasis that Forster and I placed on quality teaching not only helped develop a better balance at Guelph after the rapid growth and vast expansion of research and graduate activities that occurred in the 1960s and 1970s but it also encouraged the realization that the university is not about "teaching versus research" but about learning at all levels, and about "the development of intellectual, moral, and aesthetic maturity," as the report put it. The subsequent creation of the Advisory Committee on Liberal Education (the immediate response of a university to an important issue is inevitably the creation of a committee!) helped keep this issue at the forefront for the next few years, and the committee then became central to the development in the mid-1980s of a new version of the Aims and Objectives of the University of Guelph, which will be described in a subsequent chapter.

University and Society

The fourth key issue that dominated my time at Guelph is that of the relationship between the university and society. My previous experiences had shown me universities that were essentially separated from the society about them. Yes, an institution such as UBC exists within a society – in fact, within the society that provides virtually all the resources for the university – and, yes, the faculty, staff, and students are all individuals living within that society. But the life that goes on within the university, or at least the life that went on thirty to forty years ago, was essentially separated from and had little direct link with the world about it. Chemistry was presented to students largely as a theoretical subject with scarcely a mention of chemical industry or the applications of chemistry to everyday life, and other subjects were treated similarly. The university was seen as concerned only with the search for truth and knowledge, and the applications of knowledge were left to someone else.

Traditionally, however, one group of universities has always been quite different, namely, those with an agricultural background. One has only to consider the original purpose and present role of the land grant universities in the US to appreciate this difference, a difference that has been at the heart of the low regard that, for example, other Ontario universities have felt for Guelph. When I left Western, even my good chemistry colleagues expressed this when they presented me with a pair of wellingtons, "gumboots" as they are called in New Zealand. But agriculturally oriented universities, whether in the US, Canada, the Netherlands, or New Zealand, long ago achieved the productive and highly regarded links with their communities that Canadian universities have been struggling to develop in the 1980s and 1990s. The US land grant universities and their sister institutions elsewhere have provided, in many cases for over a hundred years, the most productive examples of technology transfer – the rapid and efficient transfer of new research knowledge to the economy – to be found to date. The "green revolution" that transformed agricultural production in both developed and developing countries in the 1950s and 1960s stemmed directly from research in these institutions, and the rapidly growing output of genetically modified foodstuffs continues that transfer today. The University of Guelph has a long record of involvement in such technology transfer, which before 1964 was largely carried out through the Ontario Agricultural College as part of the provincial government. Since 1964, the university has continued to play a major role in agricultural research and extension, and with the recent transfer to Guelph of responsibility for the five provincial agricultural colleges as well as most of the extension programs, this role is now considerable.

What is important in the present context, however, is the impact that such community-linked activities have on the culture of the university. In the first place, it has meant that many faculty members at Guelph are in direct and often frequent communication with those involved in agriculture in ways that rub off immediately on students. This communication may be in the form of a telephone conversation with a farmer having a particular technical problem, or a meeting with industry representatives, or a presentation of a report on current research to a group of industry and government persons. And while these involvements are most directly those of faculty in the agricultural and veterinary colleges, the fact that they occur, and the knowledge of them and the obvious presence on campus of numerous visitors and agricultural groups, subtly influences the atmosphere and culture on campus. There is unquestionably a greater recognition at Guelph than at other institutions that the university exists to serve its community.

The existence of these linkages and the early and continuing involvement of faculty in technology transfer also helped Guelph develop through the 1970s and 1980s good institutional policies on issues such as the ownership of intellectual property, commercialization, and conflict of interest. By and large, these are similar to those now in place at most Canadian universities, but Guelph's early start in their development and implementation helped it avoid most of the problems that have appeared in other institutions. Nor, it should be stressed, are these community linkages restricted to agriculture or technology transfer. Over the last twenty to thirty years, a number of Canadian universities have periodically held "open houses," hoping to give the public a greater understanding of what a university is and what it does. None has matched the University of Guelph, which annually since the 1920s has held a remarkably successful open house known as "College Royal," often attracting 25,000-30,000 visitors per year. Moreover, College Royal is a student-run event, although it regularly receives widespread and enthusiastic support from faculty members across the university, and family and friends of students travel considerable distances from across Ontario to attend. The entire university is linked solidly to the community, and has especially strong links with rural and semi-rural communities.

When I arrived at Guelph in 1976, one of my first visitors introduced himself as the director of the Kellogg-funded Rural Development Outreach Project, and stated that he reported to me. This was a little unsettling for an academic chemist who had no conception of what rural development might be. It turned out, however, that this was an extremely interesting project undertaken to explore ways in which a university could assist and encourage the long-term development of rural communities, and it helped lead to the creation of a new School of Rural Planning and Development. It provided many lessons for those of us within the university, not least the fact that there really is still a great gulf between those who live in small, often isolated rural communities and those regarded as intellectuals who inhabit a university. And while the ideal form of rural development would have a community decide how it wishes to develop, the difficulty in achieving this can too easily lead to the academic telling the community what is best for it!

In many ways, my experiences at Guelph brought home to me the considerable need for Canadian universities to devote much greater effort to working with their communities, however they may be defined. Traditionally, even an activity as valuable as extension education has been seen as an extra, and with the considerable value attached to research and research productivity over the past fifty years, such extras receive less and less attention from faculty in most universities. Of course, such activities can reduce the time available for research, but the survival of universities as they now exist will depend on sympathetic and understanding support from society in general, which even in the year 2002, still provides the greater portion of financial support. Strengthening of ties with the community and provision of more community-directed programs can only increase that sympathy and understanding.

Finally, a most important aspect of outreach at Guelph, an aspect that had been identified in the 1972 aims and objectives document and one that President Winegard had encouraged, concerned international involvement. Guelph was well ahead of its time, at least compared with other Canadian universities, in its early recognition of the importance of internationalization. To some degree, this reflected the fact that agriculture and veterinary science had very direct and immediate relevance to international development, but Winegard had also insisted that such international involvements be accepted as institutional commitments. In too many instances, international projects have been initiated enthusiastically by a small handful of faculty members, with the university becoming aware of its commitment only when a contract arrives for signature.

When the Canadian International Development Agency (CIDA) introduced a new program in the late 1960s that encouraged Canadian universities to develop partnerships with institutions in Third World countries, Guelph was at the forefront and undertook such a partnership with the University of Ghana. To develop the project and to make it an institutional commitment, Winegard insisted on leading the first team to visit Ghana himself, and also insisted that the deans of the colleges concerned accompany him. This helped ensure the success of the project, which has maintained informal links between Ghana and Guelph for over thirty years. The university has since participated in numerous such international linkages in a wide variety of countries, and until CIDA substantially reduced its funding for such programs in the late 1980s, they engaged the attention of numerous faculty and students at Guelph.

I took great interest in these projects since they appeared to have the potential to dramatically increase the international character of Canadian universities, a character that globalization was going to make more and more important for universities. In the early 1980s, we developed an overall strategy for such international involvements consisting of three elements: (1) a wholly owned corporation that would engage in international development projects on a contractual basis with agencies such as CIDA, the World Bank, the regional development banks, and so on; (2) smaller, probably more fundamental projects that would be managed by the university's International Development Office and that might help enhance the institution's understanding of development; and (3) the offering of a coherent program of short-term courses relating to various aspects of international development.

Unfortunately, the strategy could never be fully implemented. The creation by a university of a corporation that might compete with the Canadian private sector was not welcomed by CIDA, at least at the time, and there has never been consistency of either funding or Canadian policy that might have allowed Canadian universities to become as active internationally as their sister institutions in many other countries (Australia, for example). Canada and Canadian universities have just missed the boat in achieving the degree of internationalization of which they are capable. It is true that immigration and visa students have brought a relatively strong international flavour to most Canadian universities, but a more consistent, aggressive policy such as those in Australia or New Zealand over the last two decades could have gained much greater economic benefit for Canada and could have made Canada's universities stronger and much more visible internationally.

Early in 1983, events elsewhere began to have a very direct impact on Guelph. The University of Toronto was seeking a new president, and despite repeated assertions that he had no interest in the post, Forster came under increasing pressure to consider it, and eventually succumbed. Following the announcement of his appointment at Toronto in the late spring of 1983, the Guelph Board of Governors created a search committee to seek his replacement, although given the timing, it was unlikely that an appointment would be made in time for the start of the new academic year. At the request of the board, I agreed to serve as acting president, and indeed was encouraged by many and directly nominated by others to have my name considered for the presidency.

In early August, with Forster's appointment at Toronto due to commence officially on 1 September, my wife, Joy, and I left for the Commonwealth Universities' Conference in Birmingham, UK. Within two hours of our arrival at a pleasant rural English hotel after the transatlantic flight, I received a phone call advising me that, tragically and utterly unexpectedly, Forster had died almost instantly from a severe heart attack during a business trip to Toronto that day. To return to Guelph the next day, to direct all of the preparations for the memorial service, and to deliver the eulogy were extremely difficult and painful tasks. His sudden death was a great personal loss, as it was for many of his other friends at Toronto and Guelph, and it had a major impact on universities across Canada. The University of Toronto renewed its presidential search process, and by the end of 1983 had appointed G.E. Connell, who was then president of the University of Western Ontario. G. Pedersen then moved from the presidency of the University of British Columbia to the presidency of Western, and David Strangway, who had been acting president at Toronto following Forster's death, became president of UBC. In my own case, there was considerable personal disappointment when the board announced in October that B.C. Matthews would become Guelph's next president on 1 January 1984. Matthews was a totally different personality from Forster, but although I had many early misgivings about his very different views on university issues, we found that we could work harmoniously together. Much of my remaining two to three years at Guelph was devoted to drafting a revised statement of the aims and objectives of the university, a statement in which I endeavoured to see reflected the effort that had been devoted to the key issues described in this chapter.

6
Central Themes from Guelph

In the previous chapter, several issues that became central to my decade at Guelph were outlined, and some of the ways in which a vice-president became involved in each were described. Each is worth additional discussion, however, since to understand today's Canadian universities, it is essential to be aware of the way in which attitudes towards each of these issues have evolved over the past fifty years. In the 1950s and into the 1960s, as the universities' remarkable growth in size and complexity gained momentum, there was little debate about the career role of the faculty member; we were all too occupied in coping with growth. In any event, as the large and newly recruited faculties of institutions such as the University of British Columbia or the University of Western Ontario commenced their work, we were convinced that we knew what our task was.

There was debate about whether the Canadian university should continue to be an elite ivory tower, as it had been before the Second World War, or whether its responsibility was to provide universal access for all qualified potential students. Federal and provincial governments quickly made clear that this was not to be debated; all policy directions pointed towards universal access as essential, and while a very few universities, such as Queen's and Mt. Allison, seriously attempted to limit enrollment and to develop further as elite institutions, the financial demands of a new era encouraged most to grow rapidly and the rest to increase enrollment. As young faculty members, however, we had great enthusiasm for all that we did, both the formal teaching and the research; we knew what we were about.

In my opinion, it was the rapid establishment of research-oriented science departments in the larger universities such as UBC, the University of Alberta, the University of Toronto, McGill, and so on that really steered the development of Canadian universities through those two decades. This was perhaps a natural corollary after the Second World War, which had demonstrated the overwhelming importance of scientific research for technological and economic development. For those of us who came to maturity in the 1950s, this was self-evident, as was our responsibility as new faculty members in Canadian universities to have as a priority the creation of vigorous new graduate and research programs. This occurred in most Western countries, and, not surprisingly, the most important activity of each faculty member was seen to be research and publication in refereed journals. It will be evident from the preceding chapters that this was indeed the case at UBC, at Western, and again at Guelph. The emphasis was evident first in science departments and then quickly spread across the entire university, so that research and scholarship became the raison d'être, the mantra, of the academic world.

The spread of this emphasis into some of the professional fields was, I believe, somewhat slower, occurring in fields such as business, law, physiotherapy, and social work, only in the 1970s and 1980s, but it has undoubtedly now became the central focus of the entire university. A consequence of this has already been mentioned, namely, the tendency, especially strong in the 1960s and 1970s, to see honours programs as the vehicle through which we, the faculty, could produce mirror images of ourselves. We seemed to fall into this trap unconsciously in chemistry, but it was a widespread phenomenon. I recall some twenty years ago discussing with a group of historians the issue of undergraduate "education" versus "training," and my astonishment at being told that their purpose in offering an honours program, followed by graduate work in history, was to "train" professional historians. This statement conveyed two overlapping messages. First, there was the naive expectation that many of the history graduates would become faculty members like their professors. Their own mirror images were being graduated, although the scarcity of faculty posts meant that most graduates went into quite different fields. Second, these graduates were being trained in the overly specialized fields of interest to the faculty, probably at the expense of true education.

By the late 1960s and the 1970s, the consequences of this very heavy emphasis on research were becoming evident with the rise of student activism. While much of this was politically motivated and reflected the tumult in North American society at that time, there can be little doubt that it also reflected genuine problems in many universities. Many faculty members were overly committed to research activities, and there was an unrealistic drive to create and populate an almost endless array of graduate programs; it was inevitable that at least some undergraduate students would feel neglected – and they probably were! On reflection, those of us lecturing at Canadian universities were arrogantly indifferent to student opinions about the instruction they received. We sincerely believed that we knew much better than they what the content and style of presentation should be for an undergraduate program. We were, by and large, correct in that view, but surely students had the intelligence and ability to offer constructive comment to which we should have been willing to listen, and from which we could have learned! Our best response, almost universally across Canada, was to agree reluctantly to the use of student evaluations of courses and lecturers, and even more reluctantly that the results of such evaluations could be brought before promotion and tenure committees. By 1980 or so, this had become nearly universal practice across Canada, although the development of, and agreement on, the form of questionnaire that was to be used was often achieved only with difficulty.

It was not that the heavy emphasis on research in the 1960s and 1970s was inappropriate in itself. Given the low commitment to research in both public and private sectors in Canada at that time, it was important that the country's research capabilities be greatly increased. What was wrong, however, was that the balance between the teaching and research commitments of faculty members became skewed too heavily in favour of research, and that research was given such prominence in the reward system. Even to discuss the issue in terms of "research" and "teaching" adds further confusion to the debate. Of particular importance was the firmly entrenched belief among faculty members, a belief still held tenaciously, that research in the university by its very nature enriches teaching. This has always been a given, and is rarely challenged. Yet it is a fact that the individual research or scholarship conducted by the faculty member usually bears at best only an indirect relationship to the undergraduate courses that he or she teaches. It is true that the enthusiasm and curiosity that may stimulate a faculty member's scholarship may well be carried over to enlighten and excite teaching, but not all faculty research is exciting; some (perhaps much) is routine and dull. What then of its impact on the instruction of students? In the last decade, moreover, pressures have come from governments in a number of countries for clear evidence that research does indeed enrich teaching. There has been little solid evidence to support that assertion, and studies conducted to date conclude that there is little if any such correlation.

It is more than regrettable that universities in Canada and in many other countries have allowed the debate to continue in terms of research versus teaching when the reality of academic life is very different. It is even more regrettable that the basic assumption of the academic profession, that research and teaching support and complement each other, has to date not been adequately examined and tested.

As many others have previously stated, today's university can be described as a learning institution in which there is a continuum of persons, each at a different point in the learning process, from undergraduate student to graduate student, to postdoctoral fellow, to junior and then senior faculty member. But all are learners, and the university exists, at least theoretically, as a community in which all learners assist one another. To change the emphasis from teaching to learning enables the university to be seen in quite a different light. There is, for example, immediate recognition that students learn in many contexts, of which the lecture room is just one; they can learn in informal discussions with one another, in social and sporting activities, in residences, and in the library. The essential question is how best to support and encourage that learning without relying solely on instruction through the voice of the professor. Research is learning for the faculty member who conducts the research, and publication of results validates and transmits that learning. Universities have been remarkably passive, and probably negligent, in allowing the debate to be conducted on any other terms, and could be much more aggressive in asserting the true role of the university as a learning institution.

Since the mid-1970s, there has, I believe, been a steady growth in this realization, although hindered by the continuing naive debate over teaching versus research. Faculty are now somewhat more committed to the undergraduate learning experience in Canadian universities, in part because of the recognition that undergraduate students are important both in financial terms and as customers who will attract other customers, but there is still some distance to go in accepting the full implications of the university as a learning institution. To define the university in this sense is fully consistent with traditional understandings of the nature of the university. It emphasizes that the university is a "people place" wherein each individual is important, and that the approach to learning will therefore vary between individuals and from stage to stage.

The Faculty Career and Faculty Development

Nowhere is this more important than in considering the career path of the individual faculty member, a person who will spend perhaps forty years within the university. It is totally unreasonable to expect that such an individual can, or should, follow an exactly constant and unchanging career path, always conducting and publishing first-class research and always being a stimulating teacher of much the same courses, but this is still the expectation. Within the last few years, I was told by one university president that his goal was to have every faculty member in his university be exactly like that, and continue like that throughout an academic career. Yet he and faculty members generally would be the first to assert that the university is not a production line in a factory or a financial institution, that it is indeed a "people place" where differences between individuals, differences in their interests over a period of time, and individual idiosyncrasies are not only tolerated but accepted and encouraged.

Despite that, all faculty members are expected to follow just one unchanging career path. In what other profession or career is there absolutely no concept of professional or career development? What folly! What unintelligent use of human capabilities! Surely it must be appreciated in the university that, for example, a newly appointed faculty member may wish to devote primary attention for a few years to the establishment of a scholarly record, and in fact should be encouraged to do so. But perhaps after a decade, the individual may find that the challenges of presenting to students a totally new and differently organized body of material have a particular attraction, and that primary attention should be devoted to this for a period of perhaps several years. The collegial response should not be, as it has been in all too many cases, "Where is your list of three to four refereed papers for each of the last five years?" And if in another decade the individual decides that a limited-term academic administrative appointment provides a challenging opportunity, the collegial response should be supportive and understanding. In other words, it is only consistent with the real nature of a university for there to be clear recognition that a number of career pathways are open, that such pathways will vary as individual interests change with time, and that the rewards for agreed-upon different pathways should be the same. This, after all, amounts only to recognition that the immense capabilities of the faculty can vary widely, although, of course, only within limits that are appropriate for the academic profession, that they will change with time, and that by providing equal rewards for different types of career, the university utilizes those capabilities most sensibly and efficiently.

At Guelph, by around 1980, when I had become thoroughly familiar with the workings of the Faculty Policies Committee and had seen college promotion and tenure committees in operation for a number of years, this central theme of the faculty career path became more obvious to me. Also, around that time, there was much discussion, mostly in the US about what was termed "faculty development." In many cases, this turned out to mean, "What should the university be doing to assist faculty to improve teaching capabilities?" – a question that is certainly important. The broader meaning, however, and the one we used at Guelph, is much more concerned with the nature and patterns of the faculty career path, and it was in this sense that discussions were initiated with the Faculty Association. These were both tedious and frustrating at first since the association representatives had great difficulty in accepting the good intention of the administration. We were bedevilled by the all too common but unwarranted assumption of faculty that the senior administration was always the "enemy." Eventually, we were able to agree on what were termed "Principles for Faculty Development," namely, that within agreed limits, the career of an individual faculty member could vary significantly, and that each faculty member had the right to negotiate with the departmental committee for agreement on a suitable career pattern for a number of years.[11] It might be one that, for example, for five years emphasized first-year undergraduate teaching with the intent of writing a first-year student textbook. Whatever the agreed career path was, it would be on that path that recommendations for promotion and tenure would be developed by the committee, and not on the unchanging, uniform path described earlier.

This can only be seen as a very small first step, and my understanding is that only a small number of individuals have utilized it since. The need for considerable flexibility in the career path and reward system of universities is as central as ever, however, and at the beginning of a new wave of faculty recruitment in 2000 and beyond, faculty associations, unions, and administrations must take care not to repeat the errors of the past and must ensure that such flexibility is available. Finally, let me offer two concluding comments on this issue.

Faculty members all too often assert that the university is responsible for not valuing instruction highly enough in relation to research, but in fact, in the participatory democracies that Canadian universities have now been for some thirty years, these policies regarding the criteria to be employed for promotion and tenure, and, more importantly, the way in which they are interpreted, have all been determined by faculty members. Indeed, to put it more strongly, my experience has been that even when the university states in its policies that activities such as continuing education or involvement in international projects should be taken into account in promotion and tenure considerations, departmental and faculty committees in practice tend to ignore such instructions and put prime emphasis on research. If the climate within universities, as well as the policies themselves, are to change, it is the faculty members who must change them.

And yes, faculty development in its broadest sense should address the question of what the institution should do to assist faculty members in improving instruction, and to enhance and develop all aspects of their careers. My own opinion is that every Canadian university should provide a strong continuing program of short courses on teaching skills and methods, that every new faculty member should be required to attend an introductory course that emphasizes the institution's learning objectives and faculty responsibilities towards students, and that every faculty member should be expected to take at least one such course within each five-year period. Similarly, the university should offer courses on the management of research grants and on personnel policies that affect individuals employed under research grants, and so on. These are not unreasonable expectations; faculty expect the university to assist them in developing their research program by providing extensive library resources, information technology facilities, and laboratories. They should also expect the institution to assist them in further developing their expertise in all other aspects of their responsibilities, and in return should be expected to use the opportunities provided.

Some Effects of Governance Changes

In the earlier chapters, I commented on the changes that have occurred in the governance of Canadian universities since 1950, and on some very specific issues, such as the nature and role of the position of department head or chair. Putting these together, it is clear that the very major change in the way in which universities govern themselves occurred across Canada in the period around 1968-75. The University of Western Ontario, with the introduction of the UWO Act of 1967, was one of the first, but essentially all universities quickly followed with reforms that emphasized the participatory governance of the institution, largely by faculty and to a lesser degree by students. The principal features of these changes were described in Chapter 3, although naturally there were variations from institution to institution. In general, the changes were those recommended by the Duff-Berdahl report of the 1960s, and they were enthusiastically supported by faculty across Canada.[12] Academic administrators, some of whom made arbitrary decisions and who remained in office indefinitely, were thus removed, and the collective will of the faculty reigned supreme. Any critical assessment of these changes in governance would conclude that they were overdue and in the right direction, given the nature of universities and given the societal circumstances of the 1960s. This was a time of rapid growth of universities accompanied by an at least equal growth in funding, and faculty considered that they, as the central component of the institution, should have major decision-making powers. Certainly in Canada, regardless of what occurred in some European countries, faculty did not accept that students should exercise a similar or anywhere near equal power.

There are good reasons, however, for concluding that these governance changes, while they may have been perfectly appropriate for the time, tilted the balance of power in the universities so far in the faculty's favour that the institutions now cannot cope well with markedly different circumstances. These changes might not have had such an extreme effect if university boards had sought parallel changes that could have preserved the integrity of the university. For example, while boards were probably correct in agreeing to term appointments for academic administrative posts and to a consistent use of selection committees, should they not also have insisted on adequate job descriptions for each of those positions to ensure that the administrative needs of the institution were fully met? In hindsight again, however, and recalling the mood of society in the late 1960s, when such boards were widely seen as conservative and reactionary, it seems unrealistic to expect that there would have been a different outcome.

In addition, the more minor changes that have occurred subsequently have continued to shift the balance in the same direction. Consider, for example, the manner in which university budgets have been prepared. Before around 1970, these were the exclusive prerogative of the senior administration and the board; indeed, in nearly all Canadian universities, the present empowering legislation still states unambiguously that the board or its equivalent has full and complete responsibility for all financial and property matters. When the major governance changes occurred around 1970, however, it was widely recognized by faculty and ultimately accepted by governments and boards that there is not a clear separation between academic matters and financial matters. A senate, therefore, cannot and should not deal with new program proposals without some reasonable understanding of the institution's financial position. Thus, the changes made in the 1970s usually provided for the creation of a senate budget committee or equivalent. Previously the budget would have been prepared by the senior administration and submitted, usually in confidence, for the approval of the board; presumably the board might make significant changes in at least some cases. With senate budget and finance committees in existence, budgets since 1970 are still prepared by the senior administration but now become public documents as soon as they are presented to senate committees. In some cases, such committees can make significant changes, while in others they can only comment or suggest change. In all cases, however, the result is that when the budget comes to an open meeting of the board for final approval, it is that much harder for any changes to be made in what has been a public document for some time. Even in financial matters, therefore, boards have increasingly become rubber stamps, while the faculty, through senates, have exercised steadily increasing power.

The greatest weakness of the present forms of university governance in Canada and elsewhere lies in the assumption that there is indeed a collective will of the faculty that can provide consistency and direction to governance of the institution. In the period 1955-75, the only necessary collective will was the will to grow. It was not necessary for any person, office, or committee to decide on a particular direction for growth; more than enough proposals for new initiatives came forward spontaneously and, provided there was a reasonably rigorous screening process, enough survived for growth to be vigorous. From 1975 to the present, however, all Canadian universities have experienced serious financial constraints or even reduced funding, and in such circumstances, as will be discussed fully in the next chapter, existing forms of participatory governance have been inadequate, since there is no collective will of the faculty. What *has* remained in effect, even under such changed circumstances, has been the collective will to grow! It is necessary only to look at the program offerings at any Canadian university to see the continuing stream of new program approvals at a time when imminent financial disaster is being predicted, and to appreciate that the 1970s linkage between academic and financial matters has now been conveniently forgotten. Adding any program to a university's range of offerings brings increased costs – there will always be at least minor extra administrative expenses, and certainly additional library costs – yet in every case, it seems possible to rationalize these away as insignificant. It is also the case that governing boards, which hold ultimate financial responsibility, have usually agreed to these new program initiatives despite claims of inadequate funding for existing programs.

It was at Guelph that I began to appreciate the extent to which the modern Canadian university has lost its earlier sense of community. Previously, my task had been to advance the interests of particular groups or units, be it the inorganic chemists at UBC or the entire Chemistry Department at Western. At Guelph, however, my perspective had to be that of the entire institution, and I quickly came to appreciate how disparate the goals and interests of the different components of the university were. Often, indeed, they were in direct conflict with one another, and this in a university that by history and tradition had a better sense of community than most. From time to time, the agricultural college would suggest through its dean, as a means of applying pressure, that perhaps it would really be better off if it returned to its earlier status as a part of the Ministry of Agriculture, and it was equally clear that the biological scientists had no high regard for some social science units, which in their view should be eliminated, with the funding being diverted to biology, of course. And to most, the administrative units were bloated and inefficient, and much of their work could be done by the academics in their spare time. It is easy to dismiss most of this as just the internal grumbling that occurs in any organization, but it was in fact more fundamental. What was being shown were the effects of growth and the effects of separateness that size and increased specialization had produced.

In many universities, deans of faculties provide a similar demonstration. Pressed by their faculty members and even more by department chairs, they tend to act as totally independent and highly competitive barons, fighting for whatever resources and recognition are available with no concern for anyone else or for the institution itself. At Guelph, at Forster's insistence, the deans were made to work collectively as a senior advisory committee, and have been able to provide real leadership to the university community. This could be achieved, however, only by insisting continually that they were an essential team in the administration of the institution, and that their role was not just to represent and be an advocate for their own faculty but to arrive collectively at recommendations in the best interests of the entire university.

Liberal Education and Institutional Objectives

Turning now to another major theme, and accepting that the university is better described as a learning institution, thereby avoiding the "education" versus "training" debate, it is essential for the institution to define its objectives for learning. This had been emphasized during the debate on the nature of undergraduate education in the US during the 1970s and 1980s.[13] The debate was marked by such highlights as the Harvard Plan for General Education of 1978, the strenuous efforts of an American Secretary of Education,[14] and the bestselling book by Allan Bloom.[15] Perhaps the most persuasive reports are those of the Association of American Colleges, especially the 1985 *Integrity in the College Curriculum: A Report to the Academic Community.*[16] Such a thorough and prolonged debate of perhaps the most fundamental issue for universities and colleges has had no parallel in Canada. The Association of Universities and Colleges of Canada (AUCC) did sponsor the study of undergraduate education undertaken in 1991 by Stuart Smith, but his report,[17] while fully consistent with US criticisms, was greeted unenthusiastically by AUCC members and had little if any impact on Canadian universities.

What are, or should be, the skills and attributes that the university expects a student to acquire as a result of an undergraduate education? To describe the university as a learning institution is appropriate, but it carries with it the obligation, as several of the above studies emphasize, for the university to define its learning goals and not just describe in its calendar the list of courses that compose each program. Learning objectives for undergraduate education can and should differ from institution to institution, and certainly from program to program: the learning objectives of a Bachelor of Arts program will be very different from those of a Bachelor of Engineering program. But if a university does not define those learning objectives, what then is its educational philosophy and what understanding does it have of its own mission?

The next chapter contains a more detailed discussion of university planning and of the development of mission statements and statements of aims and objectives. At Guelph in the mid-1980s, as part of such activities, we were able to develop and gain approval for a university statement of undergraduate learning objectives; indeed, Guelph is one of only a few Canadian institutions that publishes such a statement in its official calendar and intends this to be a guide as well as a commitment to students. At that level, however, a statement is inevitably fairly general, and it is only when such objectives are refined and applied at the individual program and then at the actual course level that they become really meaningful. Only small institutions of the liberal arts type, such as Alverno College in Milwaukee, have so far been able to do this with measurable success, although the consistent emphasis on learning and its defined objectives over a period of years can exert a great influence on institutional culture and produce change.

In most Canadian universities, however, there is little tradition of continued internal debate of educational philosophy and of the learning environment of the institution. During the past forty to fifty years, university senates have been largely preoccupied with the administrative requirements for the introduction of new programs and for dealing with growth, and have rarely debated philosophical issues such as the meaning of liberal education in the twentieth or twenty-first centuries. Senates have tended to become administrative rather than academic, and this trend has also been evident at the individual program level. In most universities, there is a committee that has overall responsibility for each undergraduate program, and one might reasonably expect the debate on learning objectives for that program to occur there. Such debate might well have occurred in the 1950s or 1960s, whenever the program was first conceived and introduced, but these committees have subsequently tended to become administrative, dealing primarily with mechanical details such as course changes and additions or deletions, and all too rarely debating and reconsidering the long-term learning objectives of the program. In too many Canadian universities, the senate or its equivalent has not exerted sufficient control or pressure on program committees to require such debate, although the increasing use of periodic external reviews of programs, especially undergraduate programs, should lead to insistence on the need for learning objectives to be defined and for continued review and debate to take place.

Finally, in this context, while it may be blindingly obvious to the reader, it is probably still useful to point out that when senates or committees are thus criticized, the object of the criticism is really the faculty collectively.

Connections with Society

On the fourth major issue, concerning the university's relationship with society, Guelph had much to teach from the type of outreach activity described in the previous chapter, but even more from the comprehensive manner in which most of these involvements were institutionally organized and managed. As is obvious by now, most sprang from the agricultural, rural side of the university, which had behind it a century of tradition. Before 1964, the agricultural and veterinary colleges had been part of the provincial civil service, but on the creation of the independent University of Guelph, most of the relevant research, the teaching of the Diploma in Agriculture program, and some extension and continuing education work became funded under a contract between the Ontario Ministry of Agriculture and Food and the university. These contractual arrangements, which have evolved and changed over the past thirty-five years, provide a remarkable demonstration of the intermediate and long-term benefits of such strong links. Above all, as already indicated, they are particularly significant in the development of a culture that emphasizes that the university is not an ivory tower, is not an isolated academic institution, but exists to serve society, a culture that permeates all components of the University of Guelph.

While there have been significant changes over the years, the basic framework of the contract continues and is widely viewed as being very successful. Through discussions that involve not only government and university personnel but also representatives of the farming and agriculture-related industries, specific major research objectives are identified, such as improved beef production or the development of new and improved crops. Similarly, current major agricultural problems, such as the outbreak of a specific animal disease, may become a significant theme. Each such program theme is defined and modified by an advisory committee composed of representatives of government, the private sector, and the university – a committee that periodically conducts a complete and very thorough review of that program, often with significant changes in the research direction.

While the overall issues and themes of each program are directed in this way, the numerous individual research projects that comprise it are designed and controlled by each faculty researcher. In other words, the faculty member proposes particular research projects to address specific issues within a program, and the advisory committee decides on the appropriateness of each. Academic freedom is thus protected, although of course if a faculty member chooses to conduct research on projects that do not fit into any of the programs, funding is not available under the contract to support those projects. The university has the overall responsibility for managing the contract in terms of finances, and also for ensuring that reporting deadlines and other administrative requirements are met. While such a management system could lead to an undue emphasis on short-term research in pursuit of immediate results of benefit to agriculture, in general it has led to quite balanced research programs. For example, under research in agro-meteorology, some fundamental work was conducted on theories of turbulent flow, a topic that might seem of little interest to the farming community. However, the model used in this work was that of airflow over a cornfield, and a convincing presentation by the researcher of its relevance to agriculture ensured its funding. Indeed, essentially all programs contained a balance of unfettered basic research together with applied research and development.

There is, of course, the question of whether the availability of funding under the contract distorted in an undesirable way the choice of research projects made by the faculty members. From time to time, as agricultural problems and crises emerged and evolved, there have certainly been some pressures that could have influenced those choices, but otherwise there appeared to be no evidence of such distortion. If it existed, it did not differ in any way from the effects of other government research funding programs, such as those developed by the National Research Council and the Natural Sciences and Engineering Research Council, many of which in recent years have been introduced to encourage research that can lead to economic development. In any event, the choice of research topic is left entirely to the faculty member. At the program level, however, there were some conflicts between government policy directions and research interests. For example, during my time at Guelph, no research funds were available from the contract with the Ministry of Agriculture and Food in the area of agricultural economics, since there was strong disagreement in the School of Agricultural Economics with government policy, which favoured agricultural commodity marketing boards.

The fact that the university was responsible for managing an extremely large research contract, which by the mid-1980s exceeded $30 million annually, brought an early awareness of contract-related issues such as ownership of intellectual property and the principle of open publication of research results, which required Guelph to be an early leader in the development and implementation of appropriate policies. The application of research results and commercialization have never been seen at Guelph as activities in which a university should never be involved; on the contrary, they have been consistently encouraged, although the need to have suitable policies in place well in advance has been well recognized. This is not to claim that all such policies were correct when first developed, but rather to assert that the culture at Guelph, with an emphasis on service to society, ensured that policies were developed early on and willingly modified later on the basis of experience. Even matters such as some of the ethical issues that are now becoming prominent in genetic engineering in crops, foods, and animals have been under discussion at Guelph for decades, although their resolution is not necessarily easier.

Some would define the objective of a university as the search for truth and the dissemination of knowledge, but it has always interested me that the University of Guelph Act of 1964 states that the purpose of the university is "to serve society." It is this statement, coupled with the agricultural tradition and history of the institution, that makes it such a relevant leader in education and research.

Most Canadian universities have encouraged and supported closer ties with industry, businesses, and society in general, particularly over the past fifteen years or so. There is, however, a question about motive. Declining levels of government funding inevitably cause eyes to be turned in other directions and alternative sources of money to be sought. Nor is this entirely inappropriate; a closer relationship between academia and the commercial world must inevitably bring some benefits to each, including funding to the university. But to what extent is preference being given to the linkages that bring just a financial benefit, with less attention being paid to other links with the broader society? There is a vast difference between a recognition that a university exists to serve society, and those forms of service or linkage that, while perhaps ultimately of benefit to others, are motivated primarily by the self-interest of those in the academic community.

7
The University Mission, Planning, and Priorities

The inherent weakness of the present governance structures of Canadian universities is most readily apparent when the issues of institutional planning and the setting of priorities are considered. Again, universities in many countries worldwide have experienced problems similar to those described here, but it is noteworthy that outside Canada, with few exceptions, there have usually been external pressures, often from government, sometimes in the shape of formal legislation, that have forced universities to address these issues. Such external pressures, other than in the form of financial constraints, have rarely been evident in Canada.

While most Canadian universities have responded to such constraints by developing mission statements in the last two to three decades, and have often engaged in strategic planning exercises, the results have been meagre in comparison with the time and resources consumed. The mission statements have all too frequently been vague and nonspecific for the institution; any statement might apply equally to any institution. While many place great emphasis on the search for excellence, few indicate how progress towards that goal is to be determined, and virtually none identify the strengths and weaknesses of the university except in the most general terms. Above all, the relationship between such strategic planning and the allocation of resources within the university is almost nonexistent, except for the identification of some areas where all would benefit from increased expenditures. The allocation of additional resources to the library for the purchase of books and journals is typical of such a "priority."

Why have our universities demonstrated such inability to determine priorities? Why have such planning exercises so completely failed in identifying programs that are now of less importance or are academically weak? How can universities, even while complaining of the ill health of their finances, continue to add new programs while rarely terminating an existing program? Indeed, is it possible for universities to have priorities or to plan for the future?

The Loss of Community

An essential part of the answer to such questions can be found in the changed character of Canadian universities. Before the Second World War, they were generally small, often with less than a thousand students, and with limited financial and physical resources. But each tended to be a real community – faculty socialized together a great deal, and they knew and were known by their students. Most had a deep interest in the welfare and survival of the institution, and certainly for the majority of faculty and for students, their first loyalty lay with the university. For all of them, the university was their community.

The events and developments of the past fifty years have wrought a complete change. While it can be argued with justification that some small universities such as Mt. Allison or Acadia have retained some sense of community, elsewhere postsecondary institutions have each become loose collections of many small, separate mini-communities, and even within these there is often not much cohesion. The university campus, or, more correctly, the individual departmental buildings, are the places where faculty members go to work, to teach, to meet students, and above all to conduct their research. There is little socializing; many departments do not even have a coffee room, and when they do, it may be used by only a minority, and in all too many cases, faculty meet together only at departmental meetings. It is no accident that at so many Canadian universities, including UBC, Western, and others, faculty clubs have disappeared, while at others they struggle to survive by opening the facilities to any who might wish to use them. In general, there is little socializing among faculty, or between faculty and students; in most cases, what there is will be among members of the same department.

Not only is today's university a collection of separate mini-communities that only rarely communicate with each other, and so do not know each other, but these mini-communities have quite different and often competing interests and objectives. The English Department and the Biochemistry Department do not know each other, and neither knows or understands the Law School; each has a different perception of what is important for career progression and for the long-term health of its own small community. When there is a lack of community, collegiality is nonexistent and institutional priorities cannot be agreed upon.

A number of factors have contributed to this fragmentation of the earlier university community. First, the growth of universities over these fifty years, although necessary to provide universal access to postsecondary education and to absorb rapidly increasing enrollments, has created large, complex bureaucratic institutions spread across large campuses. The university seems to be, and usually is, an impersonal institution in which it is impossible to sustain the personal contacts and relationships of the earlier, smaller university community. Moreover, growth occurred so rapidly, perhaps much more rapidly than was desirable, in the 1960s and 1970s that the rate of growth itself helped to destroy the sense of community. Canadian universities were not alone in this; rapid growth occurred in universities in many Western countries. But Canada was different in that so many new faculty members had to be recruited from elsewhere, and this in turn further fragmented the universities.

Second, the great emphasis that has been placed on research and scholarship since the Second World War has inevitably detracted from the importance of the purely educational mission of the university, and has contributed significantly to fragmentation and loss of community. Third, and closely related to that research emphasis, the continued specialization within each discipline and subject area has inevitably directed the interests of faculty members away from the institution. When Professor Brown is the only specialist in the history of Outer Mongolia at the University of Central Canada, he or she will be far more interested in discussions with a colleague in Florida than with the person in the next office who specializes in some aspect of modern European history. Such hyperspecialization produces experts, but it cannot produce the generalist and in too many cases does not produce the scholar. Fourth, and very importantly, e-mail and the Internet and all the effects of globalization have now made it not only possible but very easy to do exactly that: the academic community of one's scholarly specialization is now global. The combination of all these factors has produced a highly fragmented university, an institution that is today a loose federation of many mini-communities often heading in quite different and sometimes opposite directions.

While some may see this as an exaggerated description of today's university, consider this question: Does the faculty member in today's Canadian university give prime allegiance to the specific university that provides employment, to the department or school in which academic work is conducted, or to the external research community that provides the intellectual excitement and opportunity? Over the past decade, I have asked many faculty members this question, including many recognized as leaders in their fields, and I have yet to encounter a faculty member who will claim that the university has his or her first allegiance. Yes, the university provides employment and salary, but these could be provided equally well through any one of a number of other mechanisms. Many faculty members are essentially indifferent to the well-being and long-term future of their own university. A minority, often because their prime interest is in students and teaching, will assert that their loyalty lies first with the department to which they belong, and hence to the academic program in which they teach. But the majority immediately reply that their prime interest, and first loyalty, lies with the intellectual, scholarly, or research community that works in their field of specialization. And if that community has been formalized into some form of continuing network, and in a few cases into an organized formal network, their only real interest is to see that community sustained and continued regardless of the future of the university. Some of the more thoughtful have said that they would hope that a common interest in the teaching function would ensure the continued existence of the university, but that clearly was of secondary importance.

Budget Reductions and the Pressure to Plan

Nowhere has this loss of a sense of the university as a community been more apparent in the last twenty or so years than in the many attempts at university planning and priority setting. The pressures to undertake planning have varied across Canada, but in general it has been financial constraints that have forced universities into planning processes. In Ontario, for example, such constraints began in the mid-1970s, at least to the extent that, thereafter, funding increases were rarely sufficient to match inflation, and in the 1990s funding actually decreased. All other parts of Canada have had similar but not identical experiences.

To address these constraints, annual reductions have been required in base budgets. At first these were invariably applied as across-the-board reductions, extracted equally from all components of the university. Very quickly, however, the call would come to protect the academic side of the institution as much as possible, and subsequently larger budget reductions would be made to administrative and nonacademic units. Over a period of years, these cuts would further remove flexibility as the budgetary portion required to provide salaries for tenured faculty and permanent staff steadily increased. Funds for part-time lecturers, demonstrators, and visiting professors were lost, and funds to purchase equipment and supplies were annually reduced. Where possible, expenses were taken from grants and other outside sources of funding, and the incentives to increase such funds mounted annually. In most universities, the provision for salaries, even after such cuts, grew dramatically due to annual salary increases and the increasing age of faculty, so that by the 1990s the total salary cost for all faculty and staff consumed over 80 percent of the budget. In most universities, there was recognition that the library had to be protected as much as possible, since annual acquisitions costs, imposed largely by commercial publishers for journals in which faculty members published, were increasing by at least 15-25 percent per year. Otherwise, however, only scrapings were left for any new undertakings, and a faculty usually had to absorb such costs within an existing budget. This has been the situation for all Canadian universities over the past fifteen years or so: across-the-board cuts applied to all academic units, with still larger reductions being required of all other parts of the institution.

An external observer might well point out that, in any university, not all academic departments or units are of equal importance, although that importance might vary from one university to another. Similarly, every institution has groupings of faculty that, by design or by the accident of some fortunate appointments, are recognized internally and externally as superior. An observer might then suggest that surely the university's long-term future might best be developed by the closure of one or two less important units so that the academic strength of superior units could be maintained or further improved. Powerful logic would also assert that, with the enormous expansion of knowledge and research over the past fifty years, no university can be excellent in everything, and that concentrating on a few carefully selected fields in which to strive for excellence would be a better strategy. Surely, then, each university should define its specific mission and declare unambiguously its priorities. And, of course, across Canada such external observers, often from governments, have suggested that "differentiation" of the province's universities would help improve the university "system." Unfortunately, such observations fail to define "differentiation" or, alternatively, leave that to the universities themselves. In any event, there is no "system," only an aggregation of independent competing institutions.

While those within the university community have generally been unimpressed by such external observations, the arguments in favour of planning and priority setting within the institution are in fact very compelling. It is really possible to identify major areas or themes of scholarly endeavour or research, each of which will be of intellectual importance and great value for at least a decade, and which could be the priority of a particular institution. Ocean studies, specific aspects of health care or of Canadian culture, artificial intelligence, and many, many others come quickly to mind. Canadian universities have, to date, been markedly unsuccessful in identifying and claiming any such fields as priorities for their institution. This is not to suggest that within Canadian universities there are no distinguished groups of faculty conducting internationally recognized research and offering first-class graduate and undergraduate education in identifiable themes of this type. The truth is that there are many such, of which Canadians can be justifiably proud, but these have invariably arisen through the initiative of a small group of faculty, and they usually have little if any recognition from the institution. Virtually none have been created or strengthened as a result of the university's identifying the field as a priority, or as a result of deliberate planning.

This conclusion is amply reinforced by the history of the development by Dr. Fraser Mustard and his colleagues of the Canadian Institute for Advanced Research (CIAR) and by the now obviously very successful Program for Networks of Centres of Excellence put in place by the federal government. These initiatives all involved the planned identification of particular themes of scholarship and research that are presently of considerable intellectual interest, and in some case of future economic potential, and of the necessary steps to create effective Canadian groupings in these fields. The point is that these have all been planned developments, and interestingly all were initially resisted by the universities. They have come into existence and have achieved considerable success despite university opposition and despite the obvious inability and unwillingness of the universities to identify and develop such priorities or to engage in meaningful planning.

Of course, it can rightly be claimed that CIAR and the federal agencies developed these major program themes by consulting with distinguished faculty members from many Canadian universities. But it was necessary for external agencies to do this: the same faculty members within their own universities would have been quite unable to achieve the same result because of the governance structure of the institutions.

Attempts to Plan

What is it, then, about the governance of our universities that makes planning and the determination of priorities so impossible? Good illustrations come from my own experience at both Guelph and later at Dalhousie, and there are many others. Most universities have attempted very seriously to engage in such planning, and there have been significant scholarly writings on university planning. The work of Keller has been particularly influential.[18]

The first step requires the drafting of a mission statement for the institution, and participatory governance usually requires that a representative committee be struck by the senate or occasionally jointly by the senate and the board. Since the task is rightly seen as important, the resulting committee tends to be large, rarely fewer than fifteen and often twenty-five or more persons, including some students. In most instances, the committee is starting from scratch since the university has had no previous statement, although Guelph was exceptional in that an excellent statement of the university's aims and objectives had been officially approved in 1972. This statement contained many of the usual general items, including the declared intent to provide an excellent liberal education for undergraduates, but it was well ahead of its time in that it also placed an emphasis on international outreach and participation in international development, and, importantly, it identified Guelph's particular emphasis on life sciences.

By the time I arrived at Guelph in 1976, there was already recognition that there could not be unlimited growth, especially in the area of graduate programs. The Senate Committee on Academic Priorities had therefore provided the Senate with a report that recommended upper and lower limits for enrollment in each existing graduate program and suggested that only a few identified new programs should be introduced. While this had ultimately been approved by the Senate, it immediately faced the usual academic criticisms that plague all planning efforts. Those dissatisfied with the report claimed that arbitrary judgments had been made, and particularly that those who had made them had not considered all of the relevant evidence. Despite these criticisms, the report took effect and generally controlled enrollments within the approved limits for a number of years.

With changing circumstances, however, its impact was steadily eroded, and by the late 1970s, a different and more comprehensive approach to planning was required. Interestingly, a few of the deans argued strongly that priorities had to be determined in order to avoid across-the-board budget reductions, but naturally those of this view were the deans who believed that their own faculties would thereby benefit.

In 1978 information was obtained about an approach to planning that had been developed and implemented at the University of Houston in the US, an approach that appeared to be convincingly and logically sound. This attribute was particularly important since the major criticism of most planning in universities has been that arbitrary judgments are too often made about the quality of academic units. This had been the major weapon used to attack the work of the Advisory Committee on Academic Planning (ACAP) in its examination of graduate programs in Ontario universities: despite the fact that ACAP worked with those involved in a particular discipline to define the appropriate information to be used in quality assessment, its unpopular conclusions and recommendations were usually attacked on the grounds that the appropriate information had not been taken into account and that the judgments were arbitrary! A planning model based on strong internal logic was therefore an intriguing discovery. Without describing the methodology in detail, it is sufficient to indicate that it involved comparisons of academic units based on a standard set of data collected from the units concerned, and an examination of budgetary allocations to all academic units compared with average allocations in a number of comparable Canadian institutions.

It was a very detailed, logical, but time-consuming approach. While it had initially been used at Houston to examine all academic units, it had later been modified to apply almost equally to the administrative side of the university. Because it involved such time and effort, we at Guelph had no alternative but to address the academic component first, and were able to examine administrative units only after several years. In fact, while logical and sound, this planning approach had one substantial defect. This lay in the fact that planning could not have any direct impact on the budget until the entire process was complete, and the effort became so time-consuming and was so resisted that it was eventually overtaken by events. Also, like any other planning approach, the process involved the making of judgments about criteria as fundamental as "quality" and "centrality." Such judgments were made in light of masses of material and information supplied by the units concerned so as to constitute a consistent set of data to enable comparisons. Yet only in the minority of cases, where the judgments agreed with the opinions of those in that unit, were they acceptable. In all other cases, where quality or centrality were judged to be only average or less, the judgments were said to be "arbitrary" and "unsound."

In fact, however, in this case as in many other planning endeavours, the types of judgments that were made were identical to those that faculty make in arriving at grades for students. Yes, there are examination papers, term marks, test results, and so on, but eventually each faculty member makes a judgment call based on all the evidence available and assigns a mark for each student. Apparently the making of such judgments is entirely acceptable insofar as it applies to students but absolutely unacceptable if it applies to faculty. But the more fundamental conclusion that becomes obvious, as it certainly did in the prolonged debate about the application of the Houston plan at Guelph, is that faculty members' reaction to such a planning model is determined entirely by its impact on their own segment of the university, be it school or department. In all the discussions, there was little concern for the well-being of the institution as a whole; in every case, the reaction to the planning work was decided by the extent to which each unit felt threatened or even criticized. The responses were based entirely on the self-interest of each mini-community.

In terms of governance, this same attitude is reflected in the work of any large representative senate committee engaged in such planning. Each member will define a role according to the best interests of the faculty or unit that he or she represents; the widespread attitude is that they are there as representatives of each separate community and not as members of the single community of the university. It is the rare individual in today's university who, when faced with a recommendation that might adversely affect his or her own unit, but which might be sensible in terms of the institution's interests, will consider supporting it. But it is the collective behaviour of the senate or a large representative committee that determines the fate of any planning or priority recommendation. Consider what happens when, for example, a recommendation is made that might reallocate resources to a few units that are judged to be superior in quality at the expense of some seen as being of poor quality or less important to the institution. What shapes the debate within the senate or the committee?

First, one essential point must be made. In every Canadian university, those who are widely seen to be the outstanding scholars, either by reputation or because of external recognition or awards, generally pay little attention to the senate and take as little part in its work or in committee work as possible; their primary focus is entirely on their research field and its external community of scholars, and perhaps on whatever related teaching they are asked to do, or consulting activities and the like. They add to the reputation of the university but assiduously keep well away from any aspect of its governance. Those who serve on the senate or on major committees represent the more average faculty member, or those with a particular issue or concern on their minds, or those with some other political interest. There are always exceptions to this – a few highly regarded scholars who still view the institution itself as important and are willing to "sacrifice" time to participate in its governance – but they are rare, valuable exceptions.

When a planning or priority recommendation comes to the senate or a major committee, those from faculties or units directly threatened will attend in force, accompanied by any allies they can find. Immediately, those who might benefit from the recommendation may find themselves in a minority. Criticism will invariably take several forms – the criteria on which the judgments of quality were made were inappropriate, and further information can show this; those who made the quality judgments were unqualified to do so, and in fact only those actually working in the subspecialty at issue have the right qualifications; such differentiation between units is invidious in a university; and so on. And as the debate proceeds, those unaffected directly by the recommendation (some of whom may not even have bothered to attend the meeting) may feel sympathy for those threatened and also appreciate that at another time their own unit might be similarly threatened. And since there is the unstated understanding that nothing can change without faculty agreement, many will conclude that the status quo is preferable to uncertain change. When the question is called, there will probably be a close vote with a majority in favour of rejecting the recommendation and maintaining the status quo.

Many of these aspects were evident in 1983, when the Senate at Guelph established a special committee, which I as vice-president academic chaired, to review the 1972 statement on the university's aims and objectives. Naturally, participatory democracy required that it be a large and representative committee with fifteen members, but fortunately among them were several very responsible senior faculty members. The final report placed primary emphasis on the university as a learning community and recommended that key learning objectives, not only for the university but ultimately for each academic program, be developed.[19] Senate approval of these recommendations means that Guelph is now one of a very few universities that publishes in its annual calendar a clear statement of the objectives of undergraduate education, a statement that defines the learning skills that a student should expect to acquire as a result of a Guelph undergraduate experience. This emphasis on student learning, as distinct from teaching, has had a great influence on Guelph's programs over the last fifteen years and has contributed greatly to Guelph's rise to prominence during that time.

However, when the committee discussed the emphasis that the original document had placed on life sciences as a distinctive feature of Guelph, there was great disagreement. Many felt that it was invidious to identify one particular area as being special to Guelph, and, especially for those from other academic units that were widely acknowledged to be of excellent quality, such recognition of life sciences that might imply a guarantee of quality or a promise of extra resources, was unacceptable. This lack of acceptability was determined entirely by the self-interest of those faculty members and the interests of their departments or mini-communities. A resolution was reached by distinguishing between quality and responsibility, with recommendations that Guelph should "seek excellence across a wide range of programs" but also "maintain a special responsibility for agriculture and veterinary medicine." There was no question that this was the most difficult point of the committee's discussion; members were torn between their wish for their own units to be unfettered in their future growth and the often reluctant acknowledgment that Guelph does have an institutional responsibility in agriculture and veterinary medicine. There was clearly no agreement that Guelph's responsibility should be to maintain excellence in agriculture and veterinary medicine. Even an institution that is generally seen as "different" from other Ontario universities, and different in very obvious ways, still has great difficulty in identifying that difference in its mission statement.

In 1995 the University of Guelph approved a revision of its strategic plan, based again on the work of a representative committee of about thirty members that engaged in consultations with "hundreds of students, staff, and faculty, and many alumni, retirees and community leaders in the public and private sectors."[20] A revised mission statement recognizes that Guelph does have a special responsibility in agriculture and veterinary medicine, but this is then only indirectly addressed in the specific recommendations of the strategic plan. The plan describes the primary strategic directions as being "an increasingly learner-centred approach to education and the fostering of research-intensiveness." The university's priorities are stated as, first, to enhance flexibility and efficiency; second, to address strategic initiatives such as the learner-centred agenda; and third, to empower people – all of these being "priorities" that apply equally to every part of the university. While there is the expressed intent to reduce the number of courses offered across the university and to develop performance indicators, there is little evidence of progress to date.

It is fair to conclude that over the past thirty years, Guelph's experiences with the development of mission statements and strategic plans under the current participatory form of governance have involved enormous work and have consumed considerable resources, only to produce conclusions that are generally weak in specificity, that do not impact on the allocation of resources, and that generally do not touch the self-interested directions of the individual departments and units. Yet it must be emphasized that

Guelph's efforts at planning have been more substantial and serious than those at many other Canadian universities; few, if any, have achieved more specific or more concrete results. The participatory form of governance, which requires large representative committees to engage in such planning, followed by senate consideration, achieves little more than the protection of the self-interests of the individual units at the expense of the institution's ability to set some specific long-term directions.

A further planning effort at Guelph also deserves comment, since it illustrates remarkably well the sheer impossibility of universities themselves initiating and undertaking significant internal change. In using a further example from Guelph, however, I must stress, and stress again, that this institution's efforts at planning have been more extensive and genuinely serious than in most Canadian universities. I certainly have nothing but praise for the valiant efforts that have been made there. Again, however, the results clearly show a collective failure and further reinforce the conclusions reached in this discussion. The length of time and amount of effort spent on university planning have provided no guarantees of success, and the most obvious conclusion is that meaningful institutional planning is simply impossible.

One recommendation of the 1995 strategic plan required the provost and deans to develop a plan for the allocation of resources to the colleges that would be based on "rational and transparent measures of instructional effort" and on "quality of teaching, research, and service." Not surprisingly, the development of such a plan was controversial, and further delays were caused by the major budget reductions of the NDP government's "Social Contract" followed by the "Common Sense Revolution" reductions of 1996-97. While these traumatic events might have been expected to accelerate the development of an allocation model, it was not until 1999 that a proposal emerged. The proposed model would place much emphasis on enrollment at both the undergraduate and graduate levels, but carefully weighted according to the nature of the program. The weightings were not arbitrarily chosen but involved very thoughtful analysis of similar weighting schemes in the US, England, New Zealand, and Australia. The quality component was to be based largely on the seven-year undergraduate review process that had recently been mandated by the provincial government, and the model proposed an 80/20 split between the weighted enrollment and quality components. It also proposed that with each college quality assessment, 4 percent of the budget would become available for redistribution, with preference being given to colleges of higher quality. It should be noted that this model is not aimed at any institutionally identified priorities, although it provided for the protection of a specified number of faculty positions that were contractually required under the agreement with the provincial Ministry of Agriculture, Food and Rural Affairs. This, however, is a matter of recognizing a contractual responsibility rather than identifying a priority. Modest redistribution was to be determined over a number of years on the basis of enrollment and quality assessments.

This proposal from the provost and deans was first seen as a mechanism or formula to be applied annually in the budget determination, but the controversy and argument over it have been so intense that the proposal has subsequently been described only as a model for the guidance of the provost in future budget discussions. It has not been implemented as a resource allocation mechanism, and it appears most unlikely that any major reallocation of resources will occur until "new" funding arrives, presumably from the province. In other words, the status quo is to be maintained; a budgetary distribution to colleges that has been determined largely by history and accident is to be continued since there is no agreement on an alternative. Each college, and within it each department, is determined to maintain its share, if need be at the expense of others and regardless of what this may do to the institution as a whole.

Another illustration of the degree of fragmentation in today's university is found in an aspect common to both Guelph and Dalhousie, and probably observable in any Canadian university. To quote a Guelph document, "Every sector of the university believes that it is the one that has been unfairly treated relative to others; not all sectors can be correct in this belief, however passionately it is held." But it is a passionately held view, and even if incorrect in most cases, as it must be, it demonstrates well the extent to which faculty are too narrowly focused on their own unit and their own interests, with little incentive to be aware of what is happening elsewhere in the institution. This view is held at Guelph and is prevalent at Dalhousie. In this latter case, several of the vice-presidents and I spent much time personally visiting all of the departments and schools, and over the years did so several times. Repeatedly, we were told that the particular unit being visited had been dealt with more harshly than any other, but all were woefully ignorant of how other units had been treated.

In fact, all of my experiences at Dalhousie with regard to planning and the definition of the university's mission were quite consistent with those at Guelph. In the early 1980s, despite the severe financial problems that Dalhousie faced and that will be described shortly, there was at first complete unwillingness to even consider the term "priorities." Many Dalhousie faculty members, and especially some of those active in the faculty union, held strongly to the view that the concept of the university was fundamentally incompatible with that of planning, that the university's task was to engage in the search for truth, and that the scholar's task was to follow wherever that search led. Planning, therefore, was not acceptable, and priorities could not and should not be identified. Intellectually, this is a valid argument, at least as far as the scholarly work of an individual faculty member is concerned. The argument has much less validity as soon as it is applied to a grouping of faculty members in a department or faculty, or especially to the university as a whole. Not only can the search for truth lead in a number of equally challenging directions between which a choice must be made, but in any event, no department, faculty, or university can cover all fields of specialization and some choices must be made. Similarly, the search for truth in, for example, the agricultural sciences cannot become so abstract and fundamental as to be divorced from the realities of agriculture, otherwise the institution loses sight of its fundamental purposes. And again, the search for truth cannot lead to an English department being utterly obsessed with the obscurities of ancient Anglo-Saxon. Inevitably, there must be some degree of planning even at the departmental level, and it is even more essential at the institutional level.

By the mid-1980s, the Dalhousie Senate reluctantly accepted that some planning was required, and under its effective leadership at the time, eventually agreed that Dalhousie might be characterized by a small number of what were termed "areas of emphasis." Although this concept had been approved, no steps had been taken to define such areas of emphasis before my arrival there as president in 1986. My first year was preoccupied with immediate crises, but by late 1987 I was able to have a relatively small committee created to develop a mission statement based on which further planning might be undertaken. The committee had only about twelve members, and although there had been a Dalhousie tradition allowing the president to create presidential committees, I still had to ensure its representative nature to gain Senate approval. Nevertheless, I had some control of its membership and included some well-respected senior academics.

As chair of the committee, I kept a firm direction in mind and ensured that the resulting document, even though it had to be subject to widespread scrutiny, expressed a strong commitment to liberal undergraduate education of outstanding quality. While this mission statement also endorsed and encouraged the unique role of Dalhousie in the Maritimes in both graduate work and professional programs, it also identified as areas of emphasis both "ocean studies" and "health studies." Both of these do fit well with Dalhousie's role, its location, and its proportionately heavy emphasis historically on "health studies," broadly defined. Given the parlous state of the university at the time, we could not afford the luxury of prolonged debate, but here the Board of Governors unexpectedly came to the rescue. Mission statements at many universities have often run to many pages, in some cases, such as Guelph, close to twenty pages. Dalhousie board members pointed out, quite appropriately, that in the private sector a mission statement was expected to be confined to one sheet of paper – it should be specific and concise. With considerable labour, the committee was able to reduce the statement to twelve key points on one page, and its brevity helped avoid unnecessary wrangling in the Senate over the choice of words, and ultimately gained its approval.

Again, however, the real concern came from those in the university who could not be included under the rubric of either ocean studies or health studies, and who concluded that they might be disadvantaged. For them, the status quo was to be preferred. Since both of these terms can be broadly interpreted, perhaps too broadly, a sufficient number felt themselves included and so approval was gained. Given the very severe financial problems that Dalhousie faced then and well into the 1990s, only relatively small resource reallocations could be made to sustain and develop its strengths in ocean studies and health studies, although, as will be described later, some very direct actions were subsequently taken to recognize these priorities and reallocate resources. In the following years, however, as so often happens in universities with their all too rapid turnover of academic administrators, other issues became more prominent and these priorities slowly waned. It should be a concern, and indeed a responsibility, of the Board of Governors, to ensure not only that there is in place a very specific mission statement, one that defines the institution uniquely and identifies priorities, but also that even with changes of senior administrators the mission statement is adhered to consistently over a decade or so, or is revised to address changed circumstances.

From these examples, it is clear that Canadian universities (although not uniquely so) have to date demonstrated a very limited ability to determine priorities or to engage successfully in planning. Even when there is general recognition that a critical shortage of resources exists, and that it is essential to establish priorities, such efforts are always violently attacked by those threatened by the outcomes. Given a consultative, participatory, and representative mode of governance that ensures that the ultimate power lies in the hands of the faculty, resistance to change is considerable, and for the majority it is less threatening and much easier to opt to maintain the status quo. Sometimes leadership by at least a central core of senior academic administrators from the president down can be sufficiently persuasive to produce some level of change or some small degree of planning, but this is possible only by persuasion and by argument, and can all too often be undone later as senior administrators change and boards forget. As indicated earlier, even though faculty will argue that the application of a formula is not appropriate for the allocation or reallocation of resources, they will equally vigorously assert that a judgment that does not agree with their own view of quality is equally inappropriate. In a further frequent argument, they will also claim that any form of planning that might involve the making of judgments by academic administrators is equally unacceptable, since administrators invariably show poor judgment! It is particularly ironic that one of the major components of the governance reforms of the 1960s, namely, the essential right of faculty to select their own administrators, has led to a situation in which such faculty-selected administrators are no more trusted for their administrative ability or judgment than were their predecessors.

8
Down East in the Maritimes

While I had considered university presidencies in Ontario at various times in the 1980s, I was surprised when, in 1985, I was approached about the presidency of Dalhousie University in Halifax. I had little knowledge of that part of Canada or of Dalhousie. I did not appreciate initially the important place that Dalhousie occupies historically in the development of universities in Canada. Indeed, having now lived in British Columbia, Ontario, and Nova Scotia, it seems to me that across Canada the lack of knowledge of its eastern shores is deplorably widespread. Although I hesitated and gave considerable thought to this Dalhousie position, I felt strongly that I had some abilities to bring to it, so that when in early 1986 I was asked to become president, I was quite prepared to accept.

Even in early visits to Nova Scotia, I was impressed with the coastal scenery, the oceanic flavour, and the sense of history and tradition. But I had to live in Halifax for a year or so before I really appreciated how much I had subconsciously missed the presence of the ocean during those twenty or so years in Ontario. To be near the sea again gave me a personal sense of satisfaction and serenity that I had not experienced since leaving New Zealand. Also, some of the differences between Western Canada, Ontario, and the Maritimes were quickly apparent, especially in terms of the people. In British Columbia, it had seemed to me that people were informal in a Californian sense, future-oriented, with little sense of history, and entrepreneurial however one interprets that overused word. By contrast, we had found people in Ontario not unfriendly but cool, with a certain reserve, and much less inclined to show feelings or reveal personal information. In Halifax, people seemed very similar to the New Zealanders I had known in the 1940s and 1950s – very open but with some traditional formality, and quite willing to give politely a very frank opinion – in fact, much more willing to do so than in BC or Ontario. I felt quite comfortable among them and was particularly struck by the remarkable number of different, unusual, but most interesting individuals whom I met there, many more than elsewhere in Canada. People in Atlantic Canada do not flaunt their individuality, but neither do they work to hide it as those in Ontario seem to do. Above all, of course, one was struck by the obvious lack of prosperity in the Maritimes compared with central Canada, although the presence of an affluent "establishment," especially in Halifax, was also evident. Moreover, one could not help but recall what can only be described as an attitude of condescension that can be sensed in Ontario towards the Maritimes. I increasingly came to describe this in terms of what the CBC did so often when commenting on the East Coast fisheries problems during the 1990s – showing on the TV screen one or two elderly fishers out in a rowboat hauling in occasionally one or two fish by hand, a perception of the fisheries that is quite unrealistic and condescending, and that reflects only ignorance.

A final general comment is certainly in order. Having lived in Halifax for nine years, as well as in Vancouver for eight, it is quite distressing to observe how unaware most Canadians are of our country's significant maritime character. Canada has one of the longest coastlines in the world, possesses the largest archipelago of islands, and, uniquely, has extensive coastal areas on three very different oceans, the Pacific, the Atlantic, and the Arctic. Under the 1995 Convention on the Law of the Sea, Canada now has jurisdiction over areas of ocean-covered land that exceed the land mass of Canada itself. That Canadians are so unaware of this seems to be related to the fact that the bulk of the population lives inland, quite distant from oceans; of the major Canadian centres of population, only Vancouver is located on the sea, and it is tucked well up in Burrard Inlet. It is interesting in this respect to compare Canada with Australia, where all major population centres are located on the coast and where there is a much greater sense of the country as a maritime nation. In contrast, southern Ontario and Quebec, with over 50 percent of the Canadian population, are inland, with little contact with the ocean and maritime affairs.

Dalhousie History

Dalhousie University has perhaps the most fascinating history of any Canadian university. It was not the first university in what became Nova Scotia, since the University of King's College had been established in Windsor in 1798, but only members of the Anglican Church were eligible for admission to the older university. In a colony rent by sectarian rivalries, the Earl of Dalhousie, during his brief tenure as governor of Canada, created Dalhousie College in 1818 as a nonsectarian institution, and did so, moreover, using funds that had been originally American.

Some five years earlier, during the 1812-15 war between Britain and the United States, British forces had occupied the small but important coastal village of Castine in Maine. Excise taxes were carefully collected by the British during the nine-month occupation, and taken by them at war's end.

The amount, something in excess of $12,000, became known as the Castine Fund, and a portion of this American money was used by Dalhousie to erect the first building of the college named after him. Shortly thereafter, unfortunately, Dalhousie left Halifax to become governor of Upper Canada; Halifax sank back into its sectarian squabblings and, without a champion, the college languished. Indeed, it existed only as a building and a piece of legislation until 1838, when scarce funds became available and enabled teaching to commence.

The colony was not in the least generous, and by 1843 the college was again so bereft of funds that teaching had to be suspended, to commence again in 1863 and continue to the present. Dalhousie University and College, as it is legally known, has probably never known a period of affluence. Its prominence in the Maritimes and across Canada in the second half of the nineteenth century was largely due to the generosity of a Nova Scotian, George Munro, who migrated to New York, where he became very wealthy. A number of generous gifts that he made to Dalhousie University made possible the establishment of an important group of endowed chairs in the 1880s, many of the occupants of which brought considerable distinction to the institution.

Of particular importance was the early creation of the Dalhousie Law School, the first university common law school in the British Empire. While the model has now been emulated in many Canadian universities, Dalhousie as the first has seen a remarkable stream of law graduates later become outstanding jurists and lawyers, a Canadian prime minister (R.B. Bennett), and many provincial premiers, noted political figures, and highly successful business people. In my own years at Dalhousie, most of the premiers of the Atlantic provinces were Dalhousie graduates, including Joe Ghiz, John Buchanan, Richard Hatfield, and Clyde Wells. The Medical School and the Faculty of Arts and Sciences have also seen many outstanding graduates, of whom Robert Stanfield is but one example.

Because of its academic strength in the second part of the nineteenth century, Dalhousie became the prominent university of the Maritimes, providing not only undergraduate programs but over time an increasing range of both graduate and professional programs, many of which are still the only ones available in Atlantic Canada. However, Dalhousie and all its sister institutions in the region have continually had to struggle financially. All were supported entirely by tuition fees, donations, and other private funds, until in Nova Scotia in the 1960s, during the Stanfield government, substantial provincial funding began to be provided. Since 1974, that funding had been channelled through the Maritime Provinces Higher Education Commission.

When I arrived in September 1986 as the ninth president of Dalhousie University, the institution was in a parlous state. My predecessors had all demonstrated that Presbyterian energy and passion for education, and a number had been Presbyterian clergymen, whose portraits show them to have been rather dour and grim individuals. Since 1911, all had been Dalhousie graduates. The predecessor whose years as president most affected my own was Henry Hicks, president from 1963 to 1980. A native Nova Scotian, Hicks graduated from Mt. Allison University in 1936, and after a further year at Dalhousie, which gave him a B.Sc. degree, he went to Oxford on a Rhodes Scholarship, obtaining a law degree in 1939. After army service during the Second World War, he practised law in Bridgetown, Nova Scotia, but also became very active in politics, first as a Liberal member of the legislature and then as minister of education from 1949 to 1954. He was premier from 1954 to 1956, but was devastatingly defeated by Robert Stanfield. To the surprise of some and the initial consternation of the faculty, he was appointed dean of arts and sciences in 1962. An obvious candidate for the presidency, he was so appointed in 1963. The next seventeen years, during part of which (from 1972 onward) Hicks also served as a federal senator in Ottawa, saw the tumultuous transformation of Dalhousie, a transformation from which it has taken time to recover.

Henry Hicks was a colourful Maritimes character, with considerable intelligence, flair, and self-confidence. He was frank and outspoken, but these qualities, combined with his tendency to make quick judgments, made him abrupt and caused problems. His style could most succinctly be described as that of a benevolent dictator. He always cherished and flaunted his Oxford background and connections: he took snuff, wore a bowler, and often carried the British furled umbrella. He believed passionately in Dalhousie and its future, and especially in its importance to the Maritimes and the dependence of other Maritime universities on it. By the time of his retirement, however, he had alienated all other universities in the region by his continual emphasis on the superiority and uniqueness of Dalhousie. Above all, Henry Hicks was a builder, and willing to take risks; as such, the particular combination of talents that he possessed served Dalhousie well, at least during the first decade of his presidency, during an unprecedented period of growth and change. He was in the mould of Norman MacKenzie, who had been president of UBC though the 1950s, although Hicks came almost twenty years later.

As noted in earlier chapters, virtually all Canadian universities underwent substantial governance reforms in the late 1960s, moving to limited term appointments for academic administrators within a highly participatory mode of governance. Dalhousie was a notable exception, largely because it had Hicks at its helm. Hicks's term of appointment was determined in 1963 and ran officially until the 31 August after his sixty-fifth birthday – that is, until 1980 – and Hicks saw no reason to consider an early retirement. Moreover, his style of operating was very much a continuation of that which had been observed in Canadian universities in the immediate postwar period, when the president, perhaps together with the chair of the board, effectively ran the university. Donald MacInnes, a prominent Halifax lawyer, became chair of the Board of Governors in 1958, was influential in Hicks's appointment as president, and remained chair until 1980. Together Hicks and MacInnes formed a powerful combination that swept all before them for seventeen years and accomplished a great deal for Dalhousie. This was, however, the exact opposite to the tide of participatory governance that had swept across Canadian universities by 1970, and this difference created enormous frustration and bitterness among the politically minded within the Dalhousie faculty, a sour bitterness that has taken its toll on the institution right into the 1990s.

Hicks's talent was in building, and he certainly had a vision of what Dalhousie could become. When he became dean of arts and sciences in 1962, Dalhousie was a small institution with about two thousand students; by his retirement in 1980, it had been transformed into a big, spread-out university with nine thousand students. Numerous new buildings had appeared on campus, including the Student Union, the new Law School building, the Tupper Building for the Medical School, a new Dentistry School, the Killam Library, a large new science complex, new athletics facilities, and others. Dalhousie's physical assets, estimated at cost, totalled $135 million in 1980. As the official history of Dalhousie by P.B. Waite says: "Without Hicks's ingenuity, panache, passion for building, Dalhousie probably could not have kept up with the vigorous competition of universities elsewhere in Canada for physical plant."[21]

His was a very considerable accomplishment, especially in a province that is poor compared with Ontario or British Columbia. Inevitably, however, it came at great cost, which was felt primarily in two areas: that of the university's finances and that of the relationship between the university and its faculty and staff. While faculty, staff, and students have benefited from their use of the buildings he erected, there remains a resentment about the dictatorial way in which Hicks brought these about. That a different president, less flamboyant, less willing to take risks, and more inclined to listen to advice, could never have accomplished the same results, especially if constrained by the processes of participatory governance, is readily apparent but only grudgingly accepted.

Hicks's passion for building often outran his ability to ensure that the costs of construction were adequately covered. In addition to sums that the university itself could find from gifts and fund-raising, a considerable amount was committed by both federal and provincial governments, but in too many cases, construction costs escalated beyond earlier estimates, with often no immediate source of funding to close any gap. The last major building projects of the Hicks era were the new Dental School building and the new athletic centre, Dalplex, both well under way by 1978. By the late 1970s and into the 1980s, rampant inflation and soaring interest rates, combined with a government intent on controlling the universities' apparently insatiable appetite for money, caused Dalhousie's debt to multiply disastrously. By 1980, the combination of unfunded capital debt together with the accumulated deficit totalled some $40 million and, worse, the annual deficit was rapidly increasing this total.

The other cost of Hicks's dictatorial, swashbuckling style of running Dalhousie had to be paid in 1978. The relationship between the board and the faculty, and especially the Faculty Association, had deteriorated steadily over the years in the face of the exuberant, headlong enthusiasm of the Hicks-MacInnes team. In 1978, faced with some of the lowest faculty salaries in Canada at a time of rising inflation, and a president and board that appeared to pay little attention to their concerns, the Faculty Association asked the board to agree to voluntary recognition of the association, but this was refused. With mounting dissatisfaction among faculty, the association sought certification under the Labour Relations Act while Hicks and the board continued to fumble. It was known that there was a strong conservative element among the faculty opposed to certification, and in fact only 55 percent of those voting, and 41.7 percent of those eligible to vote, supported certification in the official vote, but that was enough. The issue was obviously very divisive and caused much dissension among faculty for years, but the die was cast and certification was in place.

The negotiation of the first collective agreement took much of 1979, and provided a remarkable demonstration of the way in which such negotiations had tended to occur elsewhere in Canada through the 1970s. The faculty negotiators had been carefully coached by the Canadian Association of University Teachers. They knew exactly what model clauses from other agreements they wanted included, and were equipped with a better information base than the administration. As at other universities, the administration team was not well prepared; the board had given no directions and the team was essentially in a reactive mode. Hicks left the negotiations to his vice-president, W.A. MacKay, and gave little direction. The outcome was what might be expected: a lengthy, comprehensive agreement containing thirty-three articles in highly legalistic language, in which, with only one or two exceptions, the association must have gained virtually everything that might have been on their original wish list. It is certain that the board did not realize the extent to which the agreement constrained their authority, nor did it recognize that collective bargaining meant that once a clause was included in such an agreement, it could be removed only through further bargaining and different concessions. It is also very likely that only a few on either side could see the extent to which collective bargaining assumes and encourages a confrontational situation, and so diminishes or destroys the traditional collegial basis of a university. And as later events confirmed, few of the faculty really understood the implications of the collective agreement, or were prepared for the emphasis that would be placed on legal process in the future. Certainly, the great majority could not conceive that issues between the association and the university might eventually lead to a strike.

Nor were the troubles with the faculty the only labour problem faced by Dalhousie. Also in 1979, the Canadian Union of Public Employees (CUPE) local representing the cleaners, caretakers, and drivers, which had experienced bitter negotiations during its previous contract, went on strike. In a shrewd move that angered and alienated not only CUPE but also labour groups across the province as well as many faculty and other supporters of Dalhousie, the administration brought in a cleaning company to supervise operations, and although the strike eventually gave the union the money it had sought, it left a considerable residue of bitterness and anger. All in all, the last two years of the Hicks era were unhappy and strife-ridden.

When he retired in 1980, W.A. MacKay, who had been dean of the Law School and then Hicks's vice-president academic since 1969, was appointed president, although not before Dalhousie had been embarrassed by the publication of the "confidential" shortlist of candidates. A much-respected person of considerable integrity, MacKay was in an impossible position. He had quietly acted as a backstop for Hicks in the preceding eleven years, during much of which Hicks had been travelling back and forth to the Senate in Ottawa; it is probable that quite a number of Hicks's successes depended more on MacKay's quiet and careful work behind the scenes. In every sense of the word, he had been Hicks's right-hand man, and when he became president, that was exactly how he was seen. He therefore inherited immediately all of the frustration that had accumulated over the previous seventeen years; worse still, he inherited the financial consequences of the Hicks era, compounded in the early 1980s by high interest rates and declining government support.

Again, MacKay's style was quiet and thorough; he wanted to see both sides of the question before making a decision, all in complete contrast to Hicks's informality and benign dictatorship. Moreover, MacKay had to deal with all of the bureaucracy and complications of new collective agreements at a time when the university's financial circumstances called for decisive, imaginative, but probably very painful action. The apparently overnight transition from the flamboyance and expansionism of the Hicks era, with new buildings sprouting all over the campus, to a financial crisis of such magnitude caught all unprepared, and MacKay had to carry the burden.

As part of its long history, Dalhousie also carried other governance weaknesses into the 1980s. There was no single coherent piece of legislation governing Dalhousie; at centre was the important act of 1863, but it was followed by more than twenty-five legislative additions and amendments.

A revised consolidating piece of legislation was urgently required, but since this would mean a private member's bill submitted to the legislature, no one at Dalhousie so far had been willing to risk the likelihood of undesirable amendments that legislative and public hearings might produce. The combined effect of existing legislation was to provide for a board of about fifty-five members, a size that was unwieldy and that all too easily encouraged representative factions forcing a particular viewpoint. Even the prescribed composition of the executive of the board required more than twelve members. Moreover, and still worse, the old legislation provided for a Senate composed of all full professors, which in the early 1950s gave a still reasonable Senate of about fifty members. By 1980 and later, however, with the rapid growth of the university and the continual promotion of its faculty members, it resulted in a Senate with a membership well in excess of 400. Indeed, with promotions, appointments, resignations, and other changes continually in progress, it was virtually impossible to determine the exact composition of the Senate! In practice, monthly Senate meetings might draw fifty to eighty persons, which is in itself an indication of the lack of interest taken in the work of the Senate. On the other hand, an especially controversial agenda might suddenly draw an attendance of several hundred. Even worse, the individuals who participated at the more usual meetings would change from one occasion to the next as items on the agenda varied. There was therefore no guarantee of consistency in the Senate's debates or decisions.

In the 1950s, Dalhousie was typical of Canadian universities as far as the roles of the board and the Senate were concerned. The Senate had responsibility for academic matters, or, as the Dalhousie legislation stated, "for the internal governance" of the institution. In the view of the board, which firmly regarded itself as "the supreme body" of the institution, internal governance did not include any financial information, which was kept completely confidential within the board's confines. The Senate, then, could certainly decide that a new program should be instituted, but in practice this would occur only when the president and deans supported the proposal, since only they had access to any financial information. In any event, any such Senate decision had to receive board approval since the board alone had complete and final authority and responsibility. In reality, since board members were volunteers who attended board meetings only once a month, the decisions were made by the president and the board chair, and even the latter could never have the same grasp of details as the president. Elsewhere in Canada, there was a huge shift in responsibility in the 1970s, with participatory governance giving the faculty control, or at least very powerful leverage, but the dominance of the Hicks-MacInnes partnership prevented this from happening at Dalhousie.

Nevertheless, the Senate did move slowly towards establishing what might be regarded as a parallel power. In 1967, for example, the Senate recommended that in the Faculty of Arts and Science, but interestingly not in the Faculty of Medicine, "heads" of departments should be replaced by "chairmen." The most important move occurred in 1978-79, when serious steps were undertaken to reform the Senate itself. These foundered, however, on the issue of Senate membership. An effective Senate required above all a much smaller defined membership, but to achieve that, the legislation called for a majority of all senators to be in favour of any change. When the vote was taken, a substantial majority of those voting were in favour of change, but not enough senators voted. Already, the primary interests of the faculty had turned well away from institutional governance matters towards their own more local and personal research interests. The reforms did lead to a somewhat more effective committee structure for the Senate, and especially to the creation of a committee on university planning; they also allowed for an elected chair of the Senate instead of requiring the president to serve as chair.

While these changes were being pursued, the movement towards faculty unionization was under way, and its achievement gave the union far more influence than Senate over important matters such as the conditions for appointments, tenure, and promotion. The Dalhousie history of the 1960s and 1970s did not produce, as happened elsewhere in Canada, a Senate with powers equal to or even exceeding those of the board. Rather, it led to a Senate that saw its role much more as a loyal but very critical opposition to the administration. Because of this turn of events, the faculty union became the competing power against the board at Dalhousie.

First Impressions

From this history, it should be clear that Dalhousie, unlike other Canadian universities, continued to be managed into the 1980s in a style that resembled that of the 1940s and 1950s, and that it then made the significant change to a unionized faculty almost overnight, and did so without having formally completed those other governance changes that might have created a more effective Senate, and perhaps also a stronger board. The combined effects of the forced changes, made in a relatively short period, and the resentments that had accumulated because the changes came so late, were traumatic.

When I arrived in September 1986, I was provided with every possible assistance, especially by W.A. MacKay, my predecessor. He had ensured that a voluminous book of briefing materials had been prepared, containing not only the essential organizational, administrative, and financial details but also impartial accounts of all of the critical issues then facing the institution. He also very generously devoted time to escorting me about Halifax on introductory visits to key persons in government, in the wider community, and in the other universities and institutions in the city. This was a far more extensive introduction than most other new presidents receive; I was grateful to him and could never claim that I was unaware of the circumstances at Dalhousie when I commenced there. Certainly, there were many problems that needed to be addressed urgently, and they were not confined to the financial or governance matters already discussed earlier. The following are some examples.

At the time of my appointment, I was not surprised that the board wanted a new president to live in the president's house, and I was quite willing to do so. What I was not prepared for was the intensity of the controversy surrounding the president's house. The house is a large, pleasant Victorian structure located close to the campus on reasonably extensive grounds. It was built in the 1860s and, interestingly, had been acquired in 1925 and donated as a gift to Dalhousie by R.B. Bennett, a Dalhousie graduate of 1893 who went on to become prime minister of Canada in 1930-35. When Hicks became president in 1963, since he already owned a home whose property abutted the Dalhousie property, and since he had no inclination to move, the board agreed to buy his home so that he could remain in it while he served as president, with the option that he could buy it back when he retired. Over the opposition of one or two board members and criticism of the arrangement from some faculty members, the board also agreed that the Bennett property could then be used for academic purposes, with the Psychology Department becoming its first tenants. With Hicks retiring in 1980 and a new president coming into office, the board rightly decided that it had no alternative but to restore the Bennett property to its original use as a house for the president.

After seventeen years of use and misuse by academic units, with essentially no maintenance, the old house was in deplorable condition, and to the consternation of all, the cost of renovations far exceeded the original estimates and finally totalled in excess of $400,000. Unfortunately, this information became public shortly after the dire financial circumstances of Dalhousie were fully apparent. The board was accused by government, the community, and especially the faculty unions of financial irresponsibility, and the president's house in which he had to live now became an albatross about the neck of MacKay's presidency. The unions and occasionally the media called for its sale, and it was the inevitable target of criticism right into the 1990s; any necessary expenditure on it was instantly noted and criticized as unnecessary, and it continually drew the attention of both the campus and the wider Halifax society.

In my first months at Dalhousie, I became well aware that in a city as comparatively small and traditional as Halifax, the president of Dalhousie was seen as a prominent citizen in a way that does not occur elsewhere across Canada. This was reinforced by my living in the president's house, the front of which was fully exposed to the public. No one passed without a stare, the Halifax summer sightseeing buses always stopped outside for a few minutes, and the occasional frank faculty member would tell me that he always checked the house for activity when he passed each day. While excellent for entertaining, the president's house has an uncomfortable resemblance to a fishbowl, at least for those who must live in it!

It may be evident from some of the foregoing remarks that another problem at Dalhousie concerned the maintenance of university property. Dalhousie had always been impoverished and maintenance had been difficult, but the transformation of the Hicks era, with its emphasis on building, had exacerbated this problem. Hicks was never one to be overly concerned with detail, and this attitude permeated much of the administration. It was most evident in the almost total inattention that had been given to the upkeep and maintenance of even the newest buildings. One of the necessary structures that had appeared on the campus early in the Hicks regime was the Central Services Building, built in 1965. It served as an electrical substation for the campus, and also provided telephone cables, steam for heating, and chilled water for the air-conditioning systems. In the spring of 1987, leading into my first summer at Dalhousie, I was informed that the air-conditioning capacity for the campus was virtually zero; it transpired that there had been no maintenance for the chillers since their installation in 1965, so that the aluminum fins had melted into solid aluminum blocks; the entire chiller system needed to be replaced at a cost well over $1 million, which, of course, was totally lacking.

But this was just the tip of the problem. Across the campus, there were broken windows, seats in lecture halls lay in mangled ruins, the lawns were badly cut and untended, the few small gardens lay stark and bare in summer, and snow-removal in winter was slow and messy. There was, in fact, no preventive maintenance program at all, and little attention had been paid to ensure that the Physical Plant Department had either the staff or equipment necessary. There were even two separate private companies on campus issuing keys to buildings, so that no single person had a complete set of keys for the entire campus! Almost from scratch, the Physical Plant Department had to be rebuilt and retrained, and the slow, laborious task of restoring and maintaining university property had to be undertaken as a serious and ongoing responsibility.

In general, a somewhat similar picture applied across the whole administrative side of the university, albeit with much variation from unit to unit. In the 1950s, the administration of Canadian universities had been relatively simple, requiring few staff. As happened at the University of Western Ontario, with accelerating enrollment increases, it was realized that a more sophisticated, larger, and professional administration had to be created; although at first resented and misunderstood by faculty, this had generally, perhaps grudgingly, been accepted. With the Hicks era beginning in 1963, however, this just did not happen at Dalhousie. Hicks was not interested in the details but in the grand picture, and the workings of the administrative side of the university commanded little of his attention, while his successor, MacKay, was so beset with financial and union problems that little was done. At the University of Guelph, I had enjoyed support from a particularly well-run administration whose origins had been in the provincial public service, and it was a shock to find at Dalhousie an administration that was understaffed, overworked, unappreciated, and weak compared with their counterparts elsewhere in Canada.

Until the later 1970s, little had been done in the way of introducing modern technology. After serious problems in the Registrar's Office in the early 1970s, there had been some progress with computerization, but it was only in the early 1980s, a decade after many Canadian universities, that serious efforts were made to establish a modern Computing Services Centre. When I first arrived in the President's Office in 1986, there were certainly electric typewriters, but it was a shock to find just one computer, and an obsolete one at that. Much work was needed to develop a stronger administration, comparable to those that other Canadian universities already had. This aspect was further complicated by the fact that shortly after I accepted the presidency, the vice-president finance and administration at the time advised me that he was resigning to move into the business sector. This meant that a temporary appointment had to be made for several months, but it enabled the appointment of B.G. Mason, who came to Dalhousie with considerable experience in administration, especially in labour negotiations, from Lakehead University, and who was to be a stalwart supporter during my presidency.

Externally, there were other difficulties. The previous twenty years or so had left in the provincial government, and also more widely across the Maritimes and certainly in the media, a strong perception of Dalhousie as forever demanding and forever expanding, but also financially irresponsible, as demonstrated by rising debt with little being done to control or reduce it; and, of course, there was the fiasco of the president's house. Much of this was the legacy of the Hicks regime, especially the institutional arrogance that he promoted. Dalhousie is not the only university in Nova Scotia, but Hicks had built on the historical and sectarian divisions between them dating back to 1818 by always asserting the academic superiority of Dalhousie, its unique importance to Atlantic Canada, and its stature as a national institution. He was fully supported by the faculty, the board, and the alumni. In general, they were right, but the frequent assertion of these views as unalterable fact only strengthened the unremitting hostility and resentment on the part of the other institutions, especially those in Nova Scotia. By the mid-1980s, when Dalhousie was in a financial struggle for its survival, some saw an opportunity to bring Dalhousie down to size, and were quick to seize it.

The situation was further complicated by the weakening role of the Maritime Provinces Higher Education Commission (MPHEC). Created largely by the Stanfield government in the 1960s, it had been a unique and valuable contributor to Maritime cooperation, but by the mid-1980s, the Nova Scotia government was becoming less and less supportive of it, and increasingly ignored its recommendations on funding. In 1985 a provincial Royal Commission had completed a major study of postsecondary education in the province, and had recommended the establishment of a provincial commission for the universities. As I arrived at Dalhousie in 1986, the debate on this report was at its height, and the response of the Buchanan government was awaited.[22] There was great uncertainty, which continued over a good many years, as to the views of government about the universities.

Other matters, both internal and external, not only presented challenges to an incoming president but demanded immediate attention. Some were smouldering crises. The scenario was in fact about as bad as could be imagined for anyone stepping into the presidency of any university; it was, I think, much worse than I had anticipated, even after the very thorough briefings I had been given. Slow as I am, it fortunately took quite a few years before I really appreciated this!

In summary, the atmosphere at Dalhousie had become soured and embittered. The years 1980-85 were full of difficulties for the Dalhousie community; the extent of the financial crisis became apparent but solutions were elusive. With MPHEC threatening to withhold grant funds in order to reduce the still-growing annual deficit, the board negotiated a complex arrangement utilizing a portion of Dalhousie's comparatively large endowment fund to reduce total indebtedness by about $8 million, but with the university being required to make annual repayments, with interest, to restore the endowment fund. This, together with budgetary reductions, averted the MPHEC threat but still left a debt of $33 million. Meanwhile, with severe pressures to reduce the annual deficit, the relationship between the board and the faculty union went from bad to worse; every perceived wrong was grieved by the union, producing a tally of grievances that only one or two other Canadian universities have exceeded. Many went to arbitration at considerable cost to both parties, and many were won by the union, often on procedural grounds. That a union could win arbitration awards on the grounds that its own members, acting as members of promotion and tenure committees or as chairs of departments, had not followed the correct procedures precisely seems and is bizarre, although, in fairness, there were just as many procedural errors by deans, vice-presidents, and the president. By 1985 the board had come to realize some of the consequences of unionization and to deplore the degree of antagonism that had developed, and many board members were personally offended by the union's militancy.

9
The Most Difficult Years

While it is common knowledge that every Canadian university has a president or principal, what does such a president actually do? A not insignificant number of faculty members will immediately answer that the president does nothing of importance; for students, a president is usually a remote and unknown person whom they rarely if ever meet. To those outside the university, the president is the person responsible, and to be blamed, for those outrageous remarks made by an eccentric faculty member to the local newspaper, or for the latest episode of irresponsible behaviour by students. If the president cannot be held responsible and made to take action in such cases, who can? Ironically, in such instances, the president can probably do little, and most members of the general public would be aghast at the very limited power of a university president, especially in today's universities. But if the president has so little power, and neither faculty nor students are impressed by the role of the president, what exactly does a president do?

The President's Job

It is difficult to think of any other position in the public or private sector in which the incumbent has so little real authority yet is held responsible to so many different constituencies, is so often criticized and verbally abused, and receives so little by way of remuneration or recognition. Perhaps the only comparable position might be the president of the CBC, who in any event is far better paid! But a university president has to deal with many more diverse constituencies – students, faculty, staff, alumni, donors and benefactors, both potential and real, government (provincial, federal, and even municipal), the board, the Senate, the media, the general public, and, not least, a spouse and family. Each constituency has its own interests and may have little concern for the often competing interests of other constituencies. For a new president, as I was in 1986, the immediate challenge was to determine how best I might connect with each constituency as quickly as possible, a task that was essential for one who came to Dalhousie "from away." Maritimers are indeed friendly and open, but the establishment of cordial working relationships was still essential.

A very early challenge came in trying to identify a workable means of communicating regularly with all of the Dalhousie constituencies. It had been pointed out by several board members that in recent confrontations with the Dalhousie Faculty Association (DFA), which had come close to a strike, my predecessor had found it difficult to communicate without running the risk of being accused of unfair labour practice. It was therefore important to establish and maintain a regularly used channel of communication. So began the practice of my writing a regular column in each issue of the Dalhousie newspaper, which appeared biweekly throughout the academic year. This was a real chore, but I rarely missed a deadline and it was interesting to find that for almost every issue a timely topic appeared. I had a means of expressing my views on important current issues affecting the university, and I also knew that the newspaper was read in other Maritime universities as well as in downtown Halifax, including government offices. What was surprising were the comments I received from individuals outside the university, including quite a number of presidential colleagues across the country. Especially in the early 1990s, when rationalization of the Nova Scotia universities was under active discussion with the provincial government, to have such a vehicle for the expression of Dalhousie's viewpoint was exceedingly valuable.

I experimented with several other forms of communication within the university. At one point, there was criticism, largely from faculty, that the president and vice-presidents were closeting themselves in offices and were unavailable to those with complaints or those wishing to raise a particular matter. I therefore declared that every Friday morning, I would be available in the University Club for up to two hours to anyone who wished to talk and have coffee with me. Of course, very few bothered to turn up, and after a number of such Fridays with only two or three persons visiting me, I was able to complain in my newspaper column of the lack of interest in discussing issues with me. I heard no more of the alleged complaint!

Connecting with the Board of Governors, my legal employer, was relatively straightforward: although it had over fifty members, the board met regularly each month except in July and August, with the officers of the board meeting separately and more frequently, so it did not take long to gain some perspective about each member. All had voluntarily agreed to serve on the board, but they varied greatly in their real interest and their level of attendance. Only about twenty-five or so were regular attendees, and even among them, business interests and other commitments sometimes caused absences. Particularly when some critical piece of business was on the agenda, it was often necessary to check beforehand on likely attendance rather than run the risk of defeat. In a few cases, again depending on the issue, board members could be completely unpredictable as to the opinion they would express, and some were what might be called single-issue members. Students, for example, were often concerned about an issue only insofar as it affected their own generation of students, and were often unable to see the matter from the long-term viewpoint. The level of tuition fees was a constant preoccupation, as to some degree it should have been, but to point out that their predecessors in the 1960s had paid essentially the same as they were paying in absolute dollars, even though the real costs of education had steadily risen, was for them no argument for increased fees. Other members who were appointed as representatives for a particular constituency considered their role to be just that – to represent, and not to consider the best interests of the institution as a whole. It is very likely that the sheer size of the board encouraged this view.

There was always, however, a core of the board membership consisting of reliable, thoughtful, and committed persons on whose support I could rely. This did not mean they were uncritical, but with prior discussion of difficult matters with the officers of the board, there would usually be a sufficiently strong consensus to gain board approval; otherwise, it was better to rethink the matter. Certainly, throughout almost nine years as president, I was supported ably by three board chairs, who gave me absolutely reliable, wise, and unstinting cooperation and advice. There is no question that a much smaller board would have been very much more effective, and in my last two years, we were able to move voluntarily in that direction without any risky attempt to have the governing legislation altered. With persuasion and much discussion, each of the constituencies represented on the board agreed to reduce its membership, resulting in a board of thirty-three members, still too large but a marked improvement.

Of course, as is the practice across Canada, meetings of the board were public except for the discussion of financial, personnel, or collective bargaining matters. While such open meetings are desirable and contribute substantially to public accountability, there were far too many occasions when board members were, or were dangerously close to being, in a conflict of interest situation. Student members cannot argue single-mindedly for low or zero tuition fees without compromising their responsibility as board members for the financial integrity of the institution, and faculty members similarly cannot use the board as a platform for faculty self-interest without being in a conflict of interest. Still, especially with these two constituencies, whose relationship with the board was often tense, it was better for the chair to give their representatives some latitude, even when it was abused.

Making good connections with the Senate was another matter. The Dalhousie Senate was not an effective body for the reasons described earlier, although at the time of my arrival, it was still trying hard. Its sheer size and unpredictable attendance continued to weaken it further, however, and in 1988, when the incumbent's term of office was complete, there were few volunteers for the position of chair of the Senate. Those who maintained any interest in its work still viewed the Senate as a loyal opposition to the president rather than as an academic equivalent to the board, and its activities and directions became even less predictable as it became less relevant to most faculty. In November 1988, the DFA declared a faculty strike, an event that will be described shortly, and it brought home to the union that it could easily control the Senate. By 1990, a former DFA president had been elected chair of the Senate, and meetings of the Senate tended to be dominated by those active in the union who were seeking every opportunity to harass the administration and the board. As a result, the Senate was unable to perform any really useful work, although sincere attempts were made by a few members. Only a very small minority of faculty took the Senate seriously at all, and the majority ignored it. The Senate, therefore, did not provide a means of knowing or being known by the faculty across the university.

Well before I arrived, I had decided that I would continue a practice that I had followed at Guelph, that of visiting faculty members in their own departments or units as often as possible, and of periodically meeting with faculty councils. Except when there was a very specific reason for such a visit, the agendas were completely informal. On arrival, I usually made it clear that I was there to listen, and asked what issues should be discussed. There often followed a short, hesitant pause, but someone always had a particular concern and lively, sometimes confrontational discussion ensued for as much as two hours. In almost nine years at Dalhousie, I visited most units at least two or three times and some much more frequently; all visits were of use, if only for the fact that it was an opportunity to correct the erroneous impression in each unit that it was the most badly treated unit in the university! Occasionally, a very specific complaint was raised that, on return to my office, I could immediately resolve, hopefully demonstrating that the administration was responsive and could produce results.

These visits were not welcomed by the DFA. Within my first couple of weeks at Dalhousie, I arranged to meet with the DFA president, in part as a courtesy and in part to begin addressing some major issues. In the course of a somewhat tense meeting, I mentioned that I intended to make such visits as often as possible; to my astonishment, and in an obvious attempt at intimidation, the president informed me that I had no right to do so, that I represented the "employer" and that the only contact I should have with faculty should be through the office of the president of the DFA. To hold such a view within a university seemed so ludicrous that I burst out laughing and made it clear that such visits would indeed occur. But it was on this note that my relations with the DFA began, and over the next few years there was only slow improvement.

Very few presidents in Canadian universities today have real involvement with students, except at the level of the student government; and generally students do not know even the name of the university president and do not care. Their university lives are spent at a very different level, mainly with other students and the relatively few faculty involved in the courses that they take, and perhaps a wider group of those participating in athletic activities and clubs. The students who participate in student government, especially at the institutional level, are usually drawn from those with a more political interest. Indeed, at Dalhousie a significant number were students from the Law School, and in quite a number of cases, I fully expect to see them active in political life, either provincially or federally, over the next decade or so. The Dalhousie Student Union (DSU), founded over 130 years ago, has always taken great pride in its history as one of the oldest such bodies in Canada, and has contributed a great deal to campus life over the years. Many of its leaders during my time were outstanding individuals who provided effective leadership for the student body. Some were typical of their student contemporaries, whose concerns were limited to issues that directly affected their generation of students, regardless of any impact on future students or the institution. The many often difficult debates on tuition fees tended to illustrate this, as has often been the case across Canada. Many of the other issues raised by the DSU were related to social justice. Typical issues included feminism, affirmative action for women, minorities, gays and lesbians, safety on campus, especially at night, and so on. There were several attempts to develop a continuing system of student-organized teaching evaluation of all courses, but with the annual change of student leaders and in the face of resistance from some faculty, these barely lasted one academic year and the results were rather dismal. In general, however, as at most universities, the DSU provided a good sounding board for student opinion, albeit of the more politically inclined, and the issues and concerns that the DSU have raised over the years have certainly helped strengthen university life.

Another community with which any president must connect today consists of the alumni. Prior to about 1980, Canadian universities had been far more occupied with growth and with retaining and maximizing government financial support than with paying much attention to alumni. Some institutions, such as the University of Western Ontario, did have quite active local alumni groups, but these were encouraged and given modest support largely for their role in arranging homecomings and other social events for alumni. Few inside the university saw them as a source of financial support; indeed, in the mid-1970s at Western, as government funds became more limited, there were criticisms of the university's support for the alumni association and suggestions that it should cease! The last two decades have produced a significant change of attitude.

Dalhousie has always drawn a large number of students from across Atlantic Canada, a not insignificant number from Ontario and the US, and smaller numbers from elsewhere in Canada. While most of its alumni are concentrated in Atlantic Canada, there are large numbers in most of the major Canadian cities, especially Toronto and Calgary, with smaller numbers in places such as Vancouver, New York, Boston, London, Hong Kong, Singapore, and Malaysia – in fact, scattered worldwide. It was only in the mid-1980s that serious efforts were made to cultivate alumni interest and a few gatherings were organized by the Alumni Office, largely in the Maritimes; in exceptional cases, such as in New York, the alumni themselves had organized and maintained an alumni association, but without much recognition or support from the university. I found, however, that there was an able and enthusiastic core of alumni who were eager to see the creation and growth of alumni chapters in as many centres as possible. They had recognized, as the university had not, that alumni support was going to be essential for any university, and certainly for any institution in the Maritimes. They saw that alumni activities, carried out at the local level and generally social in nature, can help keep alive the interest in the university and over time can often be translated into real financial support. This attitude has long been common in American institutions, whereas in Canada it was ignored or even stifled by the magnitude and apparent continuity of government funding until the 1980s.

Canadian universities were not alone in this, since their sister institutions in the UK, Australia, and New Zealand behaved in exactly the same way. By the end of the 1990s, however, there may have been reason to conclude that universities in those countries had been better at learning their lesson than Canadian institutions. Certainly, the best alumni magazine that I receive, and I regularly receive them from five universities, is that of Cambridge University, and the magazine from Auckland is at least comparable to any Canadian counterpart.

A significant part of my work as president was, therefore, the cultivation of alumni and the development of continuing alumni chapters at major centres across Canada and elsewhere. In this, not only I but often also the university's chancellor and sometimes the chair of the board, as well as staff of the Alumni Office were involved in extensive and frequent travel, and while the results were variable and often depended on the degree of enthusiasm of one or two local alumni, we were able to rekindle the interest and support of alumni in a good many locations. While no direct attempt was made to engage in fund-raising at alumni social functions, the financial state of health of the university was always drawn to their attention. Much greater work was also put into the Annual Fund drive, with students, faculty volunteers, and alumni involved in the task. The result was that over a four-year period, the annual total raised in this drive increased from $400,000 to over $1.5 million, an amount that was in addition to the ongoing stream of bequests and gifts throughout the year.

This increasing amount had an interesting effect on the attitudes of deans and their faculty members. In 1985, the major faculties of Arts and Science received very little from the Annual Fund, which had little significance for the faculty; at that time, the Faculty of Medicine had worked much harder to maintain the interest of its alumni and benefited most from their support. Over the next four or five years, as the annual total rose past $1.5 million, the Faculty of Arts began to receive amounts of about $100,000, which took on great significance as budget cuts became very severe. A small unit such as the Drama Department began to appreciate that an unrestricted annual amount of perhaps $5,000 from the Annual Fund gave them a degree of flexibility that was invaluable, and even the most cynical of faculty members began to appreciate the increasing value of alumni support and became involved in seeking that support.

Such fund-raising and cultivation of alumni and potential donors have become a very large part of presidential duties; some estimates suggest that many current presidents spend up to 40 percent of their time and effort on these activities. In my case, it was somewhat less but still significant. In 1986, when I became president, Dalhousie was in the middle of a five-year fund-raising campaign begun in 1984 with a target of $35 million; about $20-22 million had been raised. Unlike many Canadian universities, which did not undertake such campaigns until the 1980s or later, Dalhousie, with little provincial support until 1964, had previously engaged in a number of successful campaigns. The 1984-89 campaign had not been well planned at first, and professional fund-raising staff had not been engaged until the last moment. But with the hard work of key staff members and the support of many faithful alumni, a total of $40 million was raised within the five-year period.

Fund-raising for this campaign helped me greatly in meeting many Dalhousie alumni; it also taught me much about the difficulties and risks of raising money! In general, I thoroughly enjoyed these aspects of the president's work, in large part because of the fascinating variety of interesting individuals with whom I came in contact. It was a wonderful experience to visit a major Canadian corporation with Robert Stanfield to seek support for Dalhousie, or to meet with several hundred Dalhousie alumni, principally from the Law School, in Calgary, or to find a remarkably loyal and interested group of fifty alumni in Kuala Lumpur.

There are still other groups with which a university president must work, and at least two more deserve comment. One is the group of senior administrators within the institution: the vice-presidents and their associates or assistants, the deans, the registrar, the chief librarian, and so on. My belief has always been that this group of administrators in a Canadian university should view themselves as being a senior management group for the entire institution and be the major source of advice to the president on significant university issues. Generally, with the exception of deans, these administrators agree with this view and do constitute such a source of advice. Deans, however, see their role much more as advocate for their particular faculty and may well feel a conflict of interest in being asked to put the interests of the institution as a whole first. This attitude was well described by one dean during my first year as president. He agreed with the point that deans should indeed form part of a senior management team, but pointed out that at the time he was recommended by a selection committee to be dean, he was asked to promise that he would fight to get every last cent of funding for his faculty regardless of the welfare of anyone else in the university! This may well be perfectly natural and human, but it also reveals a high degree of fragmentation and does not say much for the university as a community of scholars.

The last sector I must mention consists of government, and through it the general public. My newspaper columns gave me a convenient means of communication, but I also had to become known to the appropriate minister and deputy minister, the premier, the chair and staff of the Maritime Provinces Higher Education Commission (MPHEC), and many others. In fact, since Dalhousie is very much a regional institution, especially with regard to Medicine, Dentistry, and some other health professions as well as some graduate fields, it was necessary for me to be known also by the premiers of the other Atlantic provinces. As well, Dalhousie occupies an unusually prominent place in Halifax and Nova Scotia; when foreign diplomats based in Ottawa made their periodic visit to Halifax, the Protocol Office often included a visit with the president of Dalhousie. And the Dalhousie president was invited to many official functions, such as the installation of the Lieutenant-Governor, the recognition of prominent lawyers as Queen's Counsel, and so on, and was expected to be seen at major social functions.

The situation in 1986 was made even more complex by the recent appearance of the *Report of the Royal Commission on Post-Secondary Education,* which advocated, among other things, the creation of a separate and permanent Nova Scotia Commission apart from MPHEC, the creation of a community college system, and some rationalization of Nova Scotia's universities. While it made for much uncertainty, with the government slow in responding to it, the report did provide an opportunity for Dalhousie to attempt some redress of problems that had been created by MPHEC in preceding years. In more than one case, MPHEC had just responded to the representations of other universities in Nova Scotia, which had been completely alienated by the condescending and arrogant attitude often displayed by Dalhousie, and particularly by President Henry Hicks. They had their own ambitions and clearly felt that Dalhousie's sense of superiority was unfounded and to be challenged. Moreover, Dalhousie's financial problems were well known and regarded as irresponsible; in their view, it was time to take

Dalhousie down a peg or two. All in all, a most challenging time to become president of Dalhousie University!

I could never suggest that before I accepted the presidency at Dalhousie I was not given full and accurate information about the existing problems; I was provided with voluminous material and extensive advice, all given thoroughly, honestly, fully, and accurately. In retrospect, however, and I do not think I am just providing myself with an excuse, I doubt that the seriousness, the magnitude, and the interconnectedness of the problems could have been appreciated by anyone until he or she was actually engaged in the situation. My first two years seemed to be spent fighting brush fires; every day a new problem seemed to emerge, each of which could be solved if only there were more money, but there was absolutely none! Many of these problems reflected weaknesses in the administrative machinery, often in quite simple matters that I had taken for granted at Western or Guelph. In other cases, obsolete equipment and practices were the cause, and in others improvements and structural changes that other Canadian universities had made long ago had just been ignored or neglected at Dalhousie. Permeating everything was the sense of frustration and the low morale that had been inherited from the Hicks era and the intervening six years, during which the magnitude of the financial problems had reluctantly been recognized. While many other Canadian universities were at that time feeling a financial pinch, few had experienced such a devastating and abrupt reversal from the expansionist Hicks years to the consequences of crushing debt and uncontrolled deficits. While other universities experienced a pinch, Dalhousie faced internal crisis and the possibility of bankruptcy.

As one small example of the extent of disarray at Dalhousie, there was the matter of the university logo and the printing of university stationery. Within one or two weeks of my arrival, I was struck by the wide variety of letterheads that seemed to be in use across the campus. A few inquiries quickly told me that there was no such thing as a standard letterhead or logo, although there did exist an official crest for Dalhousie. In the highly democratic university, the only way to address such a controversial matter was to establish a committee! This I did, and was subsequently amused to be told, in the committee's report, that over ninety different logos, letterheads, and crests were in use. The Purchasing Department and the various print shops on campus were quickly instructed to use only one logo, adapted from the official crest, and within a year, after some minor altercations, Dalhousie had a uniform logo and letterhead stationery. In my first year or so, this type of issue, minor in itself but revealing an administrative laxity and disorganization, seemed to rise to the surface almost daily.

Beyond the apparently endless stream of such daily crises and difficulties, my first few years were much occupied with, and to a marked degree dominated by, two or three fundamental issues.

The Financial Crisis

The overwhelming problem was obviously financial, and the first task was to stem the financial bleeding of an annual deficit and to balance the budget. Since the government and MPHEC were initially unsympathetic, and the DFA interested only in salary increases, pretty harsh decisions had to be made, and here the absolute steadfastness of Vice-President Finance and Administration B.G. Mason was essential. By quickly taking control of all expenditures in fall 1986, we were able to keep the deficit below $250,000 for the 1986-87 financial year, and in 1987-88 the budget was close to being balanced, with a small deficit of well under $100,000. Thereafter, for the remaining seven budget years of my presidency, the budget was in balance and occasionally produced an extremely small surplus.

This was achieved only at a considerable price. The base budget reductions in the four years from 1986 to 1990 were 3.0, 4.24, 3.6, and 2.55 percent, respectively; roughly and very imprecisely, this constitutes by simple addition a total reduction to the base of 13.34 percent; and a similar addition, for what it is worth, for the 1986-95 period of my term as president gives a total of 26.7 percent! Whatever this number really means, it at least conveys an accurate feeling of the difficulty, pain, and frustration that was experienced across the entire institution. But the discipline was essential, and without it Dalhousie might well have been bankrupt. Annual reductions of this magnitude cannot be achieved without reducing personnel, especially when salaries consume at least 80 percent of the budget. In 1986, the DFA collective agreement for the years 1985-87 contained a clause that required the board to maintain the number of faculty at the pre-1985 level; this itself illustrates the extent to which power had fallen into the hands of the DFA. We knew that substantial future budget reductions lay ahead and realized that these could not be achieved unless the faculty complement could be reduced. When the collective agreement came up for renegotiation in mid-1987, Mason, as chief negotiator for the board, was able to achieve some modification to the relevant clause that, within quite limiting conditions, gave the president the ability to reduce the numbers of faculty positions without having to invoke the cumbersome and unworkable clauses that would invoke Financial Constraint. The price paid for this came in the form of a new collective agreement that lasted for just one year, and, of course, agreement on increased salaries.

While all the details of the amended clause in the collective agreement are unimportant here, the actual application of it in each of the following seven years illustrates again the weakness of community feeling within a university. To implement this clause, the president had to advise the Senate that budgetary reductions would be necessary and that he proposed to reduce the faculty complement by a specific number in that budget year. He also proposed a distribution of that number between the various faculties.

These proposals had to be accompanied by financial information justifying the proposed level of reductions. All proposals were then considered by the Senate Budget and Finance Committee, which then made a recommendation to the Senate. Given the widely known state of Dalhousie's finances, neither the committee nor Senate could avoid the necessity of the budgetary reductions, and while there was always great unhappiness at the prospect of reducing the number of faculty positions, in every year the committee found it impossible to arrive at a different distribution of the total number. For one faculty to argue that it should be more leniently treated required another to accept a greater reduction! Annually, therefore, the committee and the Senate, in frustration had no alternative but to reluctantly accept the president's proposed distribution of reductions. Of course, these were reductions in a total complement of funded positions, and since there were annually retirements and resignations, the required reductions could usually be achieved without affecting tenured faculty members, although the numbers of part-time faculty were much reduced.

In addition, all other items in the budget – supplies, equipment, and so on – had to be cut to the maximum extent possible, although, as in other Canadian universities, the acquisitions budget of the library was protected and occasionally received increases. The administrative units had to absorb larger reductions than the academic units, but at the same time, to the extent that it might be possible, there had to be reorganization and strengthening of the administrative side of the institution. We appointed a director of physical plant who instituted a preventive maintenance program and, over opposition from an entrenched group of employees, restructured the department; similarly, the Registrar's Office underwent major alterations and received a new registrar, and the entire operation of that office was made much more friendly to students. With annual reductions necessary to restore financial health to the institution, every initiative of this sort was greeted with hostility, especially from some faculty.

There was also a fundamental problem in the funding mechanism employed by MPHEC. First, there was the annual question of how much the commission would have to distribute. When MPHEC was first established, it was assigned responsibility for recommending annually to the three Maritime provincial governments the percentage increase that would be required, and for almost a decade, the governments accepted these recommendations without question. By the mid-1980s, however, the Nova Scotia government had become quite disenchanted with MPHEC and, especially on funding, began to ignore its advice and to decide independently on a usually smaller increase. This slowly undermined the credibility of MPHEC and caused the universities to pay increasing attention to the attitudes of the Nova Scotia government.

At the same time, some of the flaws in the funding formula through which the government-determined funds were distributed to each university became more apparent. While every effort had been made to achieve equity in setting the formula for the Maritimes, the many voices of the smaller institutions in Nova Scotia had tended to drown out the lone voice of Dalhousie. Other institutions were largely undergraduate but in some cases had considerable ambitions to become much more, whereas Dalhousie provided nearly all of the professional programs and over 85 percent of the graduate programs and university research. While the funding formula in effect in 1986 weighted graduate and professional program enrollments more heavily, it did so to a lesser degree than in Ontario and also took no recognition of the underlying costs of research. Moreover, the formula provided a considerable incentive for growth in undergraduate programs, while at Dalhousie a significant portion of enrollment was in professional programs that were restricted in size and could not grow. Especially in the preceding decade, therefore, the smaller institutions in the province had benefited considerably but at a price paid by Dalhousie. My presidential colleagues at the other Nova Scotia institutions informed me that this merely compensated for the preferential treatment for Dalhousie that Hicks had been able to pry from government, and they felt that still further repayment was necessary!

Over the two-year period from 1986 to 1988, I was therefore engaged in fierce debate with these colleagues, and with active lobbying of MPHEC and the provincial government. By 1988, MPHEC had agreed to engage an external consultant, Alan Adlington, to review matters; he accepted many of Dalhousie's arguments and recommended the introduction of an interim modified formula in 1989 that substantially improved Dalhousie's funding relative to the other institutions.[23] The interim nature of the changes reflected the government's growing doubts about the continuing role of MPHEC, as well as questions raised by the 1995 Royal Commission about the long-term effectiveness of having fifteen independent postsecondary institutions in the province. While the interim formula helped Dalhousie greatly, it also signalled the beginning of the acrimonious, prolonged, and largely unproductive public debate on rationalization of the province's universities. By that time, the financial hemorrhage had been stemmed at Dalhousie and the first step taken back to financial health.

The Chancellor

On a much lighter note, but still of significance to Dalhousie, was the matter of the chancellor. The story surrounding this office has a characteristically colourful Maritime aspect. Historically, there was no provision for the office of chancellor at Dalhousie until the late 1950s, when the board created the post for its first incumbent, C.D. Howe, the most prominent federal cabinet minister through the 1940s and 1950s. A most influential person, Howe did much for the university during his short tenure, but died in 1960. The post remained vacant for some time, until in 1968 the board was able to persuade the third Lady Beaverbrook, its most generous donor at the time, to become the second chancellor. Although there was an installation ceremony, to which she brought a magnificent gold thread-embroidered chancellor's gown specially imported from Britain, as well as cases of her favourite champagne, she never carried out the ceremonial duties that chancellors of other Canadian universities regularly perform at convocation ceremonies. Each president had conducted all of those ceremonies, complicated and tiring though they were, with Hicks thoroughly enjoying himself and MacKay later enduring them with dignity and patience.

By 1986 the circumstances surrounding the post of chancellor were almost bizarre. Lady Beaverbrook had, over the eighteen years since her installation, become increasingly reclusive. She had never again been to the Dalhousie campus, and during his term, President MacKay had never met her. I was told that around 1980 the board decided that a letter should be sent to her, thanking her for her services as chancellor, but since there were expectations of further donations from her, the letter must have been worded in a most circuitous and indirect manner. Lady Beaverbrook or her secretary obviously misread it, and replied that she was delighted to be chancellor and would happily continue. Faced with no alternative, the board had reappointed her for three years, up to 1983. By 1986 Dalhousie legally had no chancellor, although it seemed clear that Lady Beaverbrook still assumed that she held that office. Fortunately, as one of his last deeds as president, MacKay managed to get her to commit a generous $2 million gift for the refurbishment of the Sir James Dunn Law Library, which had been severely damaged by fire in 1985. It was widely assumed, however, and certainly by Lady Beaverbrook, that she remained chancellor. As the new president, I wished to have the benefit of an active and prominent chancellor, but there seemed no way of delicately terminating the matter, especially as there remained substantial funds in the Dunn Foundation over which she had great influence.

There were other unusual circumstances. When I arrived at Dalhousie, I felt that I should communicate with the chancellor but was astonished to be told that this could be done only through a secretary in Montreal, and that any letter sent to the secretary had to be in large printing, double-spaced! By this peculiar route, I offered to visit Lady Beaverbrook and to bring her up-to-date on Dalhousie affairs, but this was immediately rebuffed in a letter from the secretary. In fact, I was never able to meet or communicate directly with Lady Beaverbrook. Over frequent discussions of this problem, the vice-presidents and I could find no easy solution, until in 1989 one vice-president made the suggestion that Lady Beaverbrook become Chancellor Emeritus. I seized on this with enthusiasm and wrote via the secretary thanking Lady Beaverbrook for her great contributions to Dalhousie and indicating that we would be honoured if she would agree to become Chancellor Emeritus, allowing us to appoint a new chancellor. A rather curt reply came back from the secretary, agreeing but pointedly asking that we ship back to St. Andrews, New Brunswick, the gown and the remaining cases of champagne that had been kept in a chiller at Dalhousie over the years. After some thought, I responded by suggesting that, as a personal gift to Dalhousie, Lady Beaverbrook might consider giving the gown to the university for the use of future chancellors, a suggestion that, to my delight, she accepted. A second letter then went to her secretary saying that of course we would return the remaining cases of champagne, but that because of their age, no commercial carrier would agree to take them and they would have to be transported illegally by private car across interprovincial borders, with somebody at Lady Beaverbrook's home in St. Andrews immediately available to accept delivery. The last communication I had from Lady Beaverbrook, again indirectly, said to just keep the cases. We did, and in fact opened some bottles in 1990 when we installed a new chancellor, Reuben Cohen; the champagne was well past its best, but still drinkable!

Reuben Cohen, another Law School graduate, had devoted many years in the 1980s to managing almost single-handedly Dalhousie's considerable endowment fund, including the substantial Killam bequest. He went on to be a splendid chancellor who took a deep interest in reactivating alumni interest in Dalhousie, travelling widely with me across Canada, to London, Boston, New York, and Hong Kong, always supporting the university with enthusiasm. He also attended convocations and participated as chancellor, conferring degrees at virtually all ceremonies during his term, and did so with style, panache, and a personal touch of humour, albeit from a different generation and therefore causing offence to some, but lightening occasions that too often can be lengthy and dull.

The Faculty Strike

My first years were dominated by the relationship with the faculty union, the Dalhousie Faculty Association. The legacy of the autocratic Hicks's reign remained, but there was also the fact that for decades faculty salaries at Dalhousie had lagged behind those of other Canadian institutions with which Dalhousie faculty had become accustomed to making comparisons. Moreover, the history of the board's responses to complaints about the disparities had fairly consistently suggested a degree of indifference and tardiness that had inevitably compounded the frustration. The valid board argument that Dalhousie was severely constrained within the limited resources of a weak Maritime economy, whereas the University of Toronto or Queen's University benefited from the much more robust Ontario economy, did not fit well with the claim that Dalhousie had national stature. And when the DFA asserted, often on the basis of data that differed sharply from official Association of Universities and Colleges of Canada (AUCC) data, that Dalhousie salaries lagged behind those of other Halifax institutions, the majority of faculty were quickly convinced. Additionally, the fact that the DFA had successfully pursued a number of grievances under the collective agreement gave further credence to the perception of the administration and board as arrogant and uncaring.

By the late 1980s, all of these historical and current perceptions, real or imagined, had created a confrontational and antagonistic atmosphere of an intensity that I had never encountered before. During 1987 and 1988, I visited departments as much as possible, I wrote in the university newspaper regularly, and I tried to address complaints to the extent that our critical financial situation allowed and to improve the maintenance of buildings and property. We went as far as possible in providing salary increases in 1987, but across the campus there seemed to be nothing but hostility and criticism of Dalhousie as an institution. A small illustration of the pettiness and hostility that existed came in the summer of 1987. By then, the relatively small campus of Dalhousie had an unkempt, littered appearance, with uncut grass, the exceedingly few flowerbeds empty of all but weeds, and unrepaired broken windows in more than one building. The newly arrived director of physical plant was struggling to bring order out of chaos, but I still directed him to spend the smallest amount possible in order to plant some flowers to improve the appearance of the grounds slightly, and whatever it took to get the grass cut regularly. The flowering plants cost about $300, but at the next Senate meeting I was attacked as a spendthrift and as just a continuation of an irresponsible administration!

By mid-1988, when the one-year agreement of 1987 had to be renegotiated, it quickly became clear that the DFA had every intention of bringing about a faculty strike. Futile negotiations took place during the summer, and by late October conciliation had been unsuccessfully tried. The main issue was, of course, salaries, although the first steps we had taken in late 1987 to reduce the faculty complement had also inflamed the faculty. By early November, the DFA had obtained a strike vote, and on 8 November the faculty mounted picket lines and were on strike. At the time of certification and throughout the following years, this had been the prime concern of a significant number of faculty who were totally opposed to unionization and who realized that the victims of any strike would inevitably be the students. In their opposition, they had deliberately abstained from any participation in DFA meetings and in DFA votes, thereby revealing their naivete about labour relations and leaving the field to the union supporters.

The most remarkable demonstration of the lack of understanding of unionization and the consequences of a strike came in the letter the DFA sent to faculty members before the strike, and in the responses to it. Faculty were informed that during a strike, they would be asked by the DFA to withhold their teaching services to all students and to cease any participation in administrative or committee work, but that they would of course be entirely free to continue without interruption their research and scholarship, and most importantly, would continue to receive full salary throughout the period of the strike. The faculty of a university are assumed to be of higher intelligence than average, and the fact that these reassurances were accepted uncritically can only be attributed to an astonishing lack of knowledge of the real world. The board position, which I quickly delivered, recognized that a significant number of faculty, especially in the faculties of Science, Medicine, and Dentistry, were not in sympathy with the union and had no wish to strike. Provided that each signed a statement to that effect, each would be allowed access to university property at all times, but otherwise all those who participated in the strike would be locked out. In retrospect, I doubt that we could have done otherwise at that time. If all union members had been locked out, the board would have immediately lost the support of the more loyal and conservative of the faculty. On the other hand, a complete lockout would have brought home more quickly the true realities of labour relations, and might have helped prevent a later strike in 1998.

The matter of the payment of salaries for the period of the strike was a critical issue. We discovered that, although there had already been quite a number of faculty strikes at other Canadian universities, in all but one case there had been full and complete payment of salaries. Apparently, in all such cases, the faculty unions had claimed that regardless of the strike, the faculty would inevitably cover, during the remainder of the academic year, the full and complete curriculum for every course, and administrations and boards had, quite remarkably, accepted this. Before the strike began, we determined that under no circumstances would such full salary be paid at Dalhousie. Quite apart from the principle of the matter, Nova Scotia was a small community and if we did otherwise, it would be quickly known and would further damage Dalhousie's reputation with the government and the general public.

The eleven-day strike was extremely unpleasant. The media were everywhere, seldom taking the time to obtain correct facts and often publishing statements from the DFA that had never been checked; the level of hostility was enormous, and the stress on senior administrators and members of the board was considerable. Students and parents demanded an immediate resolution, since of course it was the students who were the victims. The board generally stood firm and remained totally supportive, apart from one or two exceptions who, after a few days, felt that Dalhousie's reputation was being so damaged that we should immediately settle at any price. We did not do so, and eventually, with the provincial minister of labour intervening, a mediator was appointed. During a prolonged mediation session, all the outstanding issues were settled, the last being that of payment of salaries during the strike. The board negotiator immediately made clear that there would be no payment, and since everything else had been settled, the DFA had little alternative but to accept.

For many faculty, the most bitterly learned lesson of the strike was that they would not be paid, and it was a lesson that many could not comprehend. Some weeks after the strike, a senior and respected scholarly faculty member came to see me. He told me frankly that although he had supported the idea of a strike and had participated on the picket lines, he had kept in touch with his students, marking and giving out assignments, and had continued with his scholarly writing at home. He just could not understand, therefore, why his salary had been stopped for the period of the strike, and would I please give him some explanation. I am still not sure that he and many others ever really understood this issue; most faculty believed at the time, and perhaps still believe, that they should have all of the rights and protections of labour relations legislation, and also the guarantee of full salary throughout a strike and all of the privileges and protection that tenure provides, and that they should simultaneously have, through a participatory form of university governance, effective control of the institution as well as the right to choose their own senior administrators.

The strike covered eleven days, but its legacy in terms of bitterness and venom, as well as in terms of lessons learned by all parties, was extensive and long-lasting. Even though many students supported the faculty against what was seen as a reactionary, "establishment" board and administration, the realization that the student body was used by the union as a bargaining tool with such indifference, with little concern for the students' education and careers, brought the harsh realities home to them. Some faculty did, I believe, begin to appreciate, at least to some degree, that collective bargaining brought with it consequences they had not expected or thought about. There was certainly some damage done to Dalhousie's reputation, but given the number of strikes that have since occurred at other universities across Canada, this was not lasting.

The bitterness, however, endured among many of the staunch unionists. In 1991 the end of my six-year term was approaching, and I had indicated to the board that I would be willing to be considered for reappointment to a further term. Unlike Guelph and many other Canadian universities, and largely because appointments for term were relatively new at Dalhousie, there had been little previous experience with reappointments. Drawing on my experience elsewhere, I described to the board chair how the appropriate committee might be created with a balance of board and Senate members as well as student representation, and how it might first conduct a review of the past six years of my presidency, before deciding whether to recommend reappointment or move on to an open search for a new president. When the required Senate elections were held for the faculty representatives to this committee, it was clear that the DFA was firmly in control, with three of the four representatives being staunch DFA supporters.

For several months, the committee met and listened to the opinions of various parties. Since the meetings were confidential, I knew little of what was going on, although I could sense that I was being severely attacked. There was even a telephone call one evening from an inebriated former president of the DFA, telling me quite gleefully that they were making sure that I would not be reappointed. I was at last invited to meet with the committee, and it quickly became clear that faculty from the DFA were there for exactly that purpose. At an early stage of the meeting, to my utter disbelief, one very militant unionist blurted out to me, "You got us during the strike, now we are going to get you!" He was referring to the loss of salary, and displayed a lack of ethical professional behaviour that I have seldom seen equalled. Fortunately for me, the board was, throughout my term as president, extremely supportive and reappointed me.

Another consequence of the DFA strike was a further serious weakening of the Senate. At the commencement of the strike, a regular meeting of the Senate was due to be called, and would have considered motions to allow teaching to continue in those faculties least affected. This, of course, would not have been welcomed by the DFA, and some of its militant members were preparing to attend in order to ensure that such motions would fail and that the Senate would decree that all classes be cancelled. At the last minute, the chair decided that to avoid a further serious confrontation, the Senate meeting should be cancelled. While this led to an angry unofficial meeting on the nearby tennis courts, and prevented the DFA from achieving its goal, it unfortunately also led to the realization that, since so many faculty members ignored Senate meetings, it was quite easy for the DFA to control the Senate. After the strike, they did gain control; a former president of the DFA was elected chair of the Senate, and it was not difficult for the union to have enough supporters attend meetings and effectively control the Senate.

While this was much more easily done at Dalhousie because of the remarkable size of the Senate, the majority of whose members rarely attended meetings, it would be quite possible at other Canadian universities, and makes clear the extent to which faculty members over the past fifty years have gained control of the institution. It also emphasizes the serious conflict of interest issue that underlies such a situation. That faculty members can take strike action against a Board of Governors is based on legal rulings in the 1970s that faculty are employees and do not constitute management. Yet faculty control the academic operations of the university and can and do use their collective power as a senate to prevent the offering of classes and to enforce a strike. Such an obvious conflict of interest can be removed only by government legislation.

A Financial Strategy

In the aftermath of the strike in the fall of 1988, morale at Dalhousie was everywhere at a very low point. It was also clear to me that the financial problems were so complex and interrelated that any president trying to tackle them one at a time during a six-year term would be able to deal with only a few. What the situation demanded was an integrated attack on the entire financial health of the institution. How could the debt be reduced or eliminated? What decisions should be made about the university's large endowment? To what extent could revenues be increased and what new sources of revenues might be pursued? What increases in tuition fees were appropriate and what effect would such increases have on accessibility and enrollments? To what degree could Dalhousie increase its enrollments? How was the university to address the massive backlog in property maintenance? And given the magnitude of all these issues, how could we simultaneously plan for the future and for replacement buildings?

After much thought, I proposed to the board that a special, relatively small committee be struck consisting only of individuals prepared to devote considerable time and effort to these questions, continuing until a reasonably comprehensive plan was developed whereby Dalhousie might face a more secure future. Thus the board created what was known as the Financial Strategy Committee, and at the same time placed a moratorium on academic programs; no new program proposal would be considered by the board until the committee had produced a final report or until the board lifted its moratorium.

To the best of my knowledge, no other Canadian university has used such a vehicle, but then few, if any, have had to face the financial problems that Dalhousie then faced. The committee was struck and met for the first time in early 1989, and it continued meeting almost every week for well over two years. The energy and determination of the committee members was remarkable, and attendance was always high. While the committee produced a number of progress reports, its most important report, its seventh, came in July 1990. Well before it was submitted, the committee had gained real credibility and respect across the university. It had done so by addressing issues openly and straightforwardly, including that of morale, which the unions, including the DFA, had repeatedly raised.

Morale at a university is not easily defined and it certainly cannot be measured; even if it could, there would be total disagreement over who was responsible for morale. Indeed, is there such a thing as collective morale at all in a university? Nevertheless, the Financial Strategy Committee took this issue seriously, engaged a consultant, had surveys taken and analyzed, and engaged in extensive discussions with the unions. It was certainly the first time in decades that the board or its representatives had so obviously listened, and for a prolonged time, to complaints from its employees and had then attempted to act with sympathy. There can be no measurement of whether this itself improved morale, but I do believe that over the next years, morale at Dalhousie did improve. More importantly, the recommendations of the Financial Strategy Committee, some of which were unpopular, were received with respect and generally accepted.

It is not appropriate to recount here the work of the committee in detail, but within two to three years all of the major issues that confronted the university were addressed and the financial health and general morale of Dalhousie were restored. One of the most controversial solutions related to the future level of tuition fees. In 1988 these tuition fees were virtually the lowest in Atlantic Canada because of an agreement that the board had made in 1984. At the start of a major fund-raising campaign, the students had been persuaded to make a commitment, of $750,000 over five years, only by the board's agreeing that tuition fees during the next six years would rise annually by an amount equal to the rate of inflation less 1 percent. Unfortunately, other Canadian institutions raised their fees by amounts well in excess of inflation, so that by 1988 Dalhousie's fees were very low comparatively, and the university was losing far more each year than it gained from the student campaign "gift" of $750,000. By mid-1991, this six-year agreement with the students expired, and although they pressed for a continuation, the board approved the Financial Strategy Committee's recommendation of significant tuition fee increases commencing in 1992-93. Tuition was increased by an average of 10 percent, but it took further increases to bring Dalhousie's fees in line with those of comparable Canadian universities.

Student opposition was intense and almost became violent, but it was focused entirely on the impact of these cost increases on current students; the fact that they had benefited from lower fees in previous years because of the 1984 agreement, or that the future financial health of the institution left no alternative, meant nothing to them. Most of their arguments were couched in terms of "accessibility," a term that generates sympathy but that Canadian students too often don't bother to define. The Financial Strategy Committee had, in fact, looked very closely at the likely impact of higher tuition fees and had also recommended that 25 percent of the total tuition increase should be allocated annually for student financial support, largely in the form of bursaries, and Dalhousie was the first Canadian university to adopt such a policy. This was in contrast to the older, more common policy of simply maintaining tuition levels as low as possible, which indirectly provides unnecessary support to the more affluent students.

The work of the Financial Strategy Committee went well beyond the issue of tuition fees. Its report in July 1990 included recommendations on other possible sources of revenue that faculties should pursue, on undertaking another major fund-raising campaign, on the need to develop a policy statement of principles for student relations, on the further need to address the morale question, on specific means to reduce the debt and accumulated deficit totalling over $40 million, and many others. There is absolutely no doubt that the work of this committee enabled Dalhousie to recover and renew itself; no president alone could have accomplished so many things in a relatively short time, and the fact that the recommendations of the committee were clearly developed by the core members of the board together with the senior administration gave them a credibility and clout that could not easily be resisted.

Simultaneously, and synergistically with the work of the committee, a number of other key steps could be taken. As mentioned earlier, a brief, one-page mission statement that recognized the centrality for Dalhousie of the two areas of ocean studies and health studies, was approved by the Senate and the board; a conceptual plan for the future development of the Dalhousie campus was prepared following a highly consultative process that encouraged the participation of the university communities as well as neighbours in the surrounding residential areas; and the first major step towards the elimination of the university's debt problem was taken.

One of the items that the Financial Strategy Committee examined was the pension plan for Dalhousie employees. This was a defined benefit plan that, like so many others in the late 1980s and 1990s, produced a significant actuarial surplus. There has been considerable controversy over the legal ownership of such surpluses – does it belong to the employer, who has responsibility for the financial health of the pension plan, or is it more correctly seen as equivalent to deferred salary of the employees? Rather than engage in this fruitless debate, the committee proposed that the surplus be treated on the basis of 50/50 ownership, and this led to protracted and delicate negotiations between the board and the various employee unions and groups. Ultimately, agreement was reached on a three-year arrangement whereby a portion of the surplus would be used to allow both sides to take some form of "pension holiday." The board agreed to allocate the funds thus released to reduce debt, while the employee unions negotiated some improvements to the plan and, during those three years, paid much reduced contributions. This was a win/win situation for all, and with a subsequent renewal of the agreement for several more years, together with other repayments of debt, it enabled Dalhousie to become totally debt-free in 1999. This remarkable accomplishment has, as far as I know, never been achieved by any other Canadian university. From all points of view, the work of the Financial Strategy Committee was incredibly successful and has been fundamental to the revitalization of Dalhousie.

This period from 1987 to 1991 was extremely stressful and arduous. In that relatively short time was compressed the DFA strike, a less difficult strike of the Dalhousie Staff Association in early 1991, all of the work of the

Financial Strategy Committee and the steps towards implementation of its recommendations, the installation of a new chancellor, and many activities to increase alumni involvement and giving. At the same time, increasing pressures came from the provincial government following the *Report of the Royal Commission on Post-Secondary Education* and my own successful agitation to achieve changes to the funding formula. Both of these encouraged the government to create a Nova Scotia Council of Higher Education in mid-1989 and to engage in some form of rationalization of the province's many postsecondary institutions, but this is a matter to be discussed in the next chapter.

Academic Initiatives

The great majority of the activities described here were administrative in nature, but I was also able to take some initiatives on the academic side. One to which I attach importance was the creation of a task force to examine issues relating to Dalhousie's degree of accessibility for members of the black and Native communities in the Maritimes. Not surprisingly, we found that Dalhousie, like most Canadian universities, was seen as a cold and unfriendly place for these minority groups. Accordingly, several significant changes were made, including the provision of permanent funding for the Transition Year Program, special counselling services, and additional student financial support. Perhaps most importantly, as president I made a point of meeting several times with representatives of the black and Mi'kmaq communities for open and frank discussion, opportunities that I much appreciated and welcomed. Subsequently, Dalhousie, with the support of the federal government, was able to create a chair in black studies that focuses on the experience of the black communities in Canadian history and society.

Reflecting again my concerns about undergraduate education, Dalhousie took two interesting steps in 1988. First, a survey was conducted among students to determine how they viewed the education they were receiving, and this was followed by a university-wide symposium on undergraduate education. All the evidence and discussion at the symposium again emphasized that Dalhousie resembled other Canadian universities in the extent to which the undergraduate teaching function had been devalued relative to research activities over the previous several decades. They also emphasized that presidents have a most important leadership role to play in stressing the values of the institution and the importance of the educational function. The symposium led to the work of a small group, chaired by the vice-president academic, that reported back on a number of improvements and actions that could be (and that subsequently were) taken to address some of these issues, but it turned out that a most important step was taken when I stated that in the future I would consider no recommendations for promotion unless each was accompanied by written evidence concerning the quality of instruction. Previously, many recommendations had come forward with substantial supporting material relating to research and scholarship, but with little more than a cursory statement that the individual being recommended was also thought to be a good teacher.

My action led to more serious attention being given to teaching, and in some faculties has helped to emphasize to new faculty members that this component of their responsibilities must be taken very seriously. In other instances, however, files in support of recommendations for promotion reached my desk with fulsome letters of praise for the individual's scholarship, with the "evidence" of teaching quality consisting of a vast stack of student teaching evaluations, unanalyzed, based on questionnaires that had not been changed in a decade, and that students viewed as routine and perfunctory. I hasten to add that this was not universally so, and I recall with pleasure a number of cases where very substantial and impressive efforts were made to assess teaching quality using a variety of approaches, including classroom visits by other faculty members, new questionnaires, and written comments from students past and present.

It should not be a surprise that the collective agreement with the DFA made it exceedingly difficult, if not impossible, to initiate other steps that might ultimately create a better balance of values between the research and teaching activities of faculty. Any attempt to give outstanding teachers awards that were monetary or provided a real benefit infringed on the collective agreement. Such awards would have to be negotiated with the DFA, which was in any event firmly opposed to any form of merit salary recognition. Moreover, these are not issues that can, or should be, dealt with in the confrontational atmosphere of labour negotiations.

The foregoing description of some of the major responsibilities of a university president is less than adequate in conveying accurately all that the position entails. I have said nothing about attending external meetings such as those of the Association of Universities and Colleges of Canada, representing Dalhousie on ceremonial occasions such as the installation of presidents or chancellors at other universities across Canada, welcoming official visitors to the university, attending social functions or student sporting events, entertaining at the president's house in efforts to maintain some sense of university community, and, of course, the endless committee meetings. Since my retirement, I have often thought of the thousands of hours I spent at such meetings, and have tried unsuccessfully to relate this vast expenditure of time to the meagre results that seem in retrospect to have been achieved. It is certainly true that many of these meetings were unnecessary and accomplished little; they took place because of a participatory form of governance that pays no attention to the efficient use of resources, including people's time. On the other hand, a good portion of these meetings was devoted to the discussion of new issues, new circumstances, and new problems, which could best be addressed by open and frank discussion by a relatively small number of suitably qualified persons. Such meetings can be constructive and even exciting, but only a small minority of university meetings fit this description!

10
Finances, Rationalization, and Political Correctness

After four or five years as president of Dalhousie University, I found that my early perceptions of the position were confirmed. For one, the workload was unremittingly heavy, not only for me but for all senior administrators. For its size and complexity of program offerings, Dalhousie was seriously understaffed on the administrative side. It contrasted with other universities, such as the University of Guelph or the University of Western Ontario, where the presidents and vice-presidents had executive assistants and executive secretaries, and the level of staffing in the various administrative units was at least sufficient to cope with the essential workload. At Dalhousie, too much landed on the desks of the president and vice-presidents, with no one to whom work might be delegated. And given the financial circumstances, there was little possibility for improvement. In the private sector or government, this would not have been allowed to continue and sufficient staffing would have been provided. Not so under the participatory governance system of the university, where any attempt to increase administrative staffing, whether at Dalhousie or elsewhere, provokes immediate criticism, especially from faculty who have a peculiarly jaundiced view of administration. Perhaps the students will also claim that fees should first be lowered! In fact, the pressure of work and the resultant stress on individuals were often unreasonable, and could be tolerated only because so many in the administration were willing to make such effort. At Dalhousie and at Canadian universities generally, most of those who labour on the administrative side demonstrate a remarkable commitment and loyalty to the institution. They often show a willingness to put in long hours that keeps the university afloat and functioning smoothly, sometimes in the face of blind criticism from faculty and students.

The Financial Struggle and Program Cuts

Although repayment of the debt and accumulated deficit had begun by 1991, the annual struggle to achieve a balanced budget was continuous and unrelenting. There was temporary relief with a modified funding formula in 1989-90. To illustrate its impact, in 1988-89 government funding to universities was increased by 7.7 percent overall, with institutional increases ranging from 2 to 13 percent. Dalhousie, which constituted almost 50 percent of the Nova Scotia system, including the most expensive programs, received an increase of 3.14 percent. In 1989-90, with the modified formula in place and an overall increase of 5.3 percent, Dalhousie received 4.8 percent, a considerable improvement.

No sooner had this formula change brought some relief than, with a change in premier, the provincial government declared that the province's finances were in a disastrous state and that funding to all government-supported institutions and agencies would be reduced. This was followed very shortly by word that federal government transfers to the provinces would initially be frozen and then reduced. Even a change to a Liberal provincial government did nothing to improve provincial revenues. Fortunately, before these further constraints began, we had been able to achieve, with the help of a conciliator, a further three-year labour agreement with the Dalhousie Faculty Association in November 1990; shortly thereafter, the province legislated a three-year salary and wage freeze. Although this prevented any immediate labour difficulties, it created considerable resentment, and Dalhousie's financial prospects were still dismal.

By early 1992, the work of the Financial Strategy Committee had been completed but the university clearly faced new budget difficulties. Accordingly, I created a Budget Advisory Committee, a presidential committee over whose composition I had some control. In a series of thoughtful reports, all of which were given wide publicity, the committee advised that Dalhousie faced very major funding reductions over the 1993-96 period, even though it had already endured ten years of real and severe cuts, including five years in which faculty numbers had been reduced annually. The view was expressed very forcefully by the committee that across-the-board reductions were no longer an option and that the preservation of some areas of priority was essential. By spring 1993, the committee recommended that a three-year budget plan be implemented over the 1993-96 period so as to achieve an overall budget reduction of 15 percent; this would require selective reductions ranging from 4 to 5 percent in Medicine, to 8 percent in Science, to 20 percent in Arts and Social Sciences, and to 33 percent in Continuing Education. The committee argued that in order to achieve these reductions and still maintain strength in Arts and Social Sciences, it would be desirable to consider closing some units, and suggested that both the Theatre and Music departments be closed.

No university president enjoys receiving such recommendations, and they were especially troubling at Dalhousie. While it could certainly be argued that both of these departments were not central to the future well-being of the university, both made very significant contributions to the cultural life of Halifax and Nova Scotia. Indeed, the Dalhousie Arts Centre and the Rebecca Cohn Theatre in particular had been at the centre of theatrical, musical, and cultural life in the Nova Scotia community since their opening in 1971. To this day, the Cohn Theatre remains the only reasonable concert hall in Halifax. The suggestion that the Theatre and Music departments be closed was, therefore, extreme and controversial.

Now, these were recommendations to the president; I did not have to accept them and, in fact, could have rejected them as too extreme and then applied an across-the-board uniform set of budget cuts. It was crystal-clear, however, that a three-year reduction of 15 percent would have had to be achieved, and almost as clear that a reduction of that magnitude in professional faculties, such as Medicine, could put their accreditations at risk. In some science areas, Dalhousie had already recently lost several key faculty members to richer Canadian universities. Neither the committee nor I could identify other academic units that might more appropriately be closed, and I considered that our first priority had to be to achieve selective budget reductions with some protection offered to certain faculties. I knew also that if I recommended to the board only the selective budget reductions, these would immediately become the focus of DFA reaction and would probably lead to a grievance and subsequent arbitration. If I recommended both the selective reductions and the closure of the two departments, the faculty and students and the DFA would focus on the closures and there would certainly be a grievance.

As in so many cases, the issue of whether the president had the right to initiate such closures of academic units came down to the legal interpretation of certain clauses in the collective agreement with the DFA. Our own interpretation of one critical clause had been supported by legal counsel, and we concluded that the president did have this right. Although there were obviously other options, I concluded that I would accept all the recommendations of the Budget Advisory Committee, and at a tumultuous open meeting in the Cohn Theatre in September 1993, I made this announcement to the university community. Not surprisingly, faculty, students, and supporters were in full force at the front of the theatre, the meeting was unruly and noisy, and the board chair and I were highly unpopular. We also faced hostility from the general public, although others understood the difficult financial choices we faced, even though they did not necessarily agree with our decisions. The DFA immediately initiated the grievance process, claiming that the president was in violation of the collective agreement, but with the board's support, it was made clear that we intended to proceed immediately with the three-year budget plan, including the selective budget reductions.

There was great opposition from the Faculty of Arts and Social Sciences, which at first refused to make the required 20 percent total reduction, and it took some time and pressure for that faculty to develop an acceptable budget plan. The DFA grievance eventually went to arbitration, with the arbitrator delivering an opinion that the president had indeed breached the collective agreement. There could therefore be no departmental closures, and there is no question that this ruling substantially weakened my ability to act as president in the way that I would have wished over the remaining fifteen months of my term. However, the achievement of the selective budget reductions not only helped retain academic strength in certain faculties that are central to Dalhousie but also brought home to many both the severity of the financial crisis and the need to define priorities. For the first time, for example, the Faculty of Arts and Social Sciences had to reach agreement on how future faculty retirements and replacements would be handled in order to ensure academic viability in critical areas. Indeed, the entire exercise strengthened the backbone of the university even as the starvation diet continued. During the nine financial years over which I as president had influence, from April 1987 to March 1996, it was only in the first that a small deficit occurred; otherwise, Dalhousie recorded eight years of balanced budgets and a much-needed sense of financial responsibility. But these results, and particularly selective budget changes, were achieved only with difficulty and at a significant price.

Rationalization: The Lost Opportunity

While a president must deal with such difficult financial situations, there is at least some satisfaction in seeing a degree of success. That cannot be said for the issue that so uselessly drained away so much time during the latter half of my presidency, namely, rationalization of Nova Scotia's universities. I will make no attempt to define that ugly word "rationalization," since there was no single definition throughout the decade when it was on the tongues of all university people. That was the real problem: the government had no clear vision of what should be accomplished, and others suggested differing interpretations of the word or just preferred the status quo. So, by default, the term "rationalization" acquired meanings ranging from "eliminating program duplication," to "greater efficiency," to "amalgamation of institutions," to "government saving money." Use of the term had been encouraged by the *Report of the Royal Commission on Post-Secondary Education* in 1985, which had rightly pointed out that Nova Scotia, for historical reasons, had an excessive number (thirteen) of degree-granting institutions, seven of them in Halifax, and that government should give thought to means whereby greater efficiency could be achieved.

The Royal Commission was not the first to make this point. There had been more than one previous attempt to "rationalize" the situation, but none had succeeded. This reflected the establishment in the nineteenth century of not only Dalhousie but also Acadia, St. Francis Xavier, St. Mary's, and Mt. St. Vincent universities, along with the University of King's College. Since the 1960s, religious control had been gradually relinquished to gain government funding; Mt. St. Vincent was the last to make this change in the 1980s. Some might conclude that these sectarian differences would have disappeared or been forgotten by now. This is not so, and while this history is never referred to in open conversation, the lingering feelings of hostility and resentment are very deep and intense.

I was made to realize this early on, when I attended my first meeting with other Nova Scotia university presidents. One of these colleagues had also been newly appointed, with no previous Maritime connections, and we had arrived in the province from Ontario at about the same time. While I knew something of the inter-institutional rivalries, I came to this meeting feeling that my newly arrived colleague and I could surely have an impartial and constructive discussion of such issues – after all, we had both just arrived from that cool, dispassionate province of Ontario. To my complete astonishment, a few minutes after the meeting started, my colleague launched into a violent attack on Dalhousie, of its past arrogance and its condescending attitudes towards all other institutions, all of which were personified in Henry Hicks (whom my colleague had probably not yet met and with whom she had had no dealings). Clearly the history, the differences, the conflicts, and the hostility were neither forgotten nor forgiven, but were instead passed on from generation to generation! To talk of rationalization in such circumstances was akin to walking through a minefield.

Yet there had been previous attempts. In the early 1920s, the Carnegie Foundation of New York, which had been supporting college education in the Maritimes for some years, conducted an inquiry into higher education in the Maritime provinces and concluded that, with the help of Carnegie funds, Acadia, King's College, St. Francis Xavier, and Mt. Allison should move to the Dalhousie campus and become constituent colleges of a federated university. Remarkably, while all of the institutions were underfunded, underequipped, and understaffed, and while the costs of relocation would be covered largely by the Carnegie Foundation, Acadia, Mt. Allison, and St. Francis Xavier all declined to enter such a federation. Dalhousie supported the concept, although not with total enthusiasm, while the University of King's College, whose buildings had recently been destroyed by fire and faced closure, reluctantly accepted. This led to the relocation of King's College from Windsor to the Dalhousie campus, and to a formal agreement between the two institutions; otherwise, however, the concept of a federation was dead.

Again, in 1965, on the basis of excellent external advice, the government considered a recommendation to merge the Nova Scotia Technical College with Dalhousie, the former to become the Dalhousie Faculty of Applied Science and Engineering. There was strong support for this, including that of the National Research Council in Ottawa, but it was bitterly opposed by the other universities, which resented the idea that Dalhousie should have control of yet another professional program. No action was taken, and nothing further happened for several years. In 1969 the two institutions began a five-year trial affiliation, which must have been viewed as successful since in 1972 the Faculty of Engineering at the Technical College recommended the full integration of the college with Dalhousie. Two years later, this had been approved in principle by both Senates, possible drafts of an agreement were being discussed, cabinet approval had been given, and towards the end of that year, legislation had been introduced and was at the committee stage. At that point, again, the other universities as well as the local newspaper became vocal in their opposition, suggesting that the merger would be the first step towards a single University of Nova Scotia. The legislation was deferred and subsequently died, with the government being unwilling to face down the opposition.

Given this history, by 1988 the position of every university on any proposal for amalgamation or rationalization had already been determined. Put briefly, this meant that Dalhousie favoured such moves, since there might then be an institution in Nova Scotia of a scale that could compete nationally and internationally, while most, if not all, of the smaller institutions preferred their independence and the status quo. In 1989 the government had in its hands both the *Report of the Royal Commission on Post-Secondary Education* and the Maritime Provinces Higher Education Commission (MPHEC) consultant's report[24] that had led to a newly revised funding formula, both of which recommended strongly that some form of rationalization be pursued. The government under John Buchanan basically accepted this view, especially as it supported the conclusion that Nova Scotia should establish its own commission for higher education.

Numerous pages could be written here describing the innumerable meetings, the impassioned arguments, and the inflamed rhetoric that characterized the discussions, as well as the articles that various local newspapers were encouraged to publish and the enormous waste of time, effort, and resources that then occurred over the next five or six years. The government did create, after again bringing in external experts to advise, the Nova Scotia Council for Higher Education (NSCHE); it did become firmer and louder in its insistence that there would be some form of rationalization regardless of the opposition of some universities; and it did appoint from Ottawa a chair of the NSCHE who was given considerable latitude and authority to bring about some form of rationalization. Each institution had its own position, reflecting the way in which it might be affected by particular features of rationalization.

With the united support of the Dalhousie community, I argued strongly that, to be competitive in a knowledge-intensive economy, Nova Scotia would need at least one large comprehensive university, either a new University of Halifax or some form of a University of Nova Scotia. This was bitterly opposed by the presidents of virtually all other universities, although some quietly conceded that sooner or later some form of amalgamation would be required, although preferably not with their institution. And Dalhousie itself was under considerable attack. The *Report of the Royal Commission* had been particularly critical of the state of affairs in the province in the fields of education (in which seven institutions offered degrees), engineering (in which six institutions competed for students in the first two years of the undergraduate program), computer science (with three small programs at Acadia, Dalhousie, and the Technical University), and several other fields. The most bitter squabble, however, was over business education in Halifax, a field in which Dalhousie, St. Mary's, and Mt. St. Vincent all offered programs. The last was quite small in size, the other two larger and more comparable, but St. Mary's had long coveted business education as its own special domain and had been very effective in its public relations efforts. Since the Royal Commission and other experts were urging the case for one large, hopefully excellent business school in Halifax, St. Mary's hoped to become the sole possessor of that field at Dalhousie's expense. The argument that such a vision of one large, excellent business school might best be achieved within a united University of Halifax was politically and conceptually a much larger jump, and hence much more difficult to sell.

The presidents met collectively on innumerable occasions, but since the majority favoured the status quo, any reports that emerged were intended as stalling actions. I found this extremely frustrating. While the historical origins of these entrenched positions were understandable, it seemed to me that in the 1990s and certainly in the twenty-first century, they were indefensible. Every consultant that had been brought into Nova Scotia to examine the university situation from the 1920s onward had forcefully recommended some form of amalgamation, but after some seventy to eighty years, the universities' views and attitudes were completely unchanged and focused entirely on institutional survival.

From Dalhousie's viewpoint, although in theory the most desirable solution might be the formation of a University of Nova Scotia with a number of federated colleges, the most important immediate step concerned the relationship between Dalhousie and the Technical University of Nova Scotia (TUNS, formerly the Nova Scotia Technical College). While these often tense but fruitless meetings of presidents, with or without government representatives participating, continued endlessly, I initiated some discussions with my fellow president at TUNS in early 1989. Although we had separate institutional agendas, we found that we could work well together. After much discussion, we agreed to seek government support and participation in a feasibility study regarding the complete relocation of TUNS so that the two institutions would directly adjoin each other, enabling the sharing of many facilities and eventually leading to amalgamation. But it was to be just a feasibility study and nothing more at that point.

We discussed the idea confidentially with the chairs of both boards, who fully supported it, then approached the minister of education, who received the concept with great enthusiasm and arranged for us to meet the premier at least twice. The premier was similarly enthusiastic and stated categorically that the feasibility study would be carried out with the provincial government as a full partner. A press conference was arranged for late one afternoon immediately after the two boards had been fully briefed, and the two presidents proceeded to make all the arrangements and schedule the various meetings. One board began its meeting at noon on the set day; the other was to begin at two o'clock and the press conference was scheduled for four o'clock, with the premier participating. At one o'clock, I received a telephone call from the premier's assistant advising me that a cabinet meeting was running late and alerting me to the possibility that the premier might not be available for the press conference. Before two o'clock, he phoned again to confirm that the premier would not be at any press conference and would not have his name on any press release. One board had already been informed and the other was due to meet imminently, and my colleague and I had no alternative but to tell our boards that the premier had backed out and to issue a press release in our names only. Apparently the premier had been advised that any such proposal would be bitterly opposed, not only by some other institutions but more especially by some in the residential areas surrounding the Dalhousie campus. Without government support, this occurred. Within days our proposal died and two university presidents were hung out to dry for reasons of political expediency.

In the following years, there were other discussions between TUNS and Dalhousie, at one point identifying a limited number of areas in which the two institutions might cooperate. These ran into different types of problems. For example, since less than one mile separates the two institutions, a single physical plant department to maintain all buildings, or a single set of student services, or a single registrar's operation, might be very possible and might achieve needed efficiencies. Often, however, such an amalgamated service unit might lead to a smaller staff complement. To arrive at a recommendation for such a combined unit would then require those currently involved in providing that service to agree that their own numbers be reduced. The discussions then always foundered or never reached a conclusion, since the two institutions had not formally committed themselves to union.

Shortly after my retirement, the amalgamation of TUNS and Dalhousie did occur. While Dalhousie welcomed this enthusiastically, TUNS participation may well have resulted from government pressure. TUNS was desperately in need of new physical facilities, and the essential funding for these became available only after the amalgamation had been agreed to.

Between 1989 and 1995, rationalization meetings, debates, discussions, and arguments; the preparation of special studies and additional statistical data; supporting written arguments and reports to the Senate and the board; and representations to the NSCHE and to the minister devoured thousands of hours of my time and that of other members of the senior administration and many others across the university. The sheer waste of resources, especially of human resources, in a collection of universities already so underfunded and financially constrained compared with institutions across Canada was inexcusable and largely unnecessary. Were there any real results to offset this waste? Yes, but they were minor, and to a considerable degree arbitrary.

It had been recognized for many years that the situation in Nova Scotia with regard to teacher training was anomalous. Nova Scotia was the only remaining province to still have a free-standing Teachers' College, located in Truro; in addition, five universities provided B.Ed. degrees that led to teacher certification. Not surprisingly, there was no correlation between the number of graduates intending to enter the teaching profession and the number of teaching positions available. As mentioned earlier, education had been on the list of about six areas that the Royal Commission on Post-Secondary Education felt required urgent attention. By the late summer of 1992, the NSCHE's new chair applied pressure on the universities to address these issues. In education, external consultants were engaged, a study was undertaken, and a report was released in January 1994 recommending the closure of the Nova Scotia Teachers' College in Truro and the closure of the B.Ed. programs at Dalhousie, St. Mary's, and St. Francis Xavier. Political arguments eventually saved the program at St. Francis Xavier, but otherwise the closures were effected. In home economics, there were some minor adjustments, and in graduate studies generally, Dalhousie was encouraged to, and did, invite individual, well-qualified faculty members at other institutions to participate in graduate programs.

The fundamental problem was, as already mentioned, that there was no overall vision of what rationalization was intended to achieve. During 1993 and 1994, Dalhousie in particular, but also some other institutions, argued strongly before both the NSCHE and the government that no actions should be taken before a comprehensive vision or plan had been developed for rationalization. This was eventually undertaken by the NSCHE, but at the same time actions were taken in other fields that the Royal Commission had identified. In computing science, again after a study by external consultants, the NSCHE concluded that only TUNS and Acadia, but not Dalhousie, should offer computing science degrees, a set of recommendations that the consultants' report could justify only poorly. Eventually, in November 1994, the NSCHE released a Green Paper proposing a number of restructuring options that leaned somewhat tentatively towards the creation of a "University of Halifax," although not under that name. By that time, however, the Conservative government had been defeated; the Liberal government of Premier John Savage was in power but was completely preoccupied with attempts to restore financial health to the province's economy. The new government had little interest in rationalization, especially since direct cuts in funding to universities as well as to other agencies and organizations saved money immediately. By the end of 1995, interest in rationalization had largely evaporated, and most of Nova Scotia's universities did everything possible to hasten this.

The University and Political Correctness

One other aspect of my experiences at Dalhousie should be mentioned, because it was a common feature of Canadian university life in the 1980s and 1990s and also because Jack Granatstein and his co-authors as well as others have commented fairly extensively on it.[25] I refer to issues that fall under the general heading of the "political correction" of Canadian universities. These include gender equity, affirmative action in hiring, the development of codes governing action or speech, policies on sexual harassment, the establishment of special administrative offices to deal with these and related matters – the list could go on. Behind nearly all of these issues lies the genuine concern about inclusiveness that has preoccupied society over the last two decades. The most important issue, however, is the effect of such political correction on both the operations of the university and on some of the principles that are fundamental to any concept of a university. At this point, I will describe some of my own experiences, deferring detailed discussion to the next chapter.

There was far greater awareness of all these issues at Dalhousie than I had experienced at the University of Guelph, which is a fairly conservative institution. It took me a little time, therefore, to adapt to the politically correct forms of address that had already been introduced at Dalhousie. For example, I still feel uncomfortable with the title department "chair," which had been Dalhousie usage for more than a decade; a chair is an inanimate object, whereas a university department has a living, breathing person in its chief office. It is the total lack of humour that surrounds these issues, particularly in universities, as others have pointed out, that seems to be a distinguishing feature. In 1986 Dalhousie had already initiated moves to correct gender-related salary inequities, to implement policies on sexual harassment, and to encourage increased hiring of females to faculty positions. A Dalhousie Faculty Women's Group was active and effective, although not always seeing eye to eye with the Dalhousie Faculty Association. Dalhousie had also been one of the first, if not the first, to introduce a Transition Year Program to encourage the entry of black and Mi'kmaq students to university programs, and a similar special program for entry into the Law School. These were all needed improvements and completely warranted, but a closer examination also shows some problems.

First, there was the need to create special administrative positions to handle many of these issues. Such actions have been criticized by Granatstein and others, but certainly at Dalhousie the prominence of some of these matters as well as the time-consuming efforts required to deal with them placed such a load on a limited number of administrative staff that there seemed to be no alternative but to create special positions. Even when such positions were dealing with gender-related issues or matters concerning minority groups, and were kept part-time because of our serious lack of funds, their creation aroused both criticism and resentment. Criticism came in two forms – either the part-time position was seen as no more than a token gesture by the president, or it was seen as quite unwarranted in times of such extreme financial constraint. Resentment came from overworked staff in other administrative units that desperately needed additional personnel. In some cases, such posts were established because this appeared to be the best response to pressures from within the Dalhousie community, such as from various women's groups, but in other instances, external pressures, such as the federal legislation relating to affirmative action in employment, mandated the creation of such positions. That they consumed resources that might have been directed to academic purposes is correct, but universities are part of a wider society and must reflect, if not lead, that society in such matters.

A second and, for me personally, a very worthwhile initiative at Dalhousie was the study undertaken by a presidential committee into the extent to which Dalhousie encouraged or passively neglected the ready access of minorities to academic programs. Historically, as at all Canadian universities, this had been chiefly a matter of neglect, although in many cases it was not difficult to distinguish elements of outright discrimination. In the 1930s and 1940s, nearly every Canadian university applied strict quotas to limit the number of Jewish students admitted to professional programs such as law and medicine. Dalhousie was an exception, and as a result had very loyal alumni in the US and in Canada who had been excluded from such programs elsewhere. The long history of the black community in Nova Scotia is a sad saga of neglect and discrimination, and that of the Mi'kmaq is scarcely any better, and institutions such as Dalhousie had shown little leadership in addressing them until the past decade or so. For example, while Dalhousie had introduced the Transition Year Program in 1970, it had always been controversial, and by 1986 was largely funded by external sources. Henry Hicks had not been enthusiastic about it, although W.A. MacKay had been a supporter. It was only in 1990 that the program became fully funded by the university and that additional resources were provided. This was followed by the establishment of the Chair in Black Canadian Studies, which was intended not only to encourage study of the Canadian experience and history of the black community but also to provide a national focus and link between that community and the university.

A common regrettable trend with such ethnically oriented university posts is that they can all too easily retreat into abstract academic research and yet again lose the community link that has to be central to their function. But these developments provided opportunities to learn from and experience more of these communities. The weekend that the federal minister of citizenship and immigration visited Dalhousie to announce funding for the creation of the chair, many prominent members of the black community met with the minister in the original oak-panelled Board and Senate Room. I was close to an elderly man who gazed around the room noting the bust of Lord Dalhousie and the sombre portraits of C.D. Howe and former presidents. He said to me, "I worked as a gardener for forty years in many of the houses in south end Halifax surrounding Dalhousie, and I never thought that I would ever actually be allowed here and welcomed into the university." While solutions for many of these problems are not readily apparent, Canadian universities still have much to do to become truly open institutions.

A much more worrisome aspect of many of these political correction issues relates to the elaborate, time-consuming, and cumbersome procedures that have been developed to address complaints and, where possible, to resolve specific incidents. At Dalhousie, as in many other institutions, this effect of creeping legalism was very evident, for example, in attempts to deal with sexual harassment. Unfortunately, in many Western societies, the term has become a cliché whose first mention seems to carry with it the automatic presumption of guilt. When I first arrived at Dalhousie in 1986, a policy on sexual harassment had already been drafted and approved, but it had only grudging support from the DFA, which had refused to merge the policy with the articles in the collective agreement that dealt with disciplinary action. Reflecting what has happened in Canadian society generally, there was a steady increase in the number of allegations of sexual harassment across the university during the 1985-95 decade, and by the late 1980s, these required the full attention of a part-time staff member. The time requirement was largely determined by the sheer complexity of the approved procedures, which were legalistic in nature and devoted to concerns about fairness and natural justice as well as the maintenance of confidentiality.

While the procedural requirement for informal discussions between the various parties involved in a specific complaint may certainly have resolved a number of complaints, in cases where formal hearings were required there seemed little assurance that justice was eventually delivered. For instance, a complaint from a student about possible sexual harassment by a faculty member required first the informal procedure, then a more formal process to determine whether a full hearing should be held, then the full hearing, which might involve days or even weeks of legal-style hearings. Should the hearing panel conclude that there had indeed been sexual harassment, the president had to ask the dean of the faculty to initiate disciplinary procedures against the faculty member, but the dean might refuse and could not be ordered to do so. If the dean did take such action, there would be a full hearing, a possible appeal, a presidential decision, a DFA grievance, and ultimately an arbitration hearing. For a student complaining of sexual harassment to go through at least six repetitions of embarrassing and personally difficult evidence with no assurance as to any likely outcome is utterly unreasonable; on the other side, the inevitably ambiguous result may leave a permanent tarnish on the reputation of an innocent faculty member. Not surprisingly, few complaints progressed beyond the informal procedures. It is the preoccupation of faculty members with process and protection that has produced these procedures, many of which are close to unworkable and impose a heavy burden on the resources of the institution.

11
Universities, Governments, and Society

A university president is uniquely placed to observe the real nature and operations of the university in relation to the society that supports it and the government through which society's tax funds flow.

The Financial Relationship with Government

Because of Canada's federal form of government, the funding of universities has always been, and still is, more difficult and controversial than in many other countries. The history and politics of university financing in Canada have been well documented and analyzed by David Cameron in his book *More than an Academic Question;*[26] here I am more concerned with the internal attitudes and responses to the changing circumstances of financing.

In the nineteenth century and the first half of the twentieth century, government expenditures on universities were small and in some provinces nonexistent. Frequently, the generosity of a few benefactors enabled individual institutions to attain some degree of respectability, although in other cases it barely allowed them to survive. During that era, all in the university knew that the institution often had little financial stability, and that in itself tended to strengthen the sense of community. The late 1950s and the 1960s were utterly different, however. The postwar period was one of optimism and, it seemed, unlimited growth. The national economy grew rapidly and federal and provincial governments, unencumbered with debt or accumulated deficits, readily increased expenditures to all social services. For educational systems struggling to provide for a baby boom generation, the needed funds for growth were provided easily and generously. For those of us recruited as faculty in those decades, the rapid annual growth of the institution and its finances appeared to be the norm; we had little basis for comparison and did not appreciate that this era was the exception, as subsequent decades have shown.

These unduly optimistic expectations and attitudes, created by the remarkable funding levels of those two decades, have had at least three effects. First, the universities came to view government as the sole source of funding, as indeed they were, since tuition fees often accounted for less than 10 percent of revenues. The commonly held view was that we only had to look to governments for additional funds; there seemed no reason to look elsewhere, and certainly no reason to raise fees, since any practicable increase would have no more than a marginal impact on total revenues. Second, since such levels of annually increasing funding were seen as the norm, there was the belief that universities were being unduly punished, and were therefore "underfunded" in subsequent years, when smaller or even zero increases were provided.

The term "underfunding" is highly emotive and very effective, but has little real meaning. Underfunded relative to what? Relative to the prewar period? To universities in other countries? Can a university be "overfunded"? Is there indeed an appropriate, generally accepted level of funding? Such questions, like the original term "underfunding," are too imprecise for reasonable discussion. Nonetheless, in the decades following the 1960s and early 1970s, when similarly substantial annual increases in funding were not being provided, complaints about "underfunding" became continuous and noisy. Moreover, with the governance changes of that earlier period giving university senates a substantial budgetary role, the state of university finances has become a preoccupation of most university senates, to the detriment of their primary role in providing academic leadership to the institution. Even a cursory glance at the minutes of current senate meetings at any university will reveal that the business consists very largely of discussion of the institution's financial health, together with essentially administrative matters relating to academic programs; rarely is there sustained discussion of genuine academic issues. The discussion of "underfunding" has thus become the major preoccupation.

The third effect of the exceptionally high levels of funding in the 1960s was the move by several provincial governments towards use of a funding formula, largely to reduce political pressures over distribution. This tended to divert the direct lobbying of the individual universities towards issues concerning the fairness of the formula and attempts to have it modified, while collectively the institutions could still argue unanimously for larger annual increases in total funding. But the use of formulas for distribution has also had an effect on governments, which have to decide only on the overall level of annual increase to the university "system." With the funding distribution determined by formula, a government increasingly but incorrectly views the collectivity of universities in systemic terms, and increasingly treats all universities as equals. This was certainly my experience in Nova Scotia, where, although Dalhousie received over 40 percent of government funding, its views on general university policy issues were all too often regarded as no more than those of one institution among twelve or thirteen equals. And in Ontario, the introduction of formula financing and its resulting tendency to encourage governments to view the collective of universities as a system similarly tend to level the views of such disparate institutions as the University of Toronto and, for example, Laurentian University.

Formula financing in its early forms inevitably favoured growth, since provincial governments were primarily concerned with access and burgeoning student enrollments. This encouraged universities to further increase enrollments in order to allow for expansion and for the balancing of annual budgets, and inevitably led in too many instances to a lowering of academic entrance standards in order to maximize revenues. Even the University of Toronto was not immune to this temptation in the early 1980s. And of course a formula that encourages growth assumes that all institutions have the same growth capacity, an assumption that the Dalhousie experience in the 1970s and 1980s shows can be quite wrong.

Despite the imperfections of all formulas or other mechanisms for funding, the fact remains that the institution itself must be financially responsible. With unfunded capital debt and accumulated deficits totalling over $40 million by 1980, Dalhousie clearly had not been so responsible in the past. In other provinces, the fear of similar occurrences moved some governments to take preventive action. Ontario passed legislation that university deficits could not exceed 2 percent of the annual budget without such debt becoming a first charge on the next year's revenues, and in other cases, universities were prohibited from incurring debt at all. The pressures causing university expenditures to rise rapidly in the 1970s and 1980s included inflation and soaring interest rates, the need to increase teaching staff as enrollments continued to rise slowly, and especially the demands of faculty and staff for significant salary increases, which became more strident as unionization occurred. As mentioned earlier, in most Canadian universities, the percentage of the annual budget required for salaries increased steadily during this period to levels often well in excess of 80 percent, and by the 1990s, budgetary flexibility was minimal. Significant reductions of faculty and staff were therefore required. These were usually achieved by enriched early retirement packages and the non-filling of vacancies, and only rarely by actual layoffs.

Although the use of formula financing encouraged the view that provincial university "systems" actually existed, in fact the governing legislation in most provinces generally takes the form of separate acts, each relating to a different institution. Legislative change would require a private member's bill or a government bill amending existing legislation, or possibly new legislation overriding the existing individual acts. In Ontario, for example, the existence of separate legislation for each university, and of a royal charter for Queen's University, continues to raise legal debate about whether the provincial auditor has or has not any reporting responsibilities over the universities.

Despite such complexities, every government has a blunt but effective instrument with which to exert pressure on the universities, namely, the control of funding. In 1995 the School of Education at Dalhousie was closed. We received no written order from the government itself to close it. Although the Nova Scotia Council for Higher Education (NSCHE) did state that the program should be closed, the legislation governing Dalhousie does not in any way make the institution subservient to government; legally the Board of Governors could have chosen to continue the program, and might, with an effective public relations campaign, have gained some public support. In other words, Dalhousie could have maintained the program, enrolled more students, and ignored the NSCHE. Two things prevented this. First, the NSCHE made it clear that graduates from such a continued program would not be eligible for teacher certification in Nova Scotia, although such graduates might well have been able to teach in any other province. Second, and more important, there would be no government funding in future years for the student enrollments in such continued programs. Financially, Dalhousie had little choice but to close the program. Curtailment, or even outright withdrawal, of funding is indeed the government's blunt instrument for effecting change.

While there has been continual tinkering with funding formulas, in the last two decades, the focus has been more on the levels of funding. In the 1980s and into the 1990s, there was genuinely less government enthusiasm for the funding of universities than in the 1960s. "Underfunding" was the order of the day, and it took considerable time for universities in Canada to realize that this was in fact a direct reflection of changed public perception. Following the early 1970s, there was diminished regard for universities, perhaps largely as a backlash against the activism of the 1960s, and this continued through the 1980s and 1990s. In addition, there were the effects of governments' actions to control and reduce their own deficits, and while the public sector in all provinces was affected, the universities were relatively easy targets and thus have been constrained quite severely over the last two decades. In the last five years, however, federal and provincial governments appear to have had at least some change of heart, and through an array of targeted programs have steadily increased the funds they provide for university research. This continues at present, with some programs supporting the research infrastructure of the universities, and others, such as the Canadian Foundation for Innovation and the Canada Research Chairs Program, directly strengthening research.

By far the majority of these programs have as their primary goal the development of new technology and economic growth. While many will assert that such programs will strengthen the university as an institution, that is only indirectly their objective. As will be discussed later, in at least some cases, these programs, which are ultimately directed towards economic development, may well seriously undermine the institution of the university. Governments provided generous funding in the 1960s and 1970s because universities were seen as important educational institutions for society. After two decade of reduced and less enthusiastic funding levels, governments are again increasing funding, but this time because research in the universities can help achieve social and economic development. Universities are now regarded as a means to a more important end rather than as ends in themselves; if better means can be found, this present support will be rapidly diverted.

A further comment can be made about the relationships between universities and governments in the changed financial circumstances of the 1990s. Most Canadian universities are much less financially dependent on government than they were three or four decades ago. In the 1970s, the direct government formula funding often represented as much as 90 percent of the institutional budget. Today, with increased tuition fees and more aggressive institutional fund-raising, this has fallen to the 60-70 percent range even for large institutions, and for some small Nova Scotia universities, direct government funding is now less than 50 percent of the budget. This encourages a much greater independence from government as well as a healthy willingness to explore alternative sources of funding and, for small institutions, perhaps even privatization.

Governing Boards and the Loss of Authority

The point has already been made that the present governance and structure of universities encouraged a preoccupation with funding, and they also seem to have left the mistaken belief that there is a simple and direct relationship between the level of funding and academic excellence. "Give us more money, at least as much as major US universities have," the universities appear to claim, "and we will automatically be as excellent." But the equation is much more complex and must include numerous other factors, such as the quality of faculty, students, and student learning, the quality of facilities, even the quality of administration, and certainly the quality of elementary and secondary education. Quality is not determined solely by the amount of money that is spent, and the arguments of Canadian universities for increased funding would be infinitely more credible if they were accompanied by an increased willingness to assess quality and to be more openly accountable.

It is here that presidents and boards can and should be more assertive. They hold final responsibility for the welfare of the institution, and it is also through them that society expects the institution to be accountable. Their role is not just to seek ever greater funding from government but also to require the institution to evaluate itself regularly by both internal and external means, on the basis of international standards, and to ensure that valid tests of accountability, of value for money, are in place. University boards are structured and behave much as in the 1960s, but their authority and powers have been substantially eroded and have been yielded to the faculty who are reluctant to embrace quality assessment and accountability. Worse still, the present functioning of boards does not reflect well the societal changes that have occurred over the past fifty years, especially in terms of the expectations of accountability.

The remarkable sweep of faculty unionization across many Canadian universities since 1970 provides ample demonstration of the weakness of university boards and senior administrations. It is important, however, to place the unionization of faculty in the context of its time. The baby boom generation had come of age, and Western society was being profoundly changed in the wake of the Vietnam war and the emergence of campus radicalism. The attitudes of students and of faculty recruited then and later were markedly different from those of their predecessors. Society was restless and changing. For example, in the 1970s federal and provincial labour legislation was enacted that allowed the extension of bargaining rights to public servants and professionals, a type of change never contemplated in the 1950s. Also, the occurrence of unionization coincided in provinces such as Manitoba and, later in the decade, Ontario with the first obvious government tightening of the purse strings, and that brought the first tremors of insecurity to faculty who had experienced a remarkable period of growth and optimism. The sweep of unionization across the country, with the significant exception of Alberta and British Columbia, is evident from the fact that 1970 saw the engineering faculty at Université de Sherbrooke become the first certified faculty union, and that within ten years certification was in place at more than twenty-five institutions. Many others have followed, so that by 2000, except for four institutions in Ontario – the universities of Toronto, Waterloo, and Guelph, and McMaster University – and those in Alberta and British Columbia, the major Canadian universities all had unionized faculty. The Association of Universities and Colleges of Canada (AUCC) indicates that of its approximately ninety-five members, at least sixty are formally unionized.

In Alberta, the older universities of Alberta and Calgary had managed by the late 1970s to arrive at voluntary agreements for collective bargaining that involved forms of binding arbitration and did not fall under labour relations legislation. In 1981 these arrangements were incorporated into special provincial legislation that would, if necessary, enforce binding arbitration. Thus, faculty associations in Alberta have the security of legislative protection to bargain collectively, but the strike option is excluded. In British Columbia, as in Alberta, certified faculty unions were banned in 1977, but while there have been various moves towards voluntary collective bargaining, there has been no legislation confirming the right of faculty associations to bargain collectively outside of labour relations legislation.

In the early 1970s, when the sweep to unionization began, the full consequences of the almost simultaneous transition to participatory governance by faculty were not fully appreciated. Arguments were made as late as 1982 by the board in the case of certification at Mt. Allison University that faculty were not "employees" within the meaning of labour relations legislation, and were in fact managerial personnel. This argument had been successful in some US cases, but has been rejected by Canadian labour relations boards. Especially in Quebec, however, there was never any secret that in the moves to unionization in institutions such as Laval and UQAM (Université du Québec à Montréal), the major confrontations were concerned with the power to manage the university and to have collective peer judgment decide, for example, such important matters as the award of tenure. And of course, faculty collectively manage, through senates, the entire academic operations of the university

In retrospect, it still seems remarkable that such a dramatic change in labour relations should have occurred so quickly against the apparently firmly established authority of university boards. After all, such boards had been largely composed of highly experienced, respected, and influential members of the local communities, many of them very knowledgeable about unions and collective bargaining. The key to such rapid and widespread faculty success lay in the role of the Canadian Association of University Teachers (CAUT), which in a very short period over 1972-74 transformed itself into a powerful advocate of formalized collective bargaining, in part as a means of preventing other unions such as the Canadian Union of Public Employees (CUPE) from becoming the representatives of faculty interests. The CAUT quickly put in place guidelines for collective bargaining, developed model clauses for collective agreements (all of which favoured the transfer of authority and power to faculty), and as a national organization provided not only information but also personnel, legal advice, and support to local faculty associations engaged in bargaining with their boards. It was an aggressive and impressive strategy, especially since its main thrust was not necessarily monetary; the focus was very much on securing legal protection for the participatory governance that had so recently been gained.

On the other side, however, boards in particular, and all too often senior administrators as well, were caught unprepared and with no firm position on critical issues. To some extent, many senior academic administrators were probably sympathetic to the concept of faculty governance even though they may have opposed the thought of faculty unionization. In any event, administrators and boards lacked the support and rapid exchange of information that the CAUT provided to faculty associations. The counterpart of the CAUT, the AUCC, played a passive role so each university was essentially on its own in dealing with its faculty and with the CAUT. Worse, in too many cases negotiators for the boards arrived at negotiation meetings unprepared, as was certainly the case at Dalhousie, and this allowed the faculty to set the agenda and effectively control negotiations. In other instances, ill-advised administrative decisions or behaviour over a period of time, or the reality or perception of a remote and authoritative board, helped foster a climate of alienation that supported unionization. And ultimately the faculty, when acting under labour relations legislation, had the very effective threat of a strike on their side. For a majority of faculty, and certainly for boards and administrators, it was often inconceivable to contemplate the idea of a strike at a university, but hardliners in support of unionization did not hesitate to use the threat in negotiations.

Later on, unionization and numerous strikes dramatically changed the labour relations climate across the entire Canadian academic scene. The outcome of collective bargaining in general, given the gulf between the state of preparation and determination of the faculty side and the ambiguity and ill-preparedness of administrations and boards, could be easily predicted. By and large, faculty unions gained nearly all of their demands, and confirmed legally the forms of participatory management that had been developing over the previous few years. The boards and administrations lost much power and authority, although ironically they had to retain the ultimate responsibility for institutions that they could no longer really manage. With the passage of more than twenty years to the present, when the full consequences of those changes are more apparent, it is interesting (although certainly idle) to speculate on whether labour relations boards or courts would still conclude that faculty are only employees and not also management.

When the movement towards faculty unionization began in the early 1970s, there was ample warning of what might ensue. In 1971 the AUCC president sponsored a study of the likely consequences. The results are found in the Adell-Carter Report, in which the two authors all too prophetically stated that "'Creeping Legalism' is unfortunately inherent in the adversary nature of the collective bargaining relationship, and can be kept under control only by the constant use of common sense on both sides."[27] Unfortunately, by its very nature, the university is not a place where common sense is necessarily encouraged; individualism and even eccentricity are, but not common sense. Creeping legalism has in fact become the heavy price now being paid in many Canadian universities, although its cause is less obvious. It may well have developed as a reaction to the decline in the sense of community within the university, and hence a decline in trust. The influence of US litigiousness may also have been a factor, as well as the common belief that the only available mechanism to deal with controversial issues is through yet another committee.

The Adell-Carter Report also drew attention to the inevitable conflict of interest that must arise when faculty effectively run the university while at the same time setting their own terms and conditions of employment. This conflict now exists in most Canadian universities, but few seem to recognize or admit it. To take just one example, the argument that faculty members should participate directly as board members seemed reasonable at the time, since most expected that their primary concern would be the welfare of the institution. And certainly during bargaining with the faculty union, most such members today withdraw from board meetings, although only for those items directly related to negotiations, thus apparently removing any conflict. But because of the indifference and lack of participation of many faculty members, such board members, elected from the faculty, all too often tend to be staunch unionists who use their time on the board to criticize administrative decisions with which the union disagrees and to promote neither the welfare of the institution nor of the faculty generally, but only the interests of the union. There is indeed a conflict of interest here, and it has helped to weaken governing boards even further since the 1970s.

There are other equally negative outcomes of faculty unionization. Consider the matter of granting tenure and promotion. Canadian universities have never taken the very hard line on tenure decisions that the best American universities took, where commonly only a fraction of those hired in tenure-stream appointments are granted tenure. The general experience across Canada during the 1960s and into the 1970s was probably that a high 80-90 percent usually received tenure; since faculty unionization, the figure has risen further and is now probably well in excess of 95 percent. There has been a very similar increase in the rate of faculty promotions. The period of time between initial appointment and promotion has decreased, and once departmental recommendations have been made, only a handful are rejected. Those which are rejected are almost invariably appealed, and the outcome of most appeals favours the faculty member. The application of collective agreements now often places more emphasis on whether there is sufficient evidence to support a negative recommendation that will inevitably be appealed than on any requirement for evidence for a positive recommendation. All too often, evidence to support a negative recommendation is lacking: personnel files tend to contain only positive material, since department chairs are members of the union who are untrained in personnel management and who are on short-term appointments. They thus have little inclination or incentive to document unpleasant facts and evidence that are necessary to support a case in arbitration or in a court of law. The consequence of faculty unionization has been that universities now have to justify the denial of tenure or denial of promotion, and have to bear the onus of proof in cases of dismissal for cause. And even when such proof is substantial and convincing, universities have lost many such cases on appeal because faculty members involved in the various stages have not followed due process! There is no question that collective agreements, by requiring this reverse onus and because of the need for procedures to be followed to the letter, have lowered the standards for both tenure and promotion.

Worse still, they have invariably led to salary schemes for faculty members that are based on seniority and certainly not on merit. Typically, the Dalhousie agreement provides for an annual fixed-sum increase for each faculty member, a so-called selective increment, which is applied automatically except in cases where the faculty dean can show reason for it to be withheld. If it is withheld, there is inevitably a grievance. Not surprisingly, there are few such exceptions, what with the requirement that there be sufficient evidence to sustain a negative decision, coupled with the fact that a labour arbitrator may eventually overrule such a decision. At the same time, at Dalhousie and also at some other Canadian universities, there is no monetary reward for an outstanding faculty member, one who may have received international recognition, prizes, and awards. There is simply no salary recognition of merit. At Dalhousie, even if such a person received the Nobel Prize, no salary recognition could be provided by the university except in circumstances where the Nobel laureate was in receipt of an attractive written offer from another institution and about to resign. Under these conditions, the DFA would first have to agree to such a salary increase for it to be legally offered, and if this was likely to create too great an exception compared with others, the DFA might well withhold agreement. The recognition of merit through salary increases is a concept that faculty unionists have worked successfully to destroy, and this has certainly been a major factor in the loss of many outstanding faculty members to American institutions.

To be clear on this point, the ability of staunch unionists to maintain this as the official union position does not necessarily mean that they are in a majority. At Dalhousie, for example, they probably are not; but they rely on the fact that the majority of faculty members, especially the outstanding ones, do not make the effort to regularly attend faculty union meetings or to express their opposing views forcefully and consistently. On several occasions, groups of faculty at Dalhousie have pressed for the introduction of some form of merit salary recognition, but have never been aggressive or consistent enough in their tactics to overcome the refusal of unionists.

While labour relations boards in the 1970s accepted the arguments that faculty were not management, the situation had changed enormously by the end of the 1990s. Collectively, faculty members at Canadian universities now have control of strategic planning, the setting of priorities (or, more accurately, the non-setting of priorities), the management of enrollments, hirings and all appointments, all academic programs, and all academic administrative appointments, and if they do not control budgeting they certainly have great influence over it. It can and usually is argued that in all of these areas, the collective will of faculty members leads only to recommendations that senior administrators and boards can approve or reject, and that it is the senior administrators and boards that actually make the decisions. But senior administrators and boards, under many collective agreements, have no legal right to make academic appointments or promotions unless they have been recommended at the departmental level, nor can they initiate or eliminate academic programs except as recommended by a senate controlled by faculty; and while boards do confirm strategic plans and mission statements, they very rarely initiate the process and seldom do anything other than rubber-stamp such statements.

In all these areas and others, the most that a board might do today is refer the matter back to the senior administration for reconsideration – back to senior administrators who have been selected by the faculty. Such referrals happen only occasionally, and resubmission with minor changes usually results in approval. Even on financial matters, where by legislation boards have ultimate authority, there has usually been great prior faculty input into budgets before they reach boards. Indeed, as discussed earlier, what is most remarkable is that while in the 1960s faculty argued strongly that academic decisions must be based on an understanding of the institution's financial position, thus justifying the considerable role of senates in financial affairs, today both senates and boards are approving new academic programs almost regardless of the financial position. Although it is argued at many a board meeting that the introduction of a new program will involve minimal extra cost, it is highly likely, when ten or a dozen such programs have thus gained approval, that the total incremental cost is substantial. Faculty, senates, and even senior administrators today are avoiding the 1970s truth that new academic programs require real new money.

The attempt at Dalhousie in 1993 to close programs in drama and music failed because the faculty union argued, and the arbitrator agreed, that the clause invoked in the collective agreement allowed for such closure only on purely academic grounds and that financial circumstances could not be taken into account. If program closure was necessary on financial grounds, so it was argued, then a different article in the collective agreement dealing with financial constraint would have had to be invoked, involving a complex and time-consuming procedure that had been shown in 1981 to be unworkable. Collective agreements, therefore, have, on the one hand, cast in stone the tremendous involvement of faculty in governance and, on the other hand, have so effectively separated academic and financial decision making with regard to program introduction and closure that faculty have full freedom and almost unlimited security. However the present situation is examined, it is clear that the faculty unionization of the 1970s and 1980s, building on the participatory governance changes of the 1960s, has given the faculty collective power and authority over the Canadian university, and has provided it with a degree of security that encourages the status quo and avoidance of change, diminishes accountability, and does little to recognize and reward quality and merit.

The reader might be tempted to ask why presidents and other senior administrators do not make changes, or why boards do not so instruct them. But any president faced with a collective agreement that leaves virtually no room for decision making or initiative without leading to grievances, combined with the fact that any significant decision must appear to emerge from a broadly representative faculty committee, is essentially hamstrung. The weapons available are persuasion, the power of argument and reason, and the power of personality or leadership. To make significant changes with only these approaches requires a great deal of time, which a five- or six-year appointment does not provide, and also involves a delicate balancing act where a fall may occur at any time. Nor can a Canadian university board, as presently constituted, provide the continuing firm support and direction required to adequately support a president in making necessary changes. Most board members do not consider themselves sufficiently knowledgeable about the internal workings of the university to give such direction. In any event, it is these same boards that have, over the last thirty years, consistently ceded so much power and authority.

Tenure and Job Security

To press the point further, it is worth examining what tenure now means in the Canadian university. The development of a clear concept of tenure has occurred relatively recently in Canadian universities. A comprehensive and highly regarded discussion of the history and meaning of tenure and academic freedom in Canadian universities has been provided by Horn, and this should be regarded as the essential background for my comments.[28] There is no point in my repeating here the valuable discussion that Horn has already provided; besides, my objective is much more limited, namely, to discuss the process by which tenure in Canadian universities has, for all practical purposes, become synonymous with job security.

In my first years at the University of British Columbia, although other new faculty members and I had been told that we would in due course be considered for tenure, we were not necessarily even guaranteed reappointment from year to year. Around May, each of us received a brief form letter from the president, advising us that if we had not heard to the contrary, we could assume that our services would be required for the following year. In fact, at UBC and across Canada, there had long been acceptance of the informal practice of appointment without term, or rather appointment at the pleasure of the board. Few written policies on tenure existed. Faculty were dependent on the final authority of the board, and while dismissal was theoretically possible, in practice the degree of job security was high and dismissals were rare.

It was only in the early 1960s that any move towards a more formalized and national position was taken, and the CAUT was the mover, adopting the well-known statement on the principles of tenure of the American Association of University Professors (AAUP). After further study concluded that the practice of appointments being at the pleasure of the board had no legal standing, the principles of tenure were firmly endorsed by the Duff-Berdahl Commission in 1966[29] and then promoted vigorously by the CAUT in its 1968 Policy Statement on Academic Appointments and Tenure.[30] The key principle of the AAUP statement reads as follows: "Teachers should have permanent (continuous) tenure after the expiration of a specified probationary period. Their services should be terminated only for adequate cause, except in the case of retirement for age."

But the CAUT statement went much further, and argued strongly that contractual positions, which did not lead to consideration for tenure, should be rare, and that the maximum probationary period should not exceed five years. More importantly, while the Duff-Berdahl report placed considerable emphasis on the need to ensure that appropriately high standards were the basis for positive recommendations for tenure, the CAUT statement focused much more on the process for dismissal of faculty members and said little about standards. This difference is reflected in current collective agreements. At UBC the agreement contains detailed statements about the standards that are to be applied in the granting of tenure, but many of the agreements at unionized institutions are much more concerned with the details of the process and say little if anything about the standards that are to be applied.

The CAUT statement then argued that for tenure to be effective, a university could dismiss a tenured faculty member only for "adequate cause," although what constituted "adequate cause" would have to be determined in relation to each case and would require sufficiently compelling evidence to establish that the "cause" was well grounded.[31] In the meantime, the AUCC had endorsed the concept of tenure in principle, but had to leave the determination of criteria for tenure and procedures to each institution. In the tumultuous climate of the late 1960s, with the trend towards participatory forms of university governance sweeping across the country, it was not surprising that the CAUT was able to report, based on a survey, that most universities had instituted policies much as suggested by the CAUT. A defined probationary period, usually of five years, was standard, and virtually all universities had instituted policies and procedures for dismissal of tenured faculty members along the lines suggested by the CAUT. Again, it is worth noting that the existing agreement at UBC provides for a probationary period of up to seven years and, in contrast to many agreements at unionized universities, makes a serious attempt to define "cause."

During the 1970s, such CAUT-type policies became entrenched in collective agreements that defined the necessary procedures in the minute detail that creeping legalism encouraged. By far the most important consequence, apart from the fact, as mentioned earlier, that nearly all probationary faculty members gained tenure, was the protection, carried over from the CAUT statement, against dismissal except for "adequate cause." As has been pointed out, "adequate cause" is rarely defined, and the definition of the standards and criteria that are to be employed for tenure decisions is usually left to each department or similar unit. The denial of tenure is then entirely problematic since standards may not have been defined, and the dismissal of tenured faculty is equally problematic since the onus is on the administration to provide convincing evidence that there is indeed "adequate cause" for dismissal. And such evidence must come from an administrative structure that is not trained or encouraged to collect and maintain this kind of evidence. At the time of the 1970 CAUT survey, only two institutions out of the forty-five or so surveyed claimed to regularly review the records and files of tenured faculty members; it is doubtful that a new survey would reveal any better outcome. With collective agreements guaranteeing annual salary increments automatically, and with strong faculty opposition to regular performance review, it is obvious that to establish "adequate cause" for dismissal is not just difficult but virtually impossible. Thus has tenure in Canadian universities become synonymous with job security.

This discussion should not lead to the interpretation that I am opposed to the broad concept of tenure; on the contrary, I strongly support it as an essential protection of academic freedom. I recall President Norman MacKenzie of UBC commenting at faculty meetings on the pressures he experienced, including demands that there be dismissals, when faculty members made controversial statements that drew the public ire and severe criticism in the local press. It is also reasonable to speculate about the Rushton case at the University of Western Ontario in the mid-1990s.[32] If tenure had not been a factor, would the defence of academic freedom have been so strong in resisting the considerable pressure applied from within and without the university? And I have personally listened to citizens of Halifax, and even members of government, express their outrage at similarly disruptive actions or statements by faculty members. Without the protection that tenure can provide, such pressures on presidents and boards even in today's tolerant Canada could endanger academic freedom.

This, however, requires tenure to have only its original meaning – that tenured faculty should be terminated only for cause – and not its present interpretation – that tenure means security since university structure prevents cause from being established. Tenure is an essential characteristic of the modern university, but in Canada it needs a thoughtful redefinition that can help ensure the use of high standards in granting tenure, and that, when combined with effective, regular performance reviews, can protect academic freedom without providing unlimited job security.

Governance, Governments, and Rationalization

With the foregoing comments in mind, it is not surprising that governments and society generally have perceived a lack of direction and a sense of drift in the universities. Unlike those in many other countries, however, federal and provincial governments in Canada have shown great reluctance to intrude directly into university affairs. Their counterparts in the UK, Australia, New Zealand, and many European countries, as well as elsewhere, have been much more forthright in their criticisms of universities and have legislated changes, sometimes with a heavy hand but with much less reluctance, and occasionally even with enthusiasm. In Canada, the trend seems to have been more towards the use of the funding mechanism as a way of inducing change.

To cite a particularly complex example, Cameron has described in detail the various changes made to the funding formula in Ontario since 1970 as both circumstances and governments have changed, and as the persuasive powers of the university community have ebbed and flowed.[33] The obvious trend has been towards greater use of targeted funding, whether it be funds allocated especially for northern universities, basic operating grant envelopes, access envelopes, excellence funds, faculty renewal funds, or, more recently, funding dependent on performance indicators. Other provinces, such as Alberta and Quebec, have also increased their use of targeted funding envelopes. The federal government, whose direct support of universities is aimed at research, has also created an increasing number of such targeted funds for research, some temporary and others, such as the Program for Networks of Centres of Excellence, permanent.

While such targeted funding has undoubtedly had a major directive influence on Canadian universities, perhaps best demonstrated in the extensive links that now exist between the universities, industry, and the business community, rarely have governments attempted to give more specific direction. In Ontario there have certainly been periodic political rumblings over the past fifty years about "unnecessary" duplication of university programs and of a perceived need for rationalization, but the university "system" remains a collection of autonomous competing institutions drawn together only by the common need to defend themselves against government intrusion. Only in Quebec has there been a planned government-inspired creation of a university system, although this had to incorporate the existing six independent institutions of Laval, McGill, Concordia, Montreal, Sherbrooke, and Bishop's. These, with the creation of the multi-campus

Université du Québec and the system of public colleges, or CEGEPS started in 1967, constitute the only Canadian example of a genuine university system.

Presumably, a system can also be created by the rationalization of a group of existing universities. In Ontario, there have been from time to time various suggestions that existing institutions needed to be rationalized in order to reduce duplication and increase efficiency. The most recent such move was probably the creation of the Bovey Commission, whose report appeared in 1984.[34] The commission had been specifically asked to propose "different and distinctive roles for the universities of Ontario," but it chose not to do so, at least not directly. It argued that such differentiation should best occur through the forces of institutional competition, and recommended that the universities should, over a number of years, be given flexibility to move to increased tuition fees, with the more research-intensive universities having greater flexibility in increasing those fees. Shortly after the commission released its report, there was a change in provincial government; the new government quickly rejected the idea of higher tuition fees, and the other recommendations were shelved. Only in the 1990s have the universities in Ontario been given any flexibility to increase fees, and those increases have now been substantial. Differences in fees between universities are relatively small, however, especially compared with differences in fees that now exist between different types of academic programs. The Ontario universities themselves have argued that differentiation would best be achieved through competition among existing institutions, but they reject the concept of private universities with whom competition might be much keener. To date, there is little evidence that any meaningful degree of differentiation will actually come about just by institutional competition.

The attempt to rationalize the degree-granting institutions of Nova Scotia during the 1989-96 period had much the same objectives, at least as far as they were spelled out. In Nova Scotia, however, there had been several previous well-conceived but unsuccessful attempts, so the problems were well known. Any rational consideration of the situation in the 1990s, especially in light of the changes that had already occurred elsewhere in the university world, would find it difficult to justify the continued existence of twelve autonomous degree-granting institutions in a province not well endowed with resources and with a population of only 900,000. For decades, Dalhousie had been the largest and best-known institution, with the widest range of programs. In the case of small, essentially undergraduate universities such as Acadia University and St. Francis Xavier University, a strong argument for their continued existence could easily be made on the basis of the small, residential academic community experience each provided, as well as the fact that their reputations allowed them to attract students from across Canada. On the other hand, there seemed little rationale for the continued separate existence of the Technical University of Nova Scotia (TUNS), the Nova Scotia College of Art and Design, the Atlantic Theological College, the Nova Scotia Teachers' College, and the Nova Scotia College of Agriculture, or for the offering of more and more graduate programs in the small institutions. Equally problematic was the existence of large, overlapping faculties of arts and science and business schools at St. Mary's University and Dalhousie within one mile of each other.

In relation to the rest of Canada, and indeed to higher education internationally, these were all anomalous, and their counterparts elsewhere had long ago been amalgamated into larger institutions. In every case, the arguments for such amalgamation had been essentially academic, namely, that an agricultural college, for example, thrives best not in isolation but within a larger institution in which it can be enriched and invigorated by its association with the biological, physical, and social sciences. This view was certainly expressed in the *Report of the Royal Commission on Post-Secondary Education* in 1985, when it recommended that the province create its own higher education commission and examine possibilities for rationalization of the existing institutions – that is, of creating a Nova Scotia university system. Much the same was said in the 1988 report of A.K. Adlington, which urged that policy focus on a planning process in which the universities would be required to develop and provide "planned capacity and role statements."[35]

It should be made clear that the Nova Scotia institutions had not previously ignored all of the possible benefits of closer cooperation. In the early 1980s, several of the institutions in Halifax had formed a single purchasing office, which had become so successful by the 1990s that many of the remaining Nova Scotia institutions became members. In well over fifteen years of existence, this combined operation has saved many millions of dollars. Similar joint undertakings have also proved to be highly efficient and effective, covering areas such as insurance, the maintenance of scientific equipment such as electron microscopes, and so on. But all of these have been concerned with essentially administrative areas, in which institutional rivalries and faculty members are not involved. When more academic areas are examined, there are fewer signs of success. The university libraries of Nova Scotia have had integrated catalogue systems in place for more than fifteen years, providing a valuable service especially for students, but it has not been possible to move further towards implementation of a single combined acquisitions system. Similarly, although the Dalhousie Library contains the largest and most essential collection of scholarly journals to which faculty and students from all institutions have access, there has been no success in having all institutions contribute to the cost.

There are several examples of combined academic programs, most of them in Halifax, but there are also examples of duplicate programs that two or more institutions have introduced at about the same time. When the Nova

Scotia College of Agriculture was given degree-granting status in 1975, it chose to hold these powers in abeyance and, through an affiliation agreement with Dalhousie, have its graduates receive Dalhousie degrees. This was subsequently extended to some shared master's level graduate programs, but any suggestion that the college should formally become the Faculty of Agriculture of Dalhousie University has been steadfastly rejected. Throughout the twentieth century, Acadia in particular but also St. Francis Xavier, St. Mary's, and Mt. St. Vincent have resisted, and in some cases prevented, growth and expansion at Dalhousie, which were seen as increasing the likelihood of a university system or of a "University of Nova Scotia."

During the 1989-96 rationalization process, all of these entrenched positions remained intact, and virtually all have survived the end of the process. The tangible outcomes, described previously, of that vast expenditure of time, energy, and resources were not trivial. But a Nova Scotia university system was not created and too many of the historic anomalies remain, as do duplications of programs and services. In terms of structure and governance, Nova Scotia still has an antiquated and inefficient group of universities and colleges that suffers serious disadvantages in competing with institutions across Canada and internationally.

Why has it been so difficult to bring about changes to the universities of Nova Scotia when the collectivity of institutions is so obviously out of date compared with universities elsewhere? Three factors seem to have been involved. First, there was the importance of the history of most of the institutions. In no other province in Canada, and in few other places in the world, has there been such prolonged and bitter relationships between institutions, in some cases lasting almost 150 years, all originating in the heated sectarian differences of the nineteenth century. These religious hostilities inflamed politics, education, and every facet of life in Nova Scotia in that era, and it is simply incorrect to assume that the impact of these conflicts would have disappeared by the end of the twentieth century in tolerant Canada.

The two other factors are intertwined. The Buchanan government embraced the concept of rationalization, or at least the sound of it, without making any attempt to define what it meant in policy terms. Its position was that rationalization was a "good thing" that would almost certainly save money for the government, but that it should not be the task of government to tell the universities how to rationalize themselves. The responsibility of government was to fund the universities, and if that funding could be reduced by rationalization, so much the better, but government should keep out of the business of telling the universities what to do. This was quite consistent with what seems to have been the general Canadian practice of provincial governments only very rarely intruding directly on universities, except through funding.

The intertwined third factor was that, as autonomous, independent institutions not directly under government control, universities and related institutions will never voluntarily commit suicide and willingly enter into amalgamations or other forms of rationalization. Institutional identity and survival were at stake in these negotiations, and no single institution was willing to make such a sacrifice, regardless of whether it was in the best interests of the province. There should again be no surprise at this, since it had been very evident in other jurisdictions where universities had been told to bring order to their "system." As discussed in Chapters 3 and 4, the threat by the Ontario government to intervene in the overly ambitious expansion of graduate programs in Ontario in the late 1960s brought the Advisory Committee on Academic Planning (ACAP) into existence. The work of this body did restrain ambitions, and did bring some order into the further development of graduate programs in the province, but only with difficulty. Universities value cooperation but will resist coercion; they will willingly cooperate when there is mutual benefit; where one sees an advantage, there will be competition; but first, last, and foremost, institutional survival will always determine their course of action and will override their commitment to serve society.

The combination of these factors doomed the process of rationalization in Nova Scotia; in some ways, it is remarkable that the process continued for so long and accomplished what it did. It can be argued that the Nova Scotia Council for Higher Education (NSCHE) should bear much of the blame for failure. If the NSCHE had at the outset, rather than in late 1994, produced a Green Paper outlining possible options for defining and restructuring a new university system, much greater success might have been achieved. But this would have been a risky undertaking for a completely new organization, especially because, despite many declarations by ministers and officials, the strength of the government's commitment to whatever it thought rationalization meant was uncertain and unpredictable. And the recent history of Nova Scotia governments reneging on commitments relating to university restructuring was compelling – as seen from events in 1974 and 1989 concerning the relationship between Dalhousie and the Technical University of Nova Scotia. Without clear and committed leadership from government, the NSCHE had only a weak hand to play, and the individual institutions knew from their long history that through passive resistance and long delays, they would eventually outlive both that particular government and the NSCHE.

The University Response to Social Justice Issues

Over the past fifty years, governments in Canada, in their attitudes towards and treatment of universities, have generally reflected the attitudes and perceptions of the public at large much more accurately than many academics are willing to concede. On much larger social issues relating to equity, individual human rights, and nondiscrimination, however, where profound changes in thinking have occurred since 1950, both universities and governments have been slow to provide leadership. This does not fit well with the university claim to be a self-governing community of scholars, or with its role as a critic of society. Many individual members of universities have played prominent roles in the critical rethinking of these "politically correct" issues, but the institutions themselves have seldom been at the forefront of change.

On the other hand, as has been argued previously, the university is no longer such a single community, and its faculty can only be expected to reflect the general views of society. For example, when one examines the actions that Canadian universities have taken to redress the gender imbalance in the composition of the faculty, the initial reluctance of male-dominated faculties and faculty associations to do anything at all was no different from that in society at large; the development and enforcement of policies for change took just as many years. Even as late as 1993 at Dalhousie, the federal government's much broader federal contractors' equal opportunity program was not greeted enthusiastically but was seen as so much additional bureaucracy. In more recent years, as in society at large, a backlash has been evident, and has been reinforced in universities by claims that the processes that have been developed to correct these societal imbalances threaten not only the concept of recognition of merit but also the true expression of academic freedom.

I have sympathy with both of these concerns. It is by no means clear that in attempting to correct past inequities in employment at, or even in student access to, universities, the recognition of merit has retained its centrality, and it is certainly true that "political correctness" has cast at least a shadow across the free discussion of ideas at a university. The tendency of both some students and some faculty to assert that their rights have been violated by mention or discussion of a particular issue has begun to reach the unreasonable, and to raise the spectre of censorship on many campuses. While universities, governments, and society generally must pay a price or endure some consequences to correct inequities inherited from the past, there has to be a limit, and if such corrections reduce academic freedom, the rights of all individuals in a free, democratic society are reduced.

Nearly all of the steps that Canadian universities have taken over the past fifty years to address these societal concerns have suffered because of the creeping legalism that has overtaken the institutions during this period.[36] With the transition to participatory governance of universities in the 1970s, followed by widespread faculty unionization, this creeping legalism has been more pronounced here than in many other countries. Moreover, with the considerable emphasis on application of the Canadian Charter of Rights and Freedoms that has been evident since the mid-1980s, Canadian society has tended to be at the forefront in addressing these equity-related issues. These two factors helped encourage the early development of equity and human rights policies within Canadian universities relative to other countries, often in the absence of any knowledge or experience elsewhere. In at least some cases, the resulting policies were not sufficiently balanced, and in other cases, errors were made. Moreover, too frequently the implementation of these policies, which requires a very balanced and mature understanding, was allowed to fall into the hands of those who were themselves advocates for a particular equity issue.

In this respect, universities were by no means alone, but why, then, did universities not leave all of these issues to the judicial system instead of creating and implementing their own internal policies? The explanation is that universities still claimed, erroneously, to be single communities within which, it was argued, there should be readily available mechanisms for the resolution of equity and human rights conflicts. These arguments, which at first glance may appear sound, ignored the fact that creeping legalism had already overwhelmed Canadian universities, and by the mid-1980s, it was no longer possible to devise anything but the most complex, legalistic, and time-consuming mechanisms that emphasized legal process and certainly did not offer any assurance that justice would be done. In any university today, only an exceedingly determined and courageous individual, even though armed with substantial evidence, would undertake the lengthy, repetitive process involved in a complaint of sexual harassment. If a student is involved, there is a high probability that such a case would still be unresolved by the time the complainant graduates and leaves the institution! The legalistic nature of the process is completely daunting and is almost as unfriendly to the parties involved as a case taken through the judicial system. Indeed, given the considerable resources that these processes presently consume within the institution, it can be argued that universities should have done nothing other than put in place relatively simple one-step procedures, with no legal representation allowed, to resolve such cases; if there remained dissatisfaction, the university could then insist that the parties involved take legal action outside the institution. To illustrate the problem, in recent years, Dalhousie has had to pay the legal costs of both parties in cases that, because of internal policies, involved prolonged internal legalistic procedures. There have been many similar cases elsewhere.

Universities must proclaim and demonstrate clearly and unambiguously their commitment to equity and full human rights, both in their structure and governance and in their daily operations. They must demonstrate by example that no form of discrimination will be tolerated within the university. They must show, through the allocation of resources, that they will act to correct discrimination, whether it involve access to university education or practices within the institution. They must also have mechanisms for resolving complaints. It is highly questionable, however, that they need complex, legalistic, resource-consuming internal processes that tend to duplicate the external legal processes of the wider society. Indeed, if universities insisted that such cases be transferred to the legal system after one simple internal attempt at resolution, much of the current threat to academic freedom would be removed.

12
Achievements, Comparisons, and Challenges

The Canadian university scene has undergone a remarkable transformation over the last fifty years. As an example, consider the University of Victoria in British Columbia. A small college affiliated with the University of British Columbia in the 1950s and offering only the first two years of honours programs to a handful of students, it is now a well-recognized institution internationally, with a large, modern campus, an operating budget in excess of $160 million annually, and approximately 17,000 students. Simon Fraser University did not exist in the 1950s, nor did others in many provinces, including Alberta, Manitoba, Ontario, and Quebec. The creation of the entire Université du Québec system provides a further outstanding example.

Each of the much smaller number of universities that existed in the immediate post-Second World War era is now unrecognizable from that earlier age, and the investment of resources by Canadian society has by any standards been generous and creative. Many small colleges of the 1950s that were barely known outside their own provinces have become, like the University of Victoria or the University of Calgary, major Canadian institutions and significant players on the international education scene. The number of degree-granting institutions in Canada now approaches 100, essentially all of them public institutions supported to one level or another by government. This number will continue to increase, especially if recent moves by some provinces encourage the development of private universities.

Fifty Years of Achievement

As discussed in earlier chapters, these fifty years of remarkable growth have been orderly, with few crises. Given the tremendous surge in undergraduate enrollment in the 1960s and 1970s, and the relatively short notice that many institutions had of government commitment of funding for the necessary facilities and staffing, the university community deserves great credit for all that was accomplished. It is interesting to note also that, while similar dramatic expansions occurred in other countries, such as in the United

Kingdom and in the rest of Europe, many of those governments made longer-term commitments of funding, enabling planning to proceed on a much more predictable basis than in Canada, where annual funding commitments have been the norm. Many Canadian universities took substantial risks in those decades in dealing with the crush of students, and although in nearly all cases short-term debts were ultimately covered by government funding, the example of Dalhousie's capital debt by 1980 shows that there were exceptions. Risk taking, on the assumption of continuing rapid growth, tended to be much more common then than it is now, and universities have become more cautious. Given the limited lead time that was often available, and granted that some of the buildings that were erected in those decades lack architectural distinction, the campuses of most universities are attractive and provide important economic and cultural benefits to their communities.

Of much more fundamental importance is the matter of the academic accomplishments of Canadian universities, and of their academic standards relative to those in other countries. First, there is no reason to expect that any Canadian institution can yet match the world's best universities, which are old by Canadian standards and have acquired the maturity and sophistication that only centuries of experience can bring. If the comparison is restricted to English-speaking countries, universities such as Cambridge, Oxford, Harvard, Stanford, and MIT must be rated as superior by any measure, whether it be number of Nobel Prizes won, size of endowment, or general reputation. Indeed, it can be argued that most of the genuine Ivy League institutions in the United States are perhaps superior to all Canadian universities. On the other hand, it would be equally fair to suggest that perhaps the twenty-five to thirty top-rated Canadian universities are entirely comparable with the same number of the best state universities and many of the very good private institutions in the US, and are probably superior to the older, so-called provincial or red-brick institutions in the UK. There can be absolutely no debate about their superior quality in relation to the remaining 75 percent of US institutions, or to new universities in the UK or Australia created from polytechnics.

Such opinions are, of course, regarded as subjective, since there is little agreement on criteria that might be used to provide a more objective comparison. But what is both indisputable and remarkable is that Canadian universities, by any measure, have clearly gained considerably in stature and reputation over the last forty to fifty years. Immediately after the Second World War, one might have compared only the University of Toronto or McGill University with Manchester University, whereas today perhaps twenty-five or more Canadian institutions would be placed at that level. If the comparison were extended further, one would find much similarity in standards and quality between the University of Toronto, UBC, McGill, and the universities of Sydney and Melbourne, but what is especially remarkable in

Canada is that there is relatively little difference in quality between Toronto or UBC and any of the remaining twenty or twenty-five larger institutions. Similarly, in Australia there is little difference between any of the twelve to fifteen older universities, and all are now equal, if not superior, to the older British red-brick universities. In the quality of its universities, Canada has made enormous strides over the last few decades while at the same time coping with one of the highest rates of growth in enrollment.

Undoubtedly a major factor in this achievement has been the attractiveness of Canada for immigrants, and hence the relative ease of recruiting able new faculty members, as was noted in Chapter 1. Over the last few decades, this helped Canadian universities significantly in providing good-quality undergraduate education to a vastly expanded student population. Canada now has the second highest participation rate among Western countries, second only to the US, but it has not always been easy to predict future enrollments accurately. During the 1960s, university enrollments in Canada increased from approximately 113,000 to 309,000, an enormous expansion that had been predicted from demographic projections in the early 1950s. By the end of the 1970s, total enrollment was 382,000. Particularly in the 1970s, most of the increase came from an unexpectedly large participation by females, rising to 45 percent of enrollments by 1980. In 1975, however, projections appeared to suggest that Canadian universities would experience a decline in enrollment during the 1980s, and in 1981 a loss of 3.2 percent over the next twenty years was predicted. As it turned out, between 1980 and 1990, universities experienced steady growth to a total of almost 514,000, and similar growth continued through the 1990s. Such growth during the last two decades came from still higher participation rates, caused partly by the economic downturn of the early 1990s and partly by the growing public recognition of the value of tertiary education in a globalizing world economy. By 2000, female participation exceeded male participation.

It is also important to appreciate that during the 1980s and 1990s, although enrollment continued to increase, government funding per student declined quite dramatically. In Ontario, for example, the per-student funding of $3,265 in 1976 declined to $2,669 in 1986, expressed in constant dollars, and this was followed in the 1990s by the further reductions of the "Social Contract" of the Rae government and those of the "Common Sense Revolution" of the Harris government. Most other provinces have seen similar cuts.

Over these decades, Canadian universities have continued to proclaim their academic excellence, but, while no direct measures are available, it seems unlikely that undergraduate education has been maintained at the same level of quality. Increased workloads and greater pressure on faculty, tremendously higher enrollments, and reduced funding per student must all have exacted a toll. However, since these factors have also been experienced by universities in most other countries, Canadian institutions might still have been able to remain comparable in quality.

Modelled traditionally on the British system, reinforced by the considerable recruitment of faculty members in the 1960s from Britain and other Commonwealth countries, and later from the US, the Canadian university system is markedly different from the American. It has stressed the four-year honours degree with fairly heavy specialization in the third and fourth years. Three-year degrees of a more general type have been widely available but have been viewed as weaker alternatives, so that in every academic department, the major attention has always been given to the honours stream and its courses. Not surprisingly, then, the course structure and curricula of honours programs in a Canadian university are quite similar to those that one would find in a sister university in the UK, Australia, or New Zealand, and more different from degree programs in the US. The marked uniformity of these programs across essentially all Canadian universities is noteworthy. While *Maclean's* magazine publishes an annual rating of Canadian universities that tends to convey the impression that there are really significant differences between institutions (which, of course, change significantly within each twelve-month period, thereby allowing an annual list to be published!), the honours degree programs in chemistry, for example, at UBC, Simon Fraser, Calgary, Manitoba, McMaster, Toronto, Western Ontario, Guelph, Waterloo, Queen's, McGill, Laval, Montreal, Dalhousie, Memorial, and a number of other universities are essentially identical and of very much the same quality.

The same is true in many other disciplines. Canadian undergraduate education, as in the UK, Australia, and New Zealand at least, is noteworthy for its uniformity and high standards by any international benchmark. Undergraduate education in the US displays much greater diversity of character and quality. These differences obviously stem from the fact that in Canada, the UK, Australia, and New Zealand, university education has been developed from a common tradition and as a public undertaking consistently supported by governments, while in the US, both public and private institutions have developed, with far greater variety among them.

Another accomplishment of Canadian universities over the past half-century has been the creation of a vast array of high-quality graduate programs in essentially every field of academic significance. Canadian students no longer need travel to the US, the UK, or elsewhere for graduate education; rather, international students are attracted in considerable numbers to excellent graduate programs in Canada. In the graduate field, moreover, Canada has been a leader in developing its own methods for assuring quality. The continuing periodic appraisals system operated by the Ontario Council for Graduate Studies commencing in the 1970s is unique and highly regarded internationally. It must be recognized, however, that this system was put in place not by the universities' concern for accountability but to ward off the threat of more direct government intervention and control. Also, the fact that differentiation at the graduate program level is now apparent among Canadian universities, with most graduate education being concentrated at about thirty of the country's institutions, has not resulted from institutional choice but rather from government pressure and concern about costs. The creation and work of the Advisory Committee on Academic Planning (ACAP) in Ontario in the 1970s reflects this well. Left to themselves, the faculty would by now have created a broad array of graduate programs in all universities, with little concern for need or duplication. By any measure, however, the Canadian enterprise in graduate education is now very substantial and is held in high regard internationally. It is certainly equal in scope and quality to that provided by other major Western countries – again, a considerable achievement created only over the last forty years.

The growth of graduate education necessarily follows that of research and scholarship; the engagement of university faculty in research and advancement of knowledge forms the base from which graduate education can grow. In 1950 Canadian universities, with only a handful of exceptions, were not heavily engaged in scholarly research. Indeed, in fields of pure and applied science, for example, the National Research Council (NRC) of Canada, under the leadership of presidents such as C.J. MacKenzie and E.W.R. Steacie, was developed in the 1940s and 1950s as the Canadian resource in fundamental and applied research, and was subsequently the principal catalyst for the rapid expansion of university research. Before the late 1950s, for example, institutions such as UBC and the University of Alberta had only very modest reputations for such research, yet by 1970 each had large and thriving science departments that were beginning to attract international attention. By the 1980s, the sum total of university research in an extremely wide range of disciplines was very substantial, and was increasingly recognized not only as the primary manifestation of fundamental research and scholarship in Canada but as the essential foundation for a knowledge-intensive society, far exceeding the role played earlier by the NRC and similar government bodies. Internationally, the stature and quality of Canadian research and scholarship gained increased recognition in the 1980s and 1990s, demonstrated by the awarding of several Nobel Prizes and similar distinctions to Canadians. There have been continual expressions of concern from within the universities about the adequacy of government financial support for research and scholarship, and indeed it was only in the late 1980s and the 1990s that governments genuinely embraced the research function of the universities. Nevertheless, what has been accomplished is quite exceptional, and both the university community and the country should take great pride in the current research capacity of the universities.

The list of ways whereby universities enrich Canadian society is much longer than these descriptions of their main roles in education and research. Over the past forty to fifty years, several million Canadians have become university graduates, as have many others from every part of the world, and they are now active and leading participants in their communities and significant contributors to the richness, diversity, and growth of world society. Canadian universities have been especially successful over this period, in some cases with very little foundation from which to start, in developing many professional programs that have formed the basis for professional credibility and acceptance in a variety of fields. The quality of such professional education in Canada is high, and this is reflected in the very low incidence, compared with some other countries, of professional incompetence and the generally high level of public credibility. In many of these areas, universities continue to contribute to professional qualifications and standards through the offering of continuing education programs.

Most Canadian universities have reflected the generous nature of Canadian society through participation in international development programs funded by government or nongovernment agencies, contributing to the social and economic growth of Third World countries. In the last decade or so, some universities have attempted to become more global in outlook and operations, and specifically to encourage their own Canadian students to develop a more international perspective. More recently, many universities across Canada have become less like ivory towers and significantly more involved with industry and business and with their local communities. Such involvements can enrich the educational experience of students and smooth the transition from education to career.

If broad comparisons are made of the growth of universities since 1950 in countries as diverse as the UK, the US, Canada, Australia, and some European countries, Canada and Australia would first be separated from the rest, in that universities elsewhere had been well established and well regarded for many decades previously. Of course, in these other countries, the university systems have grown enormously since 1950, with the creation of many new institutions and with significant changes in the size and character of many of the older ones, and all of these countries have made university education widely accessible. But in Canada, Australia, and New Zealand in 1950, the societies and their economies, and certainly their universities, were, comparatively speaking, young and immature, and there was a much smaller base on which the rapid changes of the next half-century could build. To be able to suggest that Canadian universities, which have grown the most, now rank collectively among the best such educational systems in the world means that they have developed and matured more rapidly and more substantially than those elsewhere.

The Price Paid

Not surprisingly, however, these accomplishments have come at a considerable price. First, the great increase in the number of institutions, in the size of each, and in their enrollments has eroded, if not destroyed, their sense of institutional identity and community. To some degree, this was a worldwide phenomenon, but Canadian universities experienced a more rapid rate of growth than those of virtually any other country, often with little by way of institutional history or tradition. The effect of growth in diminishing any sense of institutional community has therefore been that much greater, far more significant than in, say, the UK, where smaller change had a much smaller effect on the significant number of older universities.

A second worldwide phenomenon that affects universities everywhere relates to the knowledge explosion of the last sixty years, which has had the effect of fragmenting knowledge into more and more highly specialized fields. This continues to play an important role in the loss of institutional community, and is being steadily reinforced by new information and communications technologies that encourage individual faculty members to be more intimately involved within a particular international field of specialization than within the institution.

Third, as a result of aggressive federal government immigration policies leading to a rapidly increasing population, Canadian universities had a far greater need to recruit foreign faculty members than universities in other countries. In the UK, the university system was able to provide more than enough doctoral graduates to staff the expansion of the system, and in countries such as Australia and New Zealand, not only were immigration policies less aggressive but the growth of the universities came later than in Canada and was smaller in magnitude. The necessary recruitment of large numbers of faculty members from outside Canada inevitably weakened the sense of institutional identity and community to a much greater extent than elsewhere.

Fourth, since 1960 the changes in governance and internal management that have taken place in Canadian universities have been more sweeping than in almost any other country. In some American institutions, the move to participatory forms of governance was carried much further, but it is important to remember the remarkable diversity of institutions in that country, as well as the fact that the changes that occurred in the better private and public institutions were, if anything, much less dramatic than in Canada. Also, while very similar changes in internal management eventually took place in universities in the UK, Australia, and New Zealand, they occurred in institutions that tended to be more traditional and conservative, and also took place somewhat later than in Canada. This means that Canadian universities are now left with forms of governance and management that were introduced in the more expansionist and radical times of the late 1960s and 1970s, participatory forms of governance that are much less suited to the more competitive Canadian society of the early twenty-first century, with its concern for efficiency and accountability. Moreover, in virtually all countries except Canada, there have been strong government pressures or direct government intervention during the last two decades to offset or amend the earlier changes in university governance.

Fifth, these participatory forms of governance and internal management have now been in effect at Canadian universities for about twenty-five years, and their strengths and weaknesses are apparent and now need to be reassessed. They have been applied in numerous institutions with a variety of modifications, and it cannot be claimed that there is insufficient evidence to assess how successful or otherwise they have been. The fact that Canadian universities are presently unable to deal effectively with priority-setting and planning issues, largely because of participatory governance, leaves the institutions, although not necessarily the individual faculty members, in a time warp, out of touch with the current demands of society and essentially frozen and unable to change.

Sixth, these participatory forms of governance, combined with pressures for fairness and concerns about natural justice, have led to the widespread use of procedures for decision making in matters of promotion and tenure that require proof of the negative, rather than the use of high standards and criteria for which positive evidence must be presented. The holding of tenure indefinitely should not be a consequence of the difficulty of removing tenure or of dismissal. To require proof of "cause" when "cause" has not been defined does nothing to ensure high institutional standards. Institutional definition of the required standards and criteria is both more positive and an easier task, but only if governance changes are made. Similarly, the procedures now in place for dealing with these issues, as well as with the avoidance of all forms of discriminatory behaviour at all levels in the university and the guaranteeing of human rights, are so complex and so fraught with legalities that too often justice is not actually done and equality is not restored. Creeping legalism has thus had an insidious effect on the institution.

Seventh, the independence, autonomy, and participatory governance by faculty of Canadian universities have all allowed the institutions to largely avoid pressure for greater accountability, for performance assessment, or for transparent processes for quality assessment. In these respects, Canada lags well behind the UK, Australia, New Zealand, and the majority of US states.

Finally, it is hard to avoid the conclusion that over the past fifty years academic standards have declined and that this has been accompanied by substantial grade inflation. The facts that participation rates have more than doubled in Canada, that expenditures per student have declined seriously over that period, and that passing rates and average class grades have increased can only be interpreted in terms of lower standards. It is perhaps important at this point to emphasize that two quite different approaches have been taken internationally to address the issue of accessibility to postsecondary education, and they produce different results.

The US provides accessibility through an array of institutions of widely different types – some public, some private, some research-intensive universities, some liberal arts colleges, some technical institutes and colleges, and so on. The best of the universities remain as they have always been, absolutely outstanding, but there is a considerable range of quality from the best to the worst of the US institutions. In Canada, Australia, New Zealand, and the UK, accessibility has largely been accomplished by the development of an increasing number of very similar institutions at roughly the same academic standard. This standard has gradually been lowered, however, either to ensure accessibility or as a result of it, while the best US institutions have maintained or raised standards, if admission grades are any criterion.

Outside the US, different types of institutions were created initially, such as polytechnics or community colleges, and with the passage of time, these have aspired to university status. In the UK and Australia, they have become universities, as have one or two in New Zealand. Even in Canada, there are similar tendencies: Ontario's community colleges have been granted the right to award applied degrees and Ryerson Polytechnic has gained university status; in BC, community colleges offer the first two years of university programs. It does not seem to have been possible in Canada and some other countries to develop and maintain the wide range of institutions that characterize the US model.

Governance Issues

When these various changes and effects are combined, the fairly obvious conclusion is that Canadian universities, especially in terms of their governance, internal management, and willingness to be accountable, are behind those in many other countries. In essentially all of these areas, the changes made in Canadian institutions tended to be more extreme, and there have been very few counter-pressures from government to make any correction that recent changes in societal and economic circumstances might require. Protected by institutional autonomy and tenure, in many cases by unionization and the security that labour relations legislation provides, and with the governance of the institution largely in the hands of the faculty, universities neither feel pressure nor have incentive to change, even as the institution itself withers and fragments further.

Many of these conclusions have been reached by others. In 1990 the Canadian Association of University Teachers (CAUT) commissioned an

Independent Study Group on University Governance, which reported in 1993.[37] This was intended to be a follow-up to the Duff-Berdahl report of 1966, which recommended and validated the dramatic changes made in Canadian university governance over the next ten years.[38] While faithfully adhering to the principles of participatory governance recommended by the Duff-Berdahl Commission, the 1993 report recognizes many of the current criticisms of university governance that I and others offer, with chapter titles such as "Isn't It All Too Cumbersome?"; the admission that in too many Canadian universities, the senate has failed to realize the potential expected of it in the 1960s, and will not take hard decisions; and the recognition that boards are too often seen as weak and ineffectual. The CAUT report also recognizes the frustration of administrators who feel unable to lead because of unwieldy and uncertain committee structures, and notes the frustration of faculty who expect leadership. It identifies many of the same failures of governance that I discussed in earlier chapters, and in considering solutions, it concludes that further reform with still greater participatory management by faculty is the only solution. The report rejects the corporate management model, although it recognizes that senior administrators, but presumably not faculty in general, might benefit from the Total Quality Management business model. It accepts the need for greater university accountability, but rejects value-for-money audits and discusses performance indicators in a most ambiguous way. Its only recommendation for universities on accountability is that "universities should engage in research about their own operations within the limits of the funding made available"!

What the CAUT report so signally fails to recognize is that by 1993 there had been twenty years of experience of the participatory forms of governance recommended by the Duff-Berdahl Commission, and that many of the report's own recommendations had already been in effect for years at a good number of Canadian institutions. What the report describes is the failure, under changed circumstances, of governance forms that had been thoroughly tested. If senates had not lived up to expectations, giving them still greater financial power would not improve matters. If a CAUT report could not offer a constructive recommendation on how universities could meet the requirements for improved accountability, the public's perceptions of universities as protectionist and defensive would only be confirmed. The existence of such perceptions today is readily apparent in newspapers, magazine articles, and other expressions of opinion.

If the report correctly describes the worsened divisions between faculty and senior administrators, all of whom had been selected by the faculty, does this mean that faculty-dominated selection committees make too many mistakes? Or does it mean that the role described for a university president, the role of bringing together by leadership alone the disparate interests of the board and the many faculty factions, is simply not possible, since there is really no longer a community of common interests? There certainly seems no reason to conclude that, just by having all faculty members vote on such selections, there would be any improvement in the quality of administrators or of university governance.

While the report does recognize that circumstances have changed dramatically since 1970, there is no willingness at all to consider anything but more of the same, even though the significant failures of participatory governance are rather reluctantly admitted. In my opinion, the report itself provides very convincing evidence of the extent to which the Canadian academic community has become separated from its own society, largely because of the isolating protection that has been provided to faculty by current forms of governance. Changes in society and in the economy between 1970 and 2000 have been far more significant, and have been experienced far more directly by the general public and hence by government, than is evident to university faculty members. Under these circumstances, more of the same simply will not do. Effective and real change is needed, and the negative effects of participatory governance on the well-being of the institution of the university, not just the positive benefits it has brought to faculty, must be appreciated.

A New Zealand Comparison

At this point, there is merit in looking again at New Zealand and examining briefly the changes that have occurred in the universities there since my own experiences in the 1950s. This, of course, will close the circle and help conclude this book by giving it some literary symmetry. There is, however, a much more important reason for doing this. In Chapter 1, I emphasized that universities in Canada and New Zealand, as well as in Britain and Australia, historically had many similarities, since all had been created and influenced in their development by their common British tradition. Because Canada, Australia, and New Zealand were quick to shed any remnants of their colonial past, especially with the end of the Second World War, it is surprising that the ways in which their universities have evolved since 1950 are still remarkably similar. Such a comparison is, of course, highly relative. The universities in these countries are very similar in contrast to, say, institutions in the US or Europe, and in this comparison they can be readily and conveniently grouped together. As soon as a detailed examination and comparison of Canadian and New Zealand universities is attempted, however, the cultural, social, political, and economic differences are quite apparent. Still, the comparison here is useful because it focuses on the need for change in university governance and on different ways of approaching this.

In 1950 the universities in New Zealand were relatively small colleges with limited government funding. They were governed through a Professorial

Board that dealt with academic matters, and a governing council that had responsibility for finances and infrastructure. During the 1950s, government grew rapidly in size and in its involvement in society and the economy, even more so than in Canada. Student grants were introduced, tuition fees that had been small to begin with were removed, and government grants to the universities began to increase, although universities did not really rank highly in the country's priorities. In 1961 the University of New Zealand was abolished and replaced by seven separate universities, each operating under its own Act of Parliament. The legislation provided for each institution to have a Professorial Board whose right to make academic decisions was guaranteed under the legislation, and it also established a governing council of twenty or so members, drawn largely from the community, who were appointed in much the same way as in Canada. Each university had an administrative and academic head appointed by the council, known as the vice-chancellor. University governance was, in other words, very similar to that in Canada at the time.

As in Canada, the 1960s and 1970s were years when intermediary bodies were in vogue; not surprisingly, the 1961 legislation provided for a University Grants Committee (UGC), much on the British model but with greater authority than, say, the Ontario Council on University Affairs. The UGC made the case to government for funding and then distributed funding to the universities, taking into account not only enrollments but also requests for special funding or for the introduction of new courses. This distribution was less formulaic and more a matter of judgment than in Canada. Effectively, the universities were regulated by the UGC, thus avoiding waste of money resulting from unnecessary duplication of effort. The UGC gave money to cover the costs of providing the courses it deemed should be taught to the number of students it deemed affordable. Although the government kept out of the universities' business in a direct sense, it nevertheless had central control through the UGC. Many in the universities found this approach very comfortable since it provided certainty, but over time it became clear that such central control stifled innovation and initiative.

During the 1960s and 1970s, New Zealand universities grew rapidly; for example, enrollment at the University of Auckland exceeded 12,000 by 1981. The late 1960s saw student demonstrations and radicalism, and as the institutions and faculty numbers grew, there were the same pressures for change in governance as in Canada. Instead of having only a single professor who was automatically and permanently head of the department, academic departments began to acquire several professors and make more use of the rank of associate professor, so that the professorial ranks became essentially North American. With this change came pressures to abolish the permanency of the head of the department; by the mid-1970s, these positions were filled, after consultation, for terms often as short as three years. At about the same time, the Professorial Board became the Senate, with a much more democratic representation, and the two or three positions on the governing council, previously restricted to heads of departments, became open to members of the lower faculty ranks by election. Of course, students had representatives on faculty councils and on both the Senate and the governing council. Committees proliferated and consumed time and resources, but a vice-chancellor probably still had greater power than university presidents in Canada. The similarities in governance were nevertheless striking, and government treatment of university funding was also similar. The 1960s and 1970s were generally seen as the golden era, whose warm glow diminished in 1980 when the government told the universities to reduce their nonacademic staff. Financial constraint or even stringency followed through the 1980s.

During that decade, New Zealand suffered severe economic problems that forced a restructuring of the public sector to an extent that has never been experienced in Canada. The government's approach to all restructuring was based on its general belief that only organizations run on business lines made efficient use of resources. After the reforming government was re-elected in 1987, it turned its attention to education, largely because of burgeoning student numbers. The University Grants Committee was abolished, universities became autonomous and able to teach whatever they wished, and funding was based on student numbers alone, although a maximum number was set each year for each university.[39] A universal and compulsory tuition fee amounting to about 8 percent of average tuition cost was introduced, and student allowances were gradually abolished, although special provisions were made for needy students. In general, more wealthy families were expected to support their children at university until the age of twenty-five.

In the early 1990s, the government announced that the annual limit on student numbers would be removed, but also that it would not increase its overall funding. All of the individual university acts were replaced with a single Act of Parliament, governing councils were overhauled and hopefully made more effective, and the legal right of Professorial Boards or Senates to control academic matters was removed. The councils thus became the governing body over academic, infrastructural, and financial matters. In Canadian terms, something close to a unicameral form of governance was adopted, with the Senate acting as the academic committee. The vice-chancellor was made the legal employer of all staff and faculty, with the intention of improving employee performance – a change that is difficult to even contemplate in Canada's unionized universities! The obvious intent was to make accountability for governance and for the quality of staff much clearer than before. Importantly, with funding related directly to student numbers, universities were given the ability to terminate the employment of faculty and staff in areas where student numbers no longer justified employment. Put succinctly, the universities were opened up to market forces, deregulation allowed full competition, and the operations of the universities were viewed as businesses.

As part of these very considerable changes, the government legislation also required that all postsecondary institutions be subject to periodic quality audits, but under pressure from the universities, the process and detailed procedures of such audits was left in the hands of the Vice-Chancellors' Committee. Since 1990, New Zealand universities have been through several cycles of such detailed review, and while these can be criticized as bureaucratic and time-consuming, they have nevertheless been highly beneficial. Both the review report for each institution, prepared by external experts, and the institution's response are public documents. While each cycle is comprehensive, focus is provided by several key themes. Thus, in the year 2000 cycle, special emphasis was placed on an examination of the realities of the relationship between research and teaching. It is interesting to speculate on how such a focused assessment might apply to Canadian universities.

Deregulation was completed in 1990 under a new government that abolished the compulsory fee and allowed the universities to set their own fees, resulting in even greater differentiation between institutions on the basis of cost as well as on courses and quality. At present, without taking into account currency exchange rates, many tuition fees at New Zealand universities are roughly comparable to those in many Canadian provinces. Indeed, the history of tuition fees in New Zealand since 1950 bears uncanny resemblances to that in Canada, although the New Zealand government has demonstrated a greater belief in the free-market system than Canadian governments. In effect, universities became corporate entities, self-governing and selling educational services. Ironically, a new government in 1999 was ideologically less accepting of market forces and raised the possibility of reducing tuition fees again. A quick reversal from full and free competition to rationalization and cooperation between institutions, is, however, most unlikely to be achieved.

Inevitably, there remains great division in New Zealand over the emphasis on the business model, which has dominated the drastic restructuring of the country's society and economy over the last two decades. Many Canadian academics would be violently opposed to the application of this model to universities, but, while some aspects of its use have been heavy-handed, there can be no doubt about the fact that this model has made New Zealand universities much more innovative and entrepreneurial. For example, over the last fifteen or so years, New Zealand universities have been much more aggressive and much more successful than Canadian universities in international education, especially in the Pacific Rim. It has been argued that universities in Western Canada naturally attract their share of students from these countries, and to a considerable degree this is so; but there is far greater realization in New Zealand of the importance of university education as an international lever, and the New Zealand universities' efforts internationally are now much better organized and proportionately much more successful than those of Canadian universities. For example, in distance education, the impact of the legislated governance changes of 1990 has made New Zealand universities highly aggressive in seeking new educational markets across the Pacific and elsewhere.

Some of the legislated changes have had negative effects, of course. The emphasis placed on student numbers in determining government grants to individual institutions has certainly made them compete more strenuously, but, as has been seen with formula financing in several Canadian provinces, this can lead too easily to compromising of academic standards in order to maintain enrollment and meet budgets. A too-direct relationship between student numbers and funding makes it too obvious to all that growth and the development of new programs is completely dependent on increasing student numbers. On the other hand, the New Zealand universities have at least been given the ability to change faculty numbers as enrollments vary over time from program to program, something that the unionized Canadian universities are unable to do because of a broad interpretation of tenure and the restrictive and often unworkable procedures embedded in collective agreements.

The stories of Canadian and New Zealand universities from 1950 to about 1990 are very similar, but over the last decade two quite different approaches have become apparent. These differences can be seen in the nature of government/university interactions and in the structure and mandate of the governing bodies of the institutions. At the working internal level, however, universities in Canada and New Zealand are much the same. Let me recount the experience of a department head in a New Zealand university in early 2000. For complex reasons, the university had overexpanded in the preceding two or three years and now had to balance its books. Under the 1990 legislation, a new vice-chancellor with a business background had complete authority over the internal governance of the institution. There had already been, however, two legal cases that faculty associations had won against vice-chancellors who were claimed to be too arbitrary. The vice-chancellor had to determine how budget reductions would be distributed and chose to do so based entirely on student enrollment experience over a defined number of years. Other than across-the-board uniform reductions, there was little alternative: the university had no clear agreement on priorities, and while the results of the quality assessment reports described earlier were available on a departmental basis, any application of them would have been entirely subjective and controversial. The department head whom

I was visiting was an academic chosen by his colleagues, with no prior administrative experience or training; he had assumed office three months earlier for only a three-year term. The department's enrollment had declined in recent years, and the head was told that its budget had to be reduced substantially and that he was to terminate the employment of about 25 percent of the faculty and staff; he had the final authority in identifying those to be terminated. This was to occur despite the fact that the department's reputation for graduate work and research was among the very best in the university. These faculty and staff terminations had just been completed when I visited, and the atmosphere and morale were appalling.

Consider what would happen in a Canadian university – perhaps Dalhousie – under comparable circumstances. First, the president does not have the same legislated authority over the institution and must engage in often fruitless committee discussions and consultations, besides being bound by the restrictive requirements of a collective agreement that predecessors and previous boards had accepted years ago. But the budget must be balanced and the president can be so directed by the board. As in New Zealand, the institution almost certainly has no clear statement of priorities that might provide a logical foundation for budget reductions, and almost the only possible option is an across-the-board uniform budget cut. These reductions have to be implemented by untrained academics serving only three years as department chairs, and there is virtually no possibility of reducing personnel except for support staff. After all, how many academic programs in Canadian universities have ever been closed or even reduced in size, except by retirements or resignations, over the past five decades?

Any outside observer, especially from the private sector, would be aghast at either scenario, Canadian or New Zealand, in terms of the lack of any ability to deal with budget reductions with an eye to the future, or on the basis of an agreed long-term plan or set of priorities; in terms of the use of untrained and often ill-prepared persons to manage the institution; and especially in terms of dealing with the individual people, the human resource of the institution. But the Canadian situation is worse: with no ability to reduce faculty numbers, it may be impossible to balance the budget, and the existing array of programs will continue indefinitely.

The Levers of Government: Finances or Legislation

Given such weaknesses in the governance and management of universities, two different approaches have been used by governments in the two countries over the last decade. In both, by about 1990 universities came under attack for lack of responsiveness and accountability; also in both, governments have respected the principles of autonomy and academic freedom and have not intervened directly in the universities' academic affairs. The similarities end there, however. In New Zealand, the government clearly wanted greater accountability but appreciated that under participatory forms of governance, the universities left to themselves would be slow to change. The government also believed, as does the Council of Ontario Universities (COU), that free-market competition can lead to greater transparency and accountability, provided that there is some independent check on maintenance of quality. Government action in New Zealand was therefore legislative: first, modify governance by clearly identifying the mandate of governing councils to be that of governance, with internal management the responsibility of the vice-chancellor, and, second, reduce the rock-solid security of tenured faculty by allowing the termination of employment on grounds of program redundancy.

Canadian governments may also have appreciated that the governance structures of universities prevented any likelihood of change, but none has acted legislatively. Provincial governments have instead continued to use the financial incentive or stick, and have moved fairly cautiously by gradually increasing the application of targeted funding. While this may be a more North American approach, it is not at all clear why provincial governments have been so reluctant to move legislatively. The irony is that although the financial lever of targeted funding has been widely used across Canada, recent moves in Ontario, in which the government has defined performance indicators to distribute funding, are a much more direct intrusion into university affairs than legislation might be. It can be argued, of course, that the Ontario government introduced its performance indicators only when the reluctance of the universities to develop their own became apparent. But the direct definition by government of what measures are to be used to assess university academic performance is a greater threat to university autonomy than if the government were to legislate that universities must introduce an acceptable mechanism to assess performance, and then give them the authority to do so, for example, through the Council of Ontario Universities. To carry out the latter, substantial legislative issues would have to be addressed, not least the fact that each university is governed by its own act. However, appropriate legislation to override these may still be far better than direct government intrusion into what will increasingly be the academic issues involved in defining performance indicators.

It is not the purpose of this book to consider in detail how the quality of university education in Canada can be best assessed, by performance indicators or other means,[40] but it is central to our discussion to consider the best approach to achieve increased accountability and to deal with the changes in governance that this will require. In New Zealand this is being done through a reasonably clear identification of the issues of accountability and governance, and the enactment of legislation. In Canada, the issue of accountability has been recognized by governments, but the inadequacies of a form of university governance that presently makes accountability very difficult have so far received much less attention.

Of considerable interest is the fact that in 1993 a Task Force on University Accountability appointed by the Ontario government produced a thoughtful and valuable report, known as the Broadhurst Report, that recognized that weaknesses in governance, especially at the board level, were at the heart of the accountability issue.[41] The solutions it recommended would be largely achieved not by legislation but by guidelines issued by the Ministry of Education and Training, although it did propose new legislation covering conflict of interest issues for governing boards. Had the government adopted the entire set of recommendations wholeheartedly and strongly, Ontario's universities would now be much stronger. This was not done, although the government did require boards to ensure that each institution had in place appropriate indicators of performance, and legislation relating to conflict of interest was passed.

With action taken on performance indicators only, and without other legislation, subsequent events (or perhaps, more accurately, the absence of them) only emphasize the governance problems of the universities. There is no question that boards have taken seriously the government's wish for greater accountability, but in every case the board has little alternative – since the issues are largely academic – but to refer the matter to the senior administration, which in turn can do little without widespread consultation with the senate and the faculty. The faculty, and certainly faculty associations and unions, have no interest in the introduction of such measures, and many actively oppose them. The result, then, has been a protracted debate that has gone on for years in some institutions with no end in sight, with boards perhaps frustrated but still seeing themselves in a more passive role than as real governors, and with little of substance achieved. It is with this background that the Ontario government has made, in the last two or three years, cautious small steps towards the use of its own performance indicators.

In 1996 the COU did act on some aspects of the Broadhurst Report by agreeing to introduce a process for periodic quality reviews of undergraduate programs at all Ontario universities, and assigned that responsibility to an Undergraduate Program Review Audit Committee, which reports to the Council of Academic Vice-Presidents. The schedule of audits began in 1997 with reviews of two universities per year. At this rate, the first full cycle will not be completed until 2004, and there is still no indication of the effectiveness or value of the process.

The Authority of the Governing Board

In my opinion, largely based on my own experiences, the Broadhurst Report has correctly put its finger on the key issue, the need to reform and strengthen the boards of universities in Canada, but I doubt that this can be achieved without legislation, and I believe that it must be accompanied by several other changes, without which board reform alone will not be successful. The changes in governance that took place in Canadian universities in the 1970s leading to faculty control were, as I have said previously, more extreme than similar changes in other countries. The very basic issue on which they focused was the separation of powers between the board and the senate, where historically the board had total financial and infrastructural control and authority, which it usually exercised in secrecy, and the senate had responsibility for purely academic matters. Faculty dissatisfaction with this form of governance grew rapidly during an era of unprecedented expansion in the 1960s, based on the premise that sound academic decisions cannot be made in the complete absence of financial information, and led to participatory forms of governance. With senates, and therefore the faculty, largely determining their own conditions of employment, with faculty having decision-making power with regard to senior academic appointments, and with senates having a major influence on financial and all budgetary matters, and, in the majority of institutions, with all this followed by faculty unionization, faculty effectively gained control of the university, which itself withered under decision-making inertia and unwillingness to change.

This has left, in the bicameral form of government of all but a few Canadian universities, a situation in which the board, in practice, is too weak and the senate and faculty too powerful, even though legally the board has ultimate authority for the institution. Whether faculty unions like it or not, the governance issue has certainly not been resolved. Senates should not be able to be involved in the financial decisions of institutions in times of expansion and growth, and still insist on a right to introduce new programs without additional funding in times of adversity and constraint. On the other hand, it is no longer appropriate for boards to see themselves just as passive trustees with little real knowledge of the internal operations of the institution and concerned chiefly with finances, an overall role that has, in any event, been seriously weakened by transfer of power to senates and faculty unions. There is, I believe, much more to be said for carefully focused debate on the issues of governance and internal management. The changes of the last fifty years, while suitable for their day, clearly have proven less suitable for times of economic constraint or times of rapid societal change, and they certainly are incompatible with the current demands for quality assurance and accountability. It is no longer useful to restrict the discussion of university governance to the question of the relationship between financial and academic matters; that question itself must be examined in terms of the assignment of responsibility for governance and for internal management.

The New Zealand situation, in which governing councils now have clearly legislated responsibility for governance, has merit. Governance is not restricted to financial matters; it must be broadly interpreted to include overall responsibility for an institution, and it is distinctly different from management. What might this mean in the Canadian context?

First and foremost, the size and composition of a board would change dramatically. Fifty years ago, to be a member of the board of a university amounted almost to an award of social recognition, a status symbol reflecting one's worth in the community. Prominent citizens might hold several such memberships on boards of universities, hospitals, or similar organizations, and attendance at only one meeting per quarter or perhaps per month, each requiring no more than a few hours, was seen simply as a social responsibility. While that perception of the board member's position has certainly evolved, with greater recognition of the importance of the task, the actual function has scarcely changed. A board member's role is still seen more as that of a passive trustee rather than that of a director of a major enterprise. Few governing boards have less than thirty or so members, and most are of a size that inhibits serious debate. Meetings are held in public, and while some do meet monthly, many still meet only quarterly. With representatives of the student body, the faculty, perhaps the staff, and the alumni, as well as a few government members, meetings tend to be regarded as political platforms, especially by students and faculty. The real work has been done, or should have been done, beforehand by senior administrators and two or three key board members, with the board, after the appropriate political gestures have been made, giving approval. This is not, as faculty unionists assert, an underhanded way for the president to pursue a hidden agenda, but a direct consequence of the fact that a board of perhaps thirty-five to forty people meeting once a month for two hours, and with conflict of interest principles often ignored, cannot handle the governance of a complex organization involving thousands of persons and hundreds of millions of dollars. There has been over the last several decades much improvement in the amount and quality of committee work for university boards, but this alone cannot substitute for an effective governing board.

In my view, a university board should have not more than twenty members. This number should include no more than two faculty members and two students, elected from their constituencies, as well as government appointees. The majority should be appointed by the board itself, and should include several alumni. The overall composition of the board should be a reasonable reflection of its society. All members must serve as individuals concerned only with the best interests of the institution and not as representatives of their particular constituencies, and they must be governed by legislated conflict of interest rules. Except for students, terms of appointment should be for not less than three years and be renewable at least once, to provide considerable continuity.

The defined responsibility of the board must be the governance of the institution, and from the outset, it must be clear that this is a considerable responsibility requiring the commitment of much time and effort. Thus, for external members, there should be some form of payment for service, perhaps on a per diem basis, as there is for service on major government boards; the position of board member should not be seen as an honorary one but as a real responsibility receiving real recognition. The time commitment will be substantial, as it is for a major board in government or in the private sector. Members should be chosen carefully for their expertise and not on the basis of representation, and there should be few, if any, restrictions on membership such as those relating to place of residence. For example, the ideal board of perhaps fifteen to eighteen persons should have several members with extensive financial experience, including investment matters and management experience. The care and careful tending of endowment and pension funds is surely not to be left in the hands of political appointees or faculty or students. There should be some members with labour relations experience, with experience in facilities management, with experience in institutional governance and management and strategic planning, and certainly with experience in university administration. The chief point here is that board members should be selected on the basis of the qualifications and experience they will bring to the board, and not just on a representational basis. It may even be that consultant assistance should be engaged in the search for new board members, as is beginning to occur with corporate boards. The greater the care taken in selecting board members for their ability and expertise, the more likely it is that board decisions will be sound and not just political.

In identifying possible members, boards should look more broadly than in the past. For example, there are many distinguished Canadians with profound academic or administrative experience of universities in the US or elsewhere who would be excellent board members without creating any conflict of interest. The board must meet frequently enough to exercise its responsibility for governance, and committee work should be substantial and serious. The board should meet in open session except when dealing with personnel matters and those pertaining to collective bargaining. The board should make financial information freely available, and this should include not only annual financial statements but also periodic reports on operating revenues and budgets, providing sufficient information for the senate to make academic decisions. The board should appoint the president and other senior administrators by processes that genuinely involve faculty and students; such processes should be recommended by the senate and ideally should not form part of collective agreements. But boards should examine and approve such recommended processes carefully and should periodically assess their effectiveness and make appropriate changes.

Boards should, through the president, insist on their management right of approving detailed job descriptions for all academic administrative appointments, should specify forms of mandatory training to be provided by the institution for such appointees, and should similarly require that appropriate performance review processes are in place for all employees. Accountability is an essential aspect of governance, and it must be the board's responsibility to ensure that appropriate measures are in place to meet this responsibility. Above all, the board must make clear within the institution that it will indeed exercise its responsibility for governance and will hold the president accountable. For example, when the board, through the president, directs the senate to provide recommended academic performance indicators, a clear and definite deadline should be set. Procrastination and interminable debate should not be possible. Clearly, if there are sound reasons why such a deadline was not met, the president must be able to persuade the board to that effect so that agreement on a reasonable extension can be reached. But the board must have final authority, and if a senate stonewalls, the board should instruct the president to act since the senate had failed to do so within a reasonable deadline. Deadlines are valuable in any organization, and a board should use them.

If boards have responsibility for governance, it is logical to conclude that this responsibility includes the definition of the parameters of the institution and the planning of its future direction. The board, in other words, must be fully responsible for the institution's mission statement and its accompanying financial and strategic plans, although the senate must clearly be involved and there must be widespread consultation. In New Zealand, the governing council is responsible for the university's charter. This is very different from current Canadian practice, under which broadly representative committees struggle for a year or two to attain campus agreement on what usually becomes a compromise, nonspecific statement of intent meaning very little. In many cases, the board plays little part other than giving a stamp of approval. When legislation gives the board responsibility for governance, such planning documents have added significance and the board is fully responsible for them. Finally, a most important consequence of legislatively giving boards full responsibility for governance is the removal of any uncertainty about the liability of board members; they would be fully liable as in any normally incorporated body, but covered by insurance. This alone identifies the seriousness of the board member's responsibilities. Nor would any of the above diminish the ability of a senate to make academic judgments, since financial information would be regularly and freely available.

Most of these suggestions are very similar to those in the Broadhurst Report, which also provides much more detail, but there is one significant difference. These suggestions, if enshrined in legislation, would, I think, force a governing board into a more active and positive role. It is one thing to point out, as the Broadhurst Report does, that an institution should have "a clear sense of institutional purpose expressed in a mission statement and supporting plans" and that these should appropriately match its choice of performance indicators, but it is quite another to specify by law that the board has the responsibility to see that these things are actually done to its satisfaction. The Broadhurst Report recommends that these changes be made by way of guidelines from government. In my opinion, this would not be sufficient, since guidelines imply a degree of possible interpretation, can allow some ambiguity, and may encourage procrastination. Achieving genuine change will require legislation. I reach this conclusion not only on the basis of the apparent need for change now to address current weaknesses in university governance but also with an eye to the future.

Take just one example. A newspaper report described the recent creation of at least two consortia, each consisting of leading English-speaking universities. One involved Cambridge, Stanford, Oxford, Yale, and other universities, and the other included UBC, the University of Toronto, McGill, University of Michigan and others. The consortia have a number of interests, including the facilitation of student exchanges, but are increasingly interested in distance-learning markets using the Internet, the size of which, outside North America, is estimated at over $15 billion. The consortia are considering joint ventures that may involve governments as well as the very large multinational media corporations. Futurists are presently thick on the ground, and attempting to predict the future with any accuracy is exceedingly difficult. What does seem clear, however, is that information technology in some form or other is likely to profoundly alter the delivery of education, and that of all institutions, universities may be the most affected. Any existing university that becomes involved in this transformation and that partners with global corporations and national governments will succeed only if it has a very different form of governance, with greater flexibility, greater receptiveness to change, and great adaptability. These are not, however, the characteristics of university governance in Canada today. Both current weaknesses and future needs suggest that legislated changes will be needed.

The Conditions of Faculty Appointments

Besides governance changes strengthening the mandates of university boards, an area where change must occur is in the terms and conditions of employment of faculty members. If the university as an institution is to have a future, there must be much greater flexibility within the organization. Influences that cannot be foreseen at present, perhaps a rapid and successful adaptation of new technology in distance education, may well force such needed flexibility upon the university, but it may then be too late to save it. Greater flexibility is needed now, but this must not be gained at the expense of academic freedom. As society and the economy become more global, the most important role that any university can play will increasingly be that of conscience and critic of society. This role will become more difficult as partnerships between universities and the private sector proliferate. Unless the principle of academic freedom is strenuously protected by governments and universities, the latter may become just a slightly different type of corporation.

There are powerful arguments that the concept and practice of tenure are essential to protect academic freedom. Such arguments can be truly convincing, however, only when tenure is accompanied by effective and periodic assessment of performance measured against well-defined criteria and high standards. Certainly, the dismissal of faculty members should require cause, and there should be one (although not more than one) institutional level for appeal that involves specified procedures and ensures due process. But dismissal should be based much more on failure to meet demanding standards as determined by a sound review process than on requirements to prove an ill-defined "cause" in a management structure that is not prepared to maintain adequate records of performance. Thus, continuing appointments (that is, with tenure) should remain, but should be subject to thorough periodic performance appraisals. Failure to meet the requirements of such an appraisal would then constitute cause for termination.

While a board should be as strong a defender of academic freedom as a senate, the board should also have the ability to require the introduction of a system of periodic reviews of all faculty, under procedures that have been developed jointly by board and senate and finally approved and, if necessary, modified by the board. Moreover, since a major part of the governance responsibilities of a board must be that of determining the institution's long-term directions, a board should have the power to require a senate to conduct periodic reviews of all program offerings, not in isolation from one another but collectively, in terms of the effectiveness of the array of programs in achieving the institution's long-term objectives. A board should have sufficient authority to question the indefinite continuance of any program that is no longer a priority for the institution, and should have the power, subject to adequate consultation with the senate, to terminate or reduce such a program, even if it means terminating the employment of some faculty and staff members. The current interpretation of tenure, which is viewed as providing complete job security, and current clauses in collective agreements that effectively prevent the closing of programs and the termination of faculty employment are unacceptable in institutions that are still largely supported by taxpayers' dollars.

At present, most Canadian universities are bound by collective agreements under labour relations legislation, and most of the remaining institutions are bound to almost the same degree by some form of special agreement. To hope that negotiations between boards and faculty unions or faculty associations might produce such changes would be naive; existing collective agreements are far too favourable to faculty, and their own self-interest would make it impossible to even consider any such changes. But what is ultimately at stake here is the survival of the institution of the university, and this should not be determined by the self-interest of a single professional group. In any event, the faculty has ample protection against arbitrary action in a variety of other forms, including tenure, academic freedom, and an effective appeal process. There should not, however, be absolute protection against change itself.

Realistically, then, given current attitudes in Canadian universities, the degree of change that is needed in governance and in internal management simply will not occur through bargaining negotiations or government guidelines, and such changes are most unlikely to be initiated by any existing board. These changes, I believe, will occur in Canada only when provincial governments, acting through legislation, recognize their dual responsibility to respect the principles of institutional autonomy and academic freedom while specifying their requirements for accountability and for the forms of governance essential to it. Many of the key principles of legislation in New Zealand are applicable in Canada, and it is interesting to note recent steps taken by the Ontario government to establish a quality assessment authority and to define more clearly through legislation the issues of conflict of interest affecting universities. While the situation in Canada lags behind those in many other countries, it may well be that over the next few years, legislative action will lead to improved governance of Canadian universities.

13
Conclusions

One type of change in universities that is just beginning to occur, but that will blossom rapidly, is that of privatization. I refer to the fact that during the last decade, and especially the last five to ten years, universities have been offered, and have accepted, increasingly large amounts of targeted funding, most of which has been directed towards research. Much of this has come from governments through new programs encouraging the development of partnerships with industry and business, which in their turn are expected to produce demonstrable economic returns within a defined time frame. These partnerships often require that the business partners themselves provide funding to match the government contribution. Others, such as the Canada Chairs Program, are less tightly framed but still give preference to disciplines and research areas that are perceived to be relevant to society's future economic needs. Major gifts from corporations and wealthy individuals have tended to follow the same pattern.

In university fund-raising campaigns and in other ways, the private sector in Canada has recently funded more and more chairs and research in the universities, but, wishing to obtain some return for this generosity, has done so with strings attached. The fields supported tend to be those of economic interest to the donor corporation, the chairs often bear the corporate name, and the general conditions of the gift and its possible continuation in the future all encourage the university to bear the donor's interests and opinions in mind as the work progresses. Even foundations have not been immune to these trends, and some are now more specific in defining the purpose of their contributions and the conditions attached. There is no doubt that all of these favour pure and applied sciences such as molecular biology, agriculture, genetics, medicine, pharmaceutical sciences, and so on, as well as business schools and closely related fields; rarely do they support the humanities or social sciences except economics. By and large, virtually all are accompanied by considerations of self-interest, which exert a subtle but considerable influence on the institution. These new sources of funding are certainly helping to revitalize the university after several decades of financial constraint, and are bringing bright, young new faculty to the institutions and opening up new research activities. But they also steer the universities in particular directions, and they place greater emphasis on the development of certain fields not because of their intellectual importance but because of potential economic returns. Their pressures for accountability and often confidentiality can be a serious risk to academic freedom.

Of course, virtually all Canadian universities now have in place good policies to avoid conflicts of interest, ensure open publication of research results (although most provide for a delay in publication to allow for the protection of intellectual property), and govern the ethical conduct of research. In numerous cases, universities have also refused such contributions from the private sector and individuals because the conditions were inconsistent with institutional policies. Nevertheless, the effects of this privatization on the institution are considerable. Over the last few years, the fastest-growing part of any research-intensive university in Canada has been in research administration, as research contracts with the private sector multiply and participation in targeted government-funded research programs increase. It should also be remembered that in most cases the primary contacts are between the individual faculty members and the industry, business, or foundation involved; the university's role is that of a corporate body that enters into contractual arrangements with the private sector sponsor, administers the funds, pays salaries and provides benefits, and ensures that contractual obligations are met. It is entirely a business arrangement between the parties, governed only by institutional policies that are intended to protect academic freedom and guarantee ethical research leading to unfettered publication of results. There should be growing concern and considerable debate within the universities about these trends and their long-term consequences.

Some voices have been raised, but I know of no case where a university senate has debated the substantive issues or considered the long-term consequences on the institution's priorities of such research participation. Specific policies have been debated, but with the current emphasis on future economic benefit from university research, and the fact that in most Canadian universities the individual researcher owns the intellectual property rights to research results, a great deal of faculty self-interest is inevitably infused into such debates, with little regard for the welfare of the institution. It is particularly interesting to note that Cambridge University has recently made a move to change policy so that the institution would become the owner of intellectual property developed by its faculty when research has been supported by the university. The debate at Cambridge is rigorous and likely to become heated, and revolves about this issue of faculty interests versus those of the university. In the Canadian context, it seems likely that there might be a far more dispassionate debate on such privatization in a well-informed board than in a faculty-dominated senate.

Many of the recent government programs have deliberately encouraged the development of formal networks of researchers across Canada, and many of them have now become corporate entities and alternative institutions to the university. The faculty members who participate in these networks increasingly owe their primary allegiance to the network, which is, in effect, their field of research specialization; there is less and less attachment to the institution of the university. Ironically also, these networks are encouraged to adopt a business model organizational structure and ethos, which is then efficiently transmitted through the graduate education that parallels the research mission of the network. There is little doubt that such programs by government and similar initiatives from the private sector are greatly strengthening Canadian research capacity, and probably also improving the quality of graduate education, at least in those fields that they support. But they are also slowly but effectively eroding further any sense of community within the university and weakening the institution itself. It is not a stretch of the imagination to say that the university is evolving towards becoming little more than a landlord that provides physical and information technology facilities for researchers, and an intermediary management body with regard to payment of salaries and other costs from funding received from third parties. However, this description does ignore the teaching function at the undergraduate level, although not necessarily at the graduate stage.

If some speculation is permitted about the long-term impact of the Internet and still newer, unanticipated technologies on the educational process, it may be very likely that undergraduate education may also become increasingly decoupled from university campuses. Of course, there will continue to be "brand value" attached to degrees obtained by distance technologies from, say, the University of British Columbia or the University of Toronto, but to gain such degrees may require little if any actual attendance on campus. The description of universities of the future as little more than management corporations that seek maximum return for such "brand value" education, and that act as intermediary contracting bodies in the provision of facilities and in partnering researchers with the private sector, may not be too far off the mark.

The irony of this is that without government intervention in forms other than the current use of targeted funding, the present governance and structure of today's Canadian universities largely guarantee that the drift in these directions will continue. Since faculty effectively control the universities, it is the faculty themselves who are allowing this privatization to occur and strengthen. As I have stated so frequently in this book, faculty feel little allegiance to the institution and far more to their research specialization. When additional funding is dangled before them that can sustain and increase those research activities in ways that may also bring economic benefit to the individual through commercialization of intellectual property, decisions are based on self-interest. It has been the willing embrace by faculty, perhaps by the majority, of these new programs and new links with the private sector that has ensured their success and discouraged debate of their impact in senates and elsewhere. Such programs are highly beneficial to the faculty, and since they can also help bring economic relief to the institution through research overheads, they are usually also encouraged by senior administration. Yet the overall effect is to further weaken the ties between the university and its faculty, to further fragment the institution, to further emphasize the management facilitation role of the senior administration, and to further reinforce the deleterious effects of the governance changes that have occurred in Canadian universities over the past fifty years. This will lead inexorably to a corporate model for the institution – inevitably and remarkably, this may well be the end result of the governance changes that have been described in earlier chapters.

So I will argue strenuously that what Canadian universities need today is not just more use of the funding lever to effect accountability but also clear legislative action from governments to specify, in principle but not detail, how universities are to be accountable and what changes in governance are needed to ensure that accountability. At the same time, governments should reaffirm their commitment to academic freedom and to institutional autonomy, and should allow and encourage completely free and open competition, regardless of whether institutions are publicly or privately owned. Smaller, more effective boards should have the ultimate responsibility for determining the long-term directions of the institution, and should provide leadership in requiring the establishment of clear policies and defined procedures for internal management. In creating these policies, the prime determinant should be the best interests of the institution, and in the internal management of that institution, the board must have sufficient authority to ensure that resources are employed with flexibility and that the future directions and well-being of the institution are always kept foremost.

Finally, in recognizing both the very significant achievements of Canadian universities over the past fifty years, and also in identifying areas of weakness or even failure, all of us who have been part of the academic community during this period must admit that we bear much responsibility. I certainly have been fully involved in the Canadian university scene over the last forty-five years. Like many others, I welcomed the governance changes of the 1960s and 1970s, believing that we would have a much stronger voice in the distribution of what seemed to be an unending flow of funds, and ultimately in the direction of the university.

I remember being convinced by arguments about the need for the Canadian Association of University Teachers to take an aggressive stand on unionization so that the Canadian Union of Public Employees would not have control over the universities, just as I remember the fierce faculty opposition to student evaluation of teaching and student representation on major committees. And above all, I remember the thousands of hours that I have sat in innumerable meetings of university committees over many years, and I realize now that, in so many instances, little of lasting value was accomplished. But we all felt it right at the time and we all bear the responsibility.

Nothing can, however, detract from the fact that I and many others, especially from Commonwealth countries, were given opportunities in Canada that we would not have had elsewhere, and that we have benefited beyond words from career opportunities in Canadian universities and from participation in Canadian life and society. My sincere hope is that our contributions to the development and achievements of Canadian universities far outweigh any problems that our time as faculty members may have left.

Notes

1 Keith Sinclair, *A History of the University of Auckland, 1883-1983* (Auckland: Auckland University Press/Oxford University Press, 1983).
2 For a fuller discussion of these issues see T.H.B. Symons, *To Know Ourselves: The Report of the Commission on Canadian Studies,* 3 volumes (Ottawa: Association of Universities and Colleges of Canada, 1975-84); R. Matthews and J. Steele, *The Struggle for the Canadian Universities* (Toronto: Toronto New Press, 1969).
3 P.B. Waite, *Lord of Point Grey: Larry MacKenzie of UBC* (Vancouver: UBC Press, 1987).
4 *Report of the Committee on New Zealand Universities* (Hughes Parry Committee) (Wellington, New Zealand, 1959).
5 J.R.W. Gwynne-Timothy, *Western's First Century* (London: University of Western Ontario, 1978).
6 Ontario, University of Western Ontario Act, 1967.
7 Sir James Duff and R.O. Berdahl, *University Government in Canada: Report of a Commission Sponsored by the Canadian Association of University Teachers and the Association of Universities and Colleges of Canada* (Toronto: University of Toronto Press, 1966).
8 Ontario, Act to Incorporate the University of Guelph, 1964.
9 *Faculty Policy Handbook,* University of Guelph, 1 January 1993, and earlier versions.
10 "Report of the Ad Hoc Committee to Study Liberal Education," Senate, University of Guelph, 1980.
11 "Faculty Development," document prepared by an ad hoc group, University of Guelph, 1981.
12 Duff and Berdahl, *University Government in Canada.*
13 An excellent overview of this debate up to 1997 can be found in Association of American Colleges and Universities, *Handbook of the Undergraduate Curriculum* (San Francisco: Jossey-Bass, 1997).
14 William Bennett, *To Reclaim a Legacy: The Humanities in Higher Education* (Washington, DC: US Department of Education, 1984).
15 Allan Bloom, *Closing of the American Mind: How Higher Education Has Failed Democracy and Impoverished the Souls of Today's Students* (New York: Simon and Schuster, 1987).
16 Association of American Colleges, *Integrity in the College Curriculum: A Report to the Academic Community* (Washington, DC: Association of American Colleges, 1985), and later reports.
17 Stuart L. Smith, *Report of the Commission of Inquiry on Canadian University Education* (Ottawa: Association of Universities and Colleges of Canada, 1991).
18 George Keller, *Academic Strategy: The Management Revolution in American Higher Education* (Baltimore, MD: Johns Hopkins University Press, 1983).
19 "Towards 2000: Aims of the University of Guelph," report of an ad hoc Senate committee, University of Guelph, 1985.
20 "Making Change: The Strategic Plan of the University of Guelph," 1995.

21 P.B. Waite, *The Lives of Dalhousie University, Vol. I, Lord Dalhousie's College* (1994); *Vol. II, 1925-1980, The Old College Transformed* (1998) (Montreal: McGill-Queen's University Press).
22 Nova Scotia, *Report of the Royal Commission on Post-Secondary Education* (Halifax: Queen's Printer, 1985).
23 Alan K. Adlington, "A Review of the Commission's Funding Formula" (Halifax: Maritime Provinces Higher Education Commission, 1988).
24 Ibid.
25 D. Bercuson, R. Bothwell, and J.L. Granatstein, *The Petrified Campus* (Toronto: Vintage Canada, 1997).
26 David M. Cameron, *More than an Academic Question* (Halifax: Institute for Research on Public Policy, 1991).
27 B. Adell and D. Carter, *Collective Bargaining for University Faculty in Canada* (Kingston, ON: Queen's University Industrial Relations Centre, 1972).
28 Michiel Horn, *Academic Freedom in Canada* (Toronto: University of Toronto Press, 1999).
29 Duff and Berdahl, *University Government in Canada.*
30 "Policy Statement on Academic Appointments and Tenure," *CAUT Bulletin,* February 1968.
31 *CAUT Handbook: Policy Statements and Guidelines* (Ottawa: Canadian Association of University Teachers, 1973).
32 Rushton, a psychologist, expressed views in both publications and lectures that were perceived by many as offensively racist. Student demonstrations, supported by many others, demanded his dismissal, which the administration resisted.
33 Cameron, *More than an Academic Question.*
34 *Ontario Universities: Options and Futures* (Toronto: Commission on the Future Development of the Universities of Ontario [Bovey Commission], 1984).
35 Adlington, "A Review of the Commission's Funding Formula."
36 Adell and Carter, *Collective Bargaining for University Faculty in Canada.*
37 *Governance and Accountability: The Report of the Independent Study Group on University Governance* (Ottawa: Canadian Association of University Teachers, 1993).
38 Duff and Berdahl, *University Government in Canada.*
39 New Zealand, Education Amendment Act 1990, to be read together with and deemed part of the Education Act 1989.
40 David C. Smith, *Report on Quality Indicators and Quality Enhancement in Universities: Issues and Experiences – "How Will I know if There Is Quality?"* (Toronto: Council of Ontario Universities, 2000).
41 *University Accountability: A Strengthened Framework* (report of the Task Force on University Accountability – Broadhurst Report) (Toronto: Ministry of Colleges and Universities, 1993).

Index

Printed and bound in Canada by Friesens
Set in Stone by Artegraphica Design Co. Ltd.
Copy editor: Francis Chow
Proofreader and indexer: Deborah Kerr